# THE PRESBYTERY CRISIS PRAYER MINISTRY

MINISTERING TO CRISIS MEMBERS IN A LOCAL CHURCH

# THE PRESBYTERY CRISIS PRAYER MINISTRY

## MINISTERING TO CRISIS MEMBERS IN A LOCAL CHURCH

**Rev. Dr. Peter Bawamakadi**

THE PRESBYTERY CRISIS PRAYER MINISTRY
Copyright © 2023 by Rev. Dr. Peter Bawamakadi

All rights reserved. Neither this publication nor any part of this publication may be reproduced or transmitted in any form or by any means, electronic or mechanical, including photocopying, recording or any information storage and retrieval system, without permission in writing from the author.

Scripture quotations marked (NIV) are taken from the Holy Bible, New International Version®, NIV®. Copyright © 1973, 1978, 1984, 2011 by Biblica, Inc.™ Used by permission of Zondervan. All rights reserved worldwide. www.zondervan.com The "NIV" and "New International Version" are trademarks registered in the United States Patent and Trademark Office by Biblica, Inc.™ • Scripture quotations marked (NKJV) taken from the New King James Version®. Copyright © 1982 by Thomas Nelson. Used by permission. All rights reserved. • Scripture quotations taken from the Amplified® Bible (AMP), Copyright © 2015 by The Lockman Foundation. Used by permission. lockman.org. • Scripture quotations marked MSG are taken from The Message, copyright © 1993, 2002, 2018 by Eugene H. Peterson. Used by permission of NavPress. All rights reserved. Represented by Tyndale House Publishers. • Scripture quotations marked (KJV) taken from the Holy Bible, King James Version, which is in the public domain. • Scripture quotations (BLB) taken from the Holy Bible, Berean Literal Bible, Copyright ©2016, 2020 by Bible Hub. Used by Permission. All Rights Reserved Worldwide. • Scripture quotations marked (RSV) are from the Revised Standard Version of the Bible, Copyright © 1946, 1952, and 1971 the Division of Christian Education of the National Council of the Churches of Christ in the United States of America. Used by permission. All rights reserved. • Scripture quotations marked (NLT) are taken from the Holy Bible, New Living Translation, copyright ©1996, 2004, 2015 by Tyndale House Foundation. Used by permission of Tyndale House Publishers, Carol Stream, Illinois 60188. All rights reserved. • Scripture quotations are from the ESV® Bible (The Holy Bible, English Standard Version®), copyright © 2001 by Crossway, a publishing ministry of Good News Publishers. Used by permission. All rights reserved. • Scripture quotations marked (ASV) taken from the American Standard Version, which is in the public domain. • Scripture quotations taken from the (NASB®) New American Standard Bible®, Copyright © 1960, 1971, 1977, 1995, 2020 by The Lockman Foundation. Used by permission. All rights reserved. lockman.org. • Scripture quotations marked (NRSVUE) are from the Revised Standard Version, Updated Edition. Copyright © 2021 National Council of Churches of Christ in the United States of America. Used by permission. All rights reserved worldwide. • Scripture quotations marked HCSB are taken from the Holman Christian Standard Bible®, Used by Permission CSB ©1999, 2000, 2002, 2003, 2009 Holman Bible Publishers. Holman Christian Standard Bible®, Holman CSB®, and HCSB® are federally registered trademarks of Holman Bible Publishers. • Scripture quotations marked (CEV) are from the Contemporary English Version Copyright © 1991, 1992, 1995 by American Bible Society. Used by Permission. • Scripture quotations marked (ICB) taken from the Holy Bible, International Children's Bible® Copyright© 1986, 1988, 1999, 2015 by Thomas Nelson. Used by permission. • Scripture quotations taken from the NET Bible® copyright ©1996-2017 by Biblical Studies Press, L.L.C. http://netbible.com All rights reserved. • Scripture quotations taken from the ISV Bible, Copyright © 1995-2014 by ISV Foundation. ALL RIGHTS RESERVED INTERNATIONALLY. Used by permission of Davidson Press, LLC. • Scripture quotations marked (GW) taken from God's Word Translation, Copyright © 1995, 2003, 2013, 2014, 2019, 2020 by God's Word to the Nations Mission Society. All rights reserved.

ISBN: 978-1-4866-2360-0
eBook ISBN: 978-1-4866-2361-7

Word Alive Press
119 De Baets Street Winnipeg, MB R2J 3R9
www.wordalivepress.ca

Cataloguing in Publication information can be obtained from Library and Archives Canada.

# Acknowledgements

THE WRITING OF this book would not have been possible without God's gracious gift of intelligence, wisdom, knowledge, and strength. I want sincerely thank God for those gifts to me.

My deepest thanks go to my family for their patience, encouragement, prayer, and financial support in my studies, ministries, and growth. Mainly I acknowledge the immense encouragement of my dear wife, Rahila Peter Bawa Makadi, as well as her honest advice and the place she occupies in my life. I thank our daughter, Dorea Peter, and our grandson, Peter Nomheiy, for their support and joy in my life and ministries. Thank you, everyone; I love all of you.

# Contents

| | |
|---|---|
| Acknowledgements | v |
| Preface | ix |
| The Presbytery Crisis Prayer Ministry Bible Text | xi |
| Introduction | xiii |

## Part One
## God's Devine Plan for Healing Human Crises

**CHAPTER ONE**
A Challenging Purpose — 3

**CHAPTER TWO**
God's Eternal Structuring Plan for Healthy Humanity — 13

**CHAPTER THREE**
God's Eternal Plan for Implementing Health — 33

## Part Two
## God's Divine Plan for Healthy Living in the Church

**CHAPTER FOUR**
The Five Approaches to Healing Sickness — 55

**CHAPTER FIVE**
Traditional and Herbal Methods of Healing — 61

**CHAPTER SIX**
Modern Scientific Medicine — 77

**CHAPTER SEVEN**
Mental Healthcare — 83

**CHAPTER EIGHT**
Religion and Spirituality — 89

**CHAPTER NINE**
The Presbytery Crisis Prayer Ministry — 127

## Part Three
## The Presbytery Faith Healing Ministry

CHAPTER TEN
Spiritual Insights Regarding James's Prayer — 139

CHAPTER ELEVEN
The Task of the Presbytery Crisis Prayer Ministry — 159

CHAPTER TWELVE
Background of the Presbytery Crisis Prayer Ministry — 193

CHAPTER THIRTEEN
Bible Characters on Crisis Prayer — 201

CHAPTER FOURTEEN
The Presbytery's Mandate for Holistic Ministry — 219

CHAPTER FIFTEEN
Defining the PCPM — 227

## Part Four
## Understanding the Cause and Effect of Sickness

CHAPTER SIXTEEN
The Cause and Effect of Crises — 239

CHAPTER SEVENTEEN
The Name of Jesus in the PCPM's Efficacy — 257

CHAPTER EIGHTEEN
The Caller's Strength in the Faith Authenticates Healing — 265

Conclusion — 275
Transforming Faith Healing Scripture — 277
About the Author — 279

# Preface

JAMES DIVINELY RECEIVED presbytery crisis prayer on behalf of the church. It is the only structural approach to healing prayer specifically intended to be used to transform the situation of an afflicted local church member. It is the Bible's best evidence-based practice for pastors, pastoral teams, teachers, chaplains, medical practitioners, mental health professionals, and church leaders on how to deal effectively with afflicted church members who call for crisis mediation and healing.

# The Presbytery Crisis Prayer Ministry Bible Text

IS ANYONE AMONG you suffering? Let him pray. Is anyone cheerful? Let him sing psalms. Is anyone among you sick? Let him call for the elders of the church, and let them pray over him, anointing him with oil in the name of the Lord. And the prayer of faith will save the sick, and the Lord will raise him up. And if he has committed sins, he will be forgiven. Confess your trespasses to one another, and pray for one another, that you may be healed. The effective, fervent prayer of a righteous man avails much. Elijah was a man with a nature like ours, and he prayed earnestly that it would not rain; and it did not rain on the land for three years and six months. And he prayed again, and the heaven gave rain, and the earth produced its fruit. (James 5:13–18, NKJV)

Is anyone among you suffering? He must pray. Is anyone joyful? He is to sing praises [to God]. Is anyone among you sick? He must call for the elders (spiritual leaders) of the church and they are to pray over him, anointing him with oil in the name of the Lord; and the prayer of faith will restore the one who is sick, and the Lord will raise him up; and if he has committed sins, he will be forgiven. Therefore, confess your sins to one another [your false steps, your offenses], and pray for one another, that you may be healed and restored. The heartfelt and persistent prayer of a righteous man (believer) can accomplish much [when put into action and made effective by God—it is dynamic and can have tremendous power]. Elijah was a man with a nature like ours [with the same physical, mental, and spiritual limitations and shortcomings], and he prayed intensely for it not to rain, and it did not rain on the earth for three years and six months. Then he prayed again, and the sky gave rain and the land produced its crops [as usual]. (James 5:13–18, AMP)

Is anyone among you in trouble? Let them pray. Is anyone happy? Let them sing songs of praise. Is anyone among you sick? Let them call the elders of the church to pray over them and anoint them with oil in the name of the Lord. And the prayer offered in faith will make the sick person well; the Lord will raise them up. If they have sinned, they will be forgiven. Therefore confess your sins to each other and pray for each other so that you may be healed. The prayer of a righteous person is powerful and effective.

Elijah was a human being, even as we are. He prayed earnestly that it would not rain, and it did not rain on the land for three and a half years. Again he prayed, and the heavens gave rain, and the earth produced its crops. (James 5:13–18, NIV)

Are you hurting? Pray. Do you feel great? Sing. Are you sick? Call the church leaders together to pray and anoint you with oil in the name of the Master. Believing-prayer will heal you, and Jesus will put you on your feet. And if you've sinned, you'll be forgiven—healed inside and out.

Make this your common practice: Confess your sins to each other and pray for each other so that you can live together whole and healed. The prayer of a person living right with God is something powerful to be reckoned with. Elijah, for instance, human just like us, prayed hard that it wouldn't rain, and it didn't—not a drop for three and a half years. Then he prayed that it would rain, and it did. The showers came and everything started growing again. (James 5:13–18, MSG)

# Introduction

> *Neglect not the gift that is in thee, which was given thee by prophecy, with the laying on of the hands of the presbytery.* (1 Timothy 4:14, KJV)

THROUGHOUT THE BIBLE, God operates out of an *if* principle when it comes to acting out his salvation, blessings, and miracles with regards to humanity. *If* you do well, shall you not be accepted? However, *if* you do not do well, sin lies at the door.

> *If you do what is right, will you not be accepted? But if you do not do what is right, sin is crouching at your door; it desires to have you, but you must rule over it.* (Genesis 4:7, NIV)

> *Jesus replied, "Truly I tell you, if you have faith and do not doubt, not only can you do what was done to the fig tree, but also you can say to this mountain, 'Go, throw yourself into the sea,' and it will be done. If you believe, you will receive whatever you ask for in prayer."* (Matthew 21:21–22)

> *"'If you can'?" said Jesus. "Everything is possible for one who believes."* (Mark 9:23)

> *Philip said, "If you believe with all your heart, you may."* (Acts 8:37)

> *If any of you lacks wisdom, you should ask God, who gives generously to all without finding fault, and it will be given to you.* (James 1:5)

If you believe… if you confess… if you have faith… This is God's divine strategy of bringing what has been done in heaven down to the earth. It's his way of accepting and turning ugly predicaments into living testimonies of enduring freedom from bondage and suffering.

Only faith in the power and authority of Jesus Christ results in genuine salvation and miracles. If the church obediently trusts God with believing faith, God will then honor his promises in the life of the church.

The power of sin and its destructive consequences on humanity can be healed by the authority and power of faith through the presbytery crisis prayer ministry (PCPM).

One of the most famous scriptures to memorize and learn in one's first year of the training as a spiritual leader, pertaining to the authenticity, inerrancy, completeness of canon, and preservation of the autographs, is 2 Timothy 3:16–17: *"All Scripture is God-breathed and is useful for teaching, rebuking, correcting and training in righteousness, so that the servant of God may be thoroughly equipped for every good work"* (NIV). This scripture lays within us the foundation of truth that God inspires every verse of the Bible. Each one is profitable for victorious Christian growth, living, and ministry.

Unfortunately, for far too long this biblical truth has been watered down in the church's liturgical life. There has been a complete neglect among the authentic members of the church to appropriate God's Word in their daily experiences.

Therefore, this book seeks to guide the PCPM in fulfilling the healing ministry of Christ in local church congregations. It provides an instructional procedure for church and parachurch leadership where it concerns the biblical direction of a believer's healing and wellness through faith prayer.

The PCPM is the divine mandate to the church stating that Jesus Christ suffered, died, was buried, and then was resurrected to save humanity. Between Christ's ascension and his glorious return to establish the New Jerusalem, the Lord Jesus Christ has given the church the mandate to accomplish his earthly ministries through his authority and power (Matthew 10:1, Mark 6:7, Ephesians 1:19–23).

This mandate has been neglected, abandoned, disbelieved, denied serious teaching attention, and considered to be a brutal biblical truth to practice.

Prayer is one of the most important biblical themes and motifs, if not the most important one, and it supplies spiritual energy and synergy to synthesize all other ministries. Many books have been written on the subject of prayer and its role in one's Christian growth and various ministries. Prayer is the one instrument God uses to with to the saints and it is the route through which all believers' burdens are made known to the throne of God.

Nevertheless, pastoral teams have neglected to precisely define the prayer that was revealed by James for the specific function of addressing the brokenness of church members. This book emphasizes the significance of such prayer ministry for afflicted believers. It also reflects many years of theological and ministerial training, pulpit ministry, and readings about the mission, ministries, and accomplishments of Jesus Christ. Prayer is the central pillar of all ministry, and healing is one of the main three. Jesus said, *"'My house shall be called a house of prayer'; but you are making it a robbers' den"* (Matthew 21:13. AMP).

Someone may ask, "Is healing a central ministry?" Although this book focuses on presbytery crisis prayer for the healing of afflicted church members, the whole ministry of Jesus Christ was meant to amend the brokenness and helplessness of man and heal the relationship between the righteous God and a sinful and lost man. The spiritual gifting of the pastor-teacher seems to be a compound gift which operates in a twofold way; preaching and teaching of the Word seems to be the same (1 Corinthians 12:11, Ephesians 4:712), but the healing ministry stands by itself.

We know that God's omnipresent, omnipotent, and sovereign character makes most prayers a *now*, spontaneous event, not just a futuristic event. Therefore, prayers contain numerous features; they are confessing, petitioning, thanksgiving, transforming, worshipping, and glorifying God.

These characteristics summarize James's presbytery prayer, making it effective and prosperous in times of need. It increases synergy within the body of Christ.

The oldest and the most challenging human problem comes in the form of afflictions. Afflictions are the result when we disobey divine leadership. Rebelling against God's divine plan for humanity is the cause of suffering.

Affliction is a painful experience because it causes an internal malfunction, and it can occur in man's spiritual, mental, or physical components. The Bible's first record of afflictions comes in Genesis 3:16–18:

> *To the woman he said, "I will make your pains in childbearing very severe; with painful labor you will give birth to children. Your desire will be for your husband, and he will rule over you."*
>
> *To Adam he said, "Because you listened to your wife and ate fruit from the tree about which I commanded you, 'You must not eat from it,' cursed is the ground because of you; through painful toil you will eat food from it all the days of your life. It will produce thorns and thistles for you, and you will eat the plants of the field." (NIV)*

This text is the beginning of all human afflictions and crises.

Note that *affliction* is a compound word that manifests in different forms and degrees throughout the human lifespan. Scientific discoveries in medicine have gone far in dealing with dysfunctionality in the human body. We have seen the unrelenting efforts of physicians, psychologists, psychiatrists, psychotherapists, and other mental health professionals to do extraordinary work remedying crises in people's bodies and minds/hearts.

However, who cares for problems in the human soul and spirit? We know that humans take their spirit and soul from the image and likeness of God and never from the spirit world, the spirits of animals, the energy of electrons, or shades of deceased human spirits, despite what many religious/spiritual healers would desire us to believe. Therefore, healing crises of the human soul, heart, and body are tentative tools and interventions.

## THE PRESBYTERY CRISIS MINISTRY

James 5:13–18 has established that the presbytery crisis ministry has been divinely given to the church to use during a crisis. The apostle Paul affirmed this divine plan in Philippians 4:6:

> *Be anxious about nothing, but in everything, by prayer and supplication with thanksgiving, let your requests be made known to God. And the peace of God, surpassing all understanding, will guard your hearts and your minds in Christ Jesus.* (BLB)

How do the realms of spirituality and scientific medicine view the healing of sickness? Scientists reject faith prayer because of the misunderstanding, confusion, and interweaving of all faith practices under the umbrella of religious traditions, diversity of theology, and spirituality. God hates human religion, religious festivities, and the worship of creation—for example, designated human beings, sun, moon, idols, angelic beings, deities, demonic spirits, carving objects in the form of gods, and aliens. However, those are the components of religious/spiritual practices.

In Amos 5 and Leviticus 1, God expresses his mindset on outward religiosity and spirituality through the use of solid words such as satiate, weary, tired, disgust, and distaste. Outward religiosity and spirituality operates on the platform of hypocrisy, falsehood, and self-righteousness; it is dependent on human philosophical and intellectualism. This religious and spiritual adventure places God outside the box.

Christianity is not a religion, and the reader should know this. It is a relationship between God and man through one intermediary, Jesus Christ. Christ is a historical figure who is also a sinless God taking human form and reaching out to reconcile sinful humanity to himself. Christ distinguishes his authority and power to heal disease and sickness from demonic religiosity and spirituality to heal through the spirit of Beelzebub. We read,

> *If a kingdom is divided against itself, that kingdom cannot stand. And if a house is divided against itself, that house cannot stand. And if Satan has risen up against himself, and is divided, he cannot stand, but has an end.* (Mark 3:24, NKJV)

> *And if I cast out demons by Beelzebub, by whom do your sons cast them out? Therefore they shall be your judges. 28 But if I cast out demons by the Spirit of God, surely the kingdom of God has come upon you.* (Matthew 12:27–28, NKJV)

# Introduction

Religion/spirituality is the search for a relationship with God conducted through human means. A religious mind searches honestly for the worship of God through intermediaries. Unfortunately, much research into the biblical record on healing comes from people whose religions are mere speculation, philosophy, ideology, and worship of creatures in the place of the Creator.

Any researcher who desires to adequately write about the authority and power of healing and health from a Christian perspective must have the presence of the indwelling Holy Spirit. The Holy Spirit illuminates the understanding of what the name of Christ can do. Such a person must undergo transformative change and enter into a person relationship with Christ.

No wonder most discussions about the relationship between science and religion are considered to be harmful. Even though many scientists have the form of God while denying the power thereof (2 Timothy 3:5), the Bible teaches that *"every good and perfect gift is from above, coming down from the Father of the heavenly lights, who does not change like shifting shadows"* (James 1:17, NIV). Every good and perfect thing a man can do is given by God, including acquiring intellectual knowledge of any branch of sciences, medicine, mental health, or traditional herbal healing.

Regenerated Christians in scientific and medical fields must rise above the test of their faith in Christ and correct the confusing notion that all religious and spiritual affiliations represent different roads that lead to the same God. This concept of religion/spirituality is a complete fallacy.

We need to provide religious and spiritual training to medical personnel so they can minister to their patients. This idea, training medical professionals to treat patients spiritually, is among the most misunderstood concepts regarding religion and spirituality. Will a doctor, nurse, psychiatrist, or psychologist who believes that the human soul is the product of reincarnation provide religious and spiritual healing to a patient who thinks the human soul is transcendent after physical death? How unrealistic would it be for a medical practitioner to use the burning of incense to heal a patient's condition, especially when such belief comes from the doctor's faith in their own object of worship? No amount of smoke can disable, move, or thwart the power of Satan and his demons from acting as agents of human suffering.

In her articles, Baumgartner writes that we must get back to the basics of human existence and strengthen spiritual ties in order to ignite our passion and guide us to our fate:

> The days of religious figures and mystics abandoning their people for the secluded voices of the gods/universe are past. Our power and energies grow best when we integrate that part of ourselves into

> society and live out our "holy" quests for meaning, purpose, and love in simple daily actions.
>
> Some pray in temples, others travel great distances to find what is no further than their doorstep. Our connections to our existence are not only found under these special circumstances.[1]

If our spiritual ties and quest for meaning, purpose, and love end only with daily actions of connecting to the nature and not the Creator, we are doomed. However, that is the tendency one could expect from medical personnel who engage in multifaith training.

This book provides practical injunctions from James, the pastor of the early church in Jerusalem. He laid out the divine foundation for presbytery ministry to the church in every generations, particularly in times of crisis.

Chapter One will outline the burden that has influenced the writing of this book, the purpose of which is to serve the church. Jesus used his divine authority and power to perform supernatural acts in his threefold ministry—preaching, teaching, and healing. He has divinely deposited his authority and capacity to every presbytery so they can effectively carry out those ministries in the church and parachurch.

Chapter Two deals with God's eternal plan for healthy humanity. We discuss God's plans in three areas: first, God's descriptive plan for humanity's perfectly healthy state; second, God's extended plan for man's healthy relationship amid the corruption of his perfect condition; and third, God's comprehensive plan for restoring man's healthy relationship in the ideal eternal state.

Chapter Three discusses the plan of God at the time of creation and describes how man ousted himself from the divine plan. The plan of God for humanity was perfect, without the presence of disease or the existence of human affliction. But man's conscious choice to disobey produced enmity between the Creator and the creature. Man's disobedience eliminated the excellent relationship between God and man. The result of this sin was sickness and suffering. To redeem the curse of sin, man chose egocentric dependency rather than theocentric dependency.

Chapter Four introduces the human approaches to healing sickness. The Bible teaches that every good and perfect gift, including healing, comes from the Creator of heaven and earth. To overcome affliction, history records that man has used five approaches: traditional/natural methods, religion/spirituality, mental healthcare, scientific medicine, and presbytery crisis prayer.

---

1. Jessica Marie Baumgartner, "Quick Ways to Connect with Nature at Home," *Llewellyn*. May 3, 2021 (https://www.llewellyn.com/journal/article/2904).

Chapter Five reviews traditional and herbal methods of healing. The discussion includes several categories of healing.

Chapter Six explains some elements of mental healthcare.

Chapter Seven reveals truths about scientific methods of healing.

Chapter Eight discusses religious/spiritual healing, including the definition and meaning of religion and spirituality. God's common grace, not any spirit in the world, empowers man to be healed. Sin causes all living creatures to get sick at a certain point, and God's common grace heals them. This chapter discusses religious and spiritual healing practices, as well as healing methods from major world religions such as Buddhism, Christianity, Hinduism, and Islam.

Chapter Nine presents the presbytery crisis prayer ministry as healing medicine. The presbytery healing prayer does not depend on the religious and spiritual worthiness of a person who prays. Instead the effect of healing comes from the authority, power, righteousness, and faith of Jesus Christ. A believer's attitudes toward righteousness, self-cleansing, and obedience to the Word of God are platforms for answered prayer.

Chapter Ten defines, explains, and applies theological terminologies related to the presbytery crisis prayer in the book of James. We will discuss the meaning of disease, sickness, the presbytery, one's calling, prayer, anointing oil, the laying on of hands, raising one's head, confessing sin, what makes a man righteous in God's eyes, and how ones gets a response from God the Father. This process will reveal that it is the Godhead who heals. Anointing oil shows the participation of the Holy Spirit, and the name of Christ is revealed as the channel through which the presbytery crisis prayer fulfills the divine standard. When believers present their requests to God the Father through Jesus Christ, it shows their trust in the Godhead's working power to redeem their affliction.

Chapter Eleven focuses fully on the presbytery crisis prayer ministry. Presbytery prayer is a carryover from the rabbinic prayer and apostolic instruction to the church. We focus our discussion on the presbytery charge, self-crisis prayer, presbytery crisis prayer for sick members of the church, and presbytery crisis prayer for other church members. We then list twenty-four confident basic promises for effective crisis prayer, as well as proactive steps one can take to be successful. Lastly, there will be a discussion on what constitutes answered prayer.

Chapter Twelve focuses on the background of James's presbytery crisis prayer message. We will discuss the authenticity of presbytery prayer ministry, the identity of James, the background of his epistle and its recipients, and his message on practical Christian living.

Chapter Thirteen examines the biblical characters who speak to the subject of crisis prayer. We will read about each crisis and learn about specific problems from naturistic, scientific, and spiritual perspectives. Finally, we will discuss how the faith prayers of some great characters from the Bible defeated affliction by carrying everything to the Lord in prayer, such as Moses, Jehoshaphat, Hezekiah, Daniel, and the apostle Paul.

Chapter Fourteen presents a discussion on the mandate of the presbytery for holistic ministry. The Trinity's holistic ministry includes preaching, teaching, and healing. The presbytery crisis prayer ministry is less emphasized in the church today. This chapter also reveals the perspective of the early church fathers on James's presbytery prayer ministry. They emphasized the practical nature of the epistle and the role of presbytery prayer in the early church's ministry of healing.

Chapter Fifteen provides an understanding and definition of presbytery crisis prayer ministry in local churches. These include its meaning, nature, character, purpose, authority and power, theology, promises, audience, and superb results.

Chapter Sixteen discusses the origin of sin, disease, and purpose as it relates to humanity. Why do we get sick and what is the reason for human suffering?

Chapter Seventeen dwells on the need for fresh revelation in understanding the greatness of Jesus Christ. We provide a concise description of presbytery crisis prayer for healing and reflect on how professionals view illness physiologically, psychologically, and spiritually. The role of diagnosis in the healing process helps the presbytery understand the precision of each prayer need. The efficacy of the name of Jesus Christ is the divine anchor for miracle-producing prayer.

Chapter Eighteen examines the faith of a church member who calls the presbytery and shows the authentication of their faith. James teaches that the crisis member must initiate the process by calling the presbytery in a time of affliction in order for this type of prayer to be effective. He reminds the church that this type of prayer calls for some practical observations, distinguishing it from other prayers. Prayers of righteousness will ascend to the throne of God when the Holy Spirit is directly interceding.

# Part One

## God's Divine Plan for Healing Human Crises

CHAPTER ONE
# A Challenging Purpose

*All this I have told you so that you will not fall away... I have told you these things, so that in me you may have peace. In this world you will have trouble. But take heart! I have overcome the world.* (John 16:1, 33, NIV)

I HAVE WRITTEN this book out of concern for the profound neglect of the practice of the presbytery crisis prayer ministry in local churches. The PCPM provides practical prayer ministry to crisis church members. However, it is a clear fact that a crisis paralyzes church members' ability to function normally—physically, spiritually, emotionally, mentally, and psychologically. As a result, the faith of many church members is devastated. It becomes dysfunctional because they face the reality of physical, mental, and spiritual crises, especially pertaining to the problem of illness.

The ministry of praying for afflicted members of the body of Christ comes second to none. Unfortunately, some mainstream denominations of the Christian faith need to pay more attention to this ministry. Some Christian ministries—not wishy-washy Christians, but those who acclaim Bible-based ministries—have picked up the faith through strong evangelistic campaigns. They have highjacked the presbytery crisis prayer ministry and turned their churches into financial business centers. Most mainstream Christian denominations have reduced the PCPM to the position of a spectator. Some denominations exist with no activity to rightly divide the Word of faith concerning presbytery crisis prayer. They need to properly appropriate the divine healing message found in the book of James.

Christian denominations that are truly orthodox and Bible-based are left to pick up the crumbs. They must engage seriously in transformational PCPM. Having prayer seminars is a good thing, but more is needed. It will benefit the faith of Bible-believers to read about how our Lord spoke, touched, and healed people with crises and sometimes anointed them with clay mixed with his saliva.

Watching congregational presbytery failure to engage practically in crisis ministry is a significant concern.

Second, this book is not an apologetic and therefore isn't intended to be a doctrinal or theological discourse on the gifts of the Holy Spirit. Instead it puts forward the challenges faced by the church in a world that exhibits confusion continuously, appears helpless, and needs to turn only to Christ for solutions to everyday human predicaments.

Jesus Christ has not changed his involvement, mercy, grace, favor, power, and authority concerning the well-being and holistic health plan for his church amidst broken humanity. He is not only concerned that souls are redeemed, taught, and nourished in the Word into maturity; he is also willing to intervene in the ill health of his children. He ensures that the healing ministry can bring about the complete well-being of crisis members.

Is our God the same miracle-working God of the first-century church? This is a question the church must answer: has our God changed, or is he changing? Why does the Bible record the threefold ministries of Christ in the gospels—preaching, teaching, and healing—while some denominations choose to emphasize and continue to uphold only the practice of preaching and teaching, neglecting the healing ministry?

Mainstream Christian denominations are in the business of training and ordaining ministers of the gospel to preach and teach for the edification of the saints, but they have abandoned the healing ministry to traditional/herbal healers, modern scientific medicine, and religious and spiritual healing.

I firmly believe that the healing ministry results in the edification of the saints. Author Elisabeth Lesser describes spirituality as an "instinct."[2] An instinct in a person helps him to eat, sleep, and play. These authors believe that person has a "spiritual instinct" to understand the world around them, knowing that life has purpose and meaning, and relax into the mysteries of life in every circumstance.

This erroneous teaching is not in line with sound biblical truth on healing, but it does express the importance of caring for the needs of a whole person.

What we call modern scientific medicine today took root in the ministry of the church. Major hospitals and medical clinics in the western world have created opportunities for "spiritual care" to be provided to patients. Other major world religions—like Buddhism, Hinduism, the Baha'i faith, and others—focus on healing meditation, especially in the area of mental health. Modern scientific medicine is now embracing meditation as a therapeutic approach to treating many mental health issues.

The Bible teaches us that our miracle-working God, in the person of the Lord Jesus Christ, is still the God of Abraham, Isaac, Jacob, Peter, and Paul. Indeed, he is the same God of every age. We need the unchanging apostolic age God in our sophisticated modern, scientific world. Such a religious mindset counts God out of the equation.

If the early church needed miracles to authenticate the mission and gospel of Jesus Christ, Jesus performed signs and wonders to propagate his message. In a world full of darkness and deep denial of the transformational gospel message of Christ, we need the Lord's revisitation. Faith in the Bible tells us that the gospel of salvation is the only means by which humanity can be reconciled to God, yet the industrialized and technological

---

2. Elizabeth Lesser, "Breaking Open Your Spirit," *Oprah.com*. January 14, 2009 (https://www.oprah.com/spirit/breaking-open-your-spirit/all).

world, because the church has abandoned the healing power of the gospel, is rejecting the redemptive work of Jesus Christ in almost every aspect of human endeavor. What will happen in Christ's church and our world, if people witness miraculous healing, deliverance, and supernatural events to stand against the works of darkness and bring glory and honor to the Lord Jesus Christ?

A third purpose of this book is to serve as a wake-up call for the mainstream denominations to return to the holistic practice of the inerrant Word of God. The twenty-first-century church (and beyond) needs to take James's message in its totality and practice its injunctions with all seriousness.

If a local church does not provide the real thing, members will have no choice but to advance to a false prayer ministry. Today, people are turning to spiritual meditation and so-called higher levels of enlightenment and awakening, as well as ancestral worship, to connect them to a higher power. People believe that by consulting with their ancestors they will get help for their sickness, affliction, and prosperity.

On the other hand, the Bible says that the fervent prayer of the righteous will not avail much until the church recognizes the authority and power of Jesus Christ's ministry, passed on through the PCPM.

Fourth, we believe in the canonicity of the Bible. A Bible-based Christian believes in the inerrancy of the autographs, in which James's epistle occupies a space. Every scripture must be given a proper place in the edification of the saints. Peter wrote, *"For prophecy never had its origin in the human will, but prophets, though human, spoke from God as they were carried along by the Holy Spirit"* (2 Peter 1:21, NIV). Paul echoed this idea: *"All Scripture is God-breathed and is useful for teaching, rebuking, correcting and training in righteousness…"* (2 Timothy 3:16, NIV)

There is debate amongst theologians regarding the spiritual gift of speaking in a new tongue. When someone speaks an unknown language in church, many insist that it must be followed by an interpretation of what God said. In contrast, others believe that the gift has ceased altogether.

However, sign gifts—miracles such as speaking in tongue, visions, healing, the raising of the dead, etc.—are among the spiritual gifts still listed in scripture among the advantages of the Holy Spirit. Therefore, every scripture is still essential and effectively edifies the saints. Furthermore, every scripture is beneficial for training and equipping the saints into righteousness, which of course includes James 5:13–18.

The emphasis of the presbytery crisis prayer ministry is not on theological and doctrinal arguments about whether sign gifts have ceased; that should be left to the Holy Spirit to operate in today's church as he wishes. Instead the PCPM focuses on God's mercy, grace, favor, authority, and power, as illustrated in Philippians 2:25–30. We read in this passage that Epaphroditus received healing because of prayer that brought forth God's mercy. As a result, the Lord healed him from a deadly sickness.

It is not enough to yell from the pulpit that members of the church must attend the Sunday morning worship service, then go for deliverance services elsewhere on Sunday evenings and to healing prayer houses on Tuesdays. Why can't the elders of every local church have a deliverance service to engage the ordeal of crises and other forces in the lives of the members? When the presbytery fails to meet the members' spiritual yearning, those members will search for satisfaction in the places that appear to display symptoms of the real thing, even if they really do not.

God still has mercy and grace for his people performing supernatural acts in his church. These acts have never ceased. The compassion and favor of God has not diminished. Human beings are wired to engage in strong spiritual quests; they are always on the move to advance their spiritual yearnings, seeking to meet their physical, psychological, and spiritual needs.

This quest is more prevalent in African Christian church, because of the people's belief that diseases and sicknesses are influenced and caused by others, especially the departed ancestral spirits. This reveals an undeniable truth that African communities are, to a large extent, health-oriented societies. They use indigenous religious rituals for healing, prosperity, and protection. The fear of disease and the existence of evil affects the whole community; it is not simply a private domain relegated to individual pastor care.[3]

When worshipers assemble in sanctuaries, they are not only carrying with them the quest for sound biblical exposition and undiluted teaching of the Word; they are also there to seek solutions to their physiological and psychological needs. They fear inflicting attacks from the ancestral spirits and want to affirm that faith in Christ provides practical solutions to the evil that comes from the ancestors. They are afraid of terrorizing reports from their spiritualists and medicating physicians.

The church must understand this and be prepared to meet the challenge. The church in Africa must contextualize biblical theology. They must practice the soteriology of Bible-believing faith and apply Christological liturgies on the physiobiological needs of the members.

So where can we find answers to this spiritual shift in church congregations? I believe that a significant reason for seeking prayer outside one's home church is that mainstream congregations have ignored or rejected James's teaching on the PCPM.

---

3. Jason Kelvin Phiri, *African Pentecostal Spirituality: A Study of the Emerging African Pentecostal Churches in Zambia*, University of Pretoria. October 2009 (https://repository.up.ac.za/bitstream/handle/2263/28976/Complete.pdf?sequence=6).

When a call is made for them to do so, the PCPM authorizes and empowers the presbytery through the Holy Spirit to pray over afflicted church members through the laying on of hands and anointing with oil. Therefore, the church should give the PCPM its rightful place in the liturgy because God has promised to act with great results if the local church leadership obeys the divine instructions.

This book calls for a return to the foundation and reawakens the divine healing power of Jesus Christ in our dying world.

As for a fifth purpose for this book, it is written to reenforce the biblical truth that God changes not, and neither does His inspired Word. It does what it says it will do. In other words, Luke 9:1–2 echoes the prediction of a spontaneous fulfillment of the message of James. It authenticates the gospel message to our generation's faithless, discourteous, and religious fallacy.

Today, the presbytery is a prototype of the disciples of Christ. Today, the church can witness spontaneous deliverance and healing. Yet the church enjoys the forgiveness of sin and salvation in the righteous prayer of the righteous presbytery.

Sixth, this book serves to remind the local presbytery that their election and calling is a high one and divinely decorated by God. Therefore, prayer for crisis members must be of the highest priority in the presbytery ministry. When a local church takes God seriously and obeys it passionately, God will act seriously and passionately in living out the truth.

Seventh, this book has been written to correct false notions among some believers regarding spontaneous healing. It is significant to say that the fervent prayer of the righteous presbytery is still influential today. Nevertheless, some believers view it with skeptical eyes. Others will witness such devotion and call it a modern, or postmodern, or cultic faith movement, dismissing it as unbiblical. There are delusions in the practice of authentic biblical faith, but they must not replace the authenticity of the faith.

Eighth, this book has also been written to acknowledge that scientific medicine has a significant role in human health. Its contributions to our wellness should be profoundly acknowledged and appreciated. However, no degree of advancement in modern scientific medicine can replace the role of faith prayer. Prayer is the divine approach to healing for spiritual, mental, and physical afflictions, while scientific medicine focuses on physical and some limited mental human afflictions.

The reader must understand that Jesus did not promise that the Christian journey would be smooth and rosy. He knew that difficult times would come and afflictions would catch up with us in this life before our sorrows, sicknesses, pains, and death were no more in the New Jerusalem. He gives us hope to remain positive in everyday life by encouraging us to take every challenge to Him in prayer. We know that God honors the prayer of his children in reversing any human condition caused by the curse of sin and works of the devil. Jesus came to destroy all the works of Satan, and He does that today through the PCPM (James 1:14, Job 2:4–5, Luke 13:11, 1 Timothy 4:1, 2 Corinthians 4:3–4, Matthew 13:19).

Ninth, Christians should distinguish faith prayer healing from the non-Christian perspective of healing through religion and spirituality. Traditional healing, religious/spiritual healing, mental healthcare, and scientific medicine have all created their own authority sources. The PCPM gets its healing power and authority from the Lord Jesus Christ.

Tenth, the presbytery crisis prayer has a threefold approach to the healthy lifestyle of church members. It doesn't only provide a reactive response to a crisis; but it also provides preventive and sustaining effects in regards to healthy living. The presbytery prays through the indwelling power of the Holy Spirit, who teaches and directs all the prayers of the saints.

The Holy Spirit knows the mind and thoughts of the Trinity. The Holy Spirit presents the prayer of the presbytery in the fashion acceptable to the Godhead to obtain the desired result. Through the leadership of God the Father, the Godhead answers prayer by examining it through the microscopic work of God the Son. The scars on Jesus's hand demonstrate the suffering and shedding of his blood for our healing (Isaiah 53:1–5). The Godhead answers faith prayer for healing because Christ took our infirmities upon Himself.

Eleventh, this book has been written to demonstrate that Christian prayer does not and should never conflict with authentic traditional medicine or scientific medicine. The relationship between them should be understood to be complementary because science studies what the Bible describes as God's creation, which includes the universe's physical, energetic, anthropological, and abstract/theoretical attributes. Science focuses not so much on the universe's spiritual and immaterial existence but on the earth's metaphysics and sufferings.

One of the main thrusts of this book is to explore not only about what causes disease and sickness but to provide a road map of how the church, not religiosity or mere human spirituality, can provide healing and restore an afflicted church member's health. The Bible does not teach that reasonable religious regulations and the practice of Christian spirituality creates disease. Neither does the course of being religious and spiritual only provide spiritual and physical healing. However, a prayerful faith that is centered on one's relationship with Christ can produce supernatural healing.

Spiritual practices and works of religiosity show how man depends on his own efforts for healing. An article for *Mana* writes that many spiritual exercises and meditations can provide healing,[4] explaining that Hinduism, Buddhism, and Taoism are not religious

---

4. "You Can Be Spiritual Without Being Religious," *Mana*. March 2, 2023 (https://manaretreat.com/you-can-be-spiritual-without-being-religious/).

per se. Although people in the west see Taoism and Buddhism as religions, they are more likely to be considered teachings in Asia. They are philosophies and practices that both work on the body (or the mind) and open the practitioner to higher awareness and ultimately help them open their hearts to the supreme reality of oneness. As a result, they feel peaceful and relaxed. That is an outcome of religion and spirituality. But spirituality acquired by good results has little to do with faith in the power and authority of Christ, which is the mark of the Christian.

Twelfth, religion and spirituality are not the best practical means of preventing oneself from getting sick—i.e., keeping the body as a temple of the Holy Spirit. One does not earn eternal salvation by practicing manufactured religiosity and spirituality. We make salvation by faith through grace in Jesus Christ, which puts us on the path of the best practice of biblical religion and spirituality. What does that mean? No one can live out healthy biblical living without having a personal relationship with the Savior and Lord Jesus Christ. In other words, one can abstain from an immoral lifestyle and remain obedient to the Word to experience health. One can be a decent man or woman without being a Christian, and one can also be a Christian without having the qualities of a decent person.

Thirteenth, God is a God of numbers. He loves numbers, pluralism, and a variety of crying voices. He wants his children to call to him as a group in a unity of faith and purpose (2 Chronicles 7:14, 1 Peter 2:9–12). He loves to be the Commander-in-Chief in leading his children to victory in times of trouble. He does this in response to the cries of the righteous. When the presbytery prays, God hears the crying of voices.

In the presbytery crisis prayer ministry, there are no individual intensive practices (works) to restore an individual's health. However, it can be accomplished through faith prayer, sometimes paired with fasting, and by acting in faith on the power and authority (promises) of Jesus Christ (Matthew 16:13–20, 17:2021, Luke 9:1–2, Philippians 2:9, James 5:13–18). Therefore, the church must rise to the challenge and distinguish itself from the pluralistic spiritual and meditation healings that are racking the church as it waits for the return of the undefeated Christ Jesus.

The fourteenth purpose of the book is to call for the church to return to the presbytery crisis prayer ministry, because it is the only divine arrangement equipped to deal with the curse of sin and disease in human history.

The Bible says that Jesus took our curse to become the righteousness of God (2 Corinthians 5:21). God made Christ, who knew no sin—in other words, he lived a sinless life here on the earth—to sin on our behalf so that we might become the righteousness of God in him. Christ became our complete curse of sin so that we can have absolute morality, redemption from sin, sickness, and eternal death.

I think it's high time we questioned why the church has embraced two of the threefold ministries of Christ, preaching and teaching, while the healing ministry appears to be theologically AWOL in many local churches. Nevertheless, we see crisis members wandering like sheep without a shepherd, in search of greener pastures to meet their needs. There can be little wonder that traditional healing and naturopathy have received such incredible attention worldwide as a significant medical resource for promoting human health. How often do we find true born-again Christian mental health professionals who engage in humanistic therapies for healing instead of trusting Christ for their total healing? Such humanistic therapies include yoga, mindfulness, acupuncture, and visiting aliens for religious and spiritual healing.

Fifteenth, the church is at a crossroads regarding the root of disease, suffering, and the role of the PCPM in human healing and health. It is disturbing to know that scientific medical practitioners and the non-Christian community have confused the Christian faith with humanistic religion and spirituality. As a result, there is a growing interest in training medical professionals to take over and provide for the spiritual needs of patients in clinics and hospitals. We seeing this happening because the church has either ignored, abandoned, neglected, or disobeyed their calling to the healing ministry of our Lord Jesus Christ.

History teaches us that modern scientific medicine started in the church. The early church provided a holistic ministry to meet the need of the total man. However, current scientific medicine has discovered that a person's effective healing must include spiritual care, because nothing can replace healing faith and dependence on the Supreme Being.

The European health sector is already looking for ways to integrate religion and spirituality into clinical practice. The first European Conference on Religion, Spirituality, and Health (ECRSH) was held on May 1–3, 2008. One of the main aims of the endeavor was to

> promote general awareness among researchers, scholars, and medical professionals of the importance of religion and spiritual issues for the human being in all aspects of health, disease, and suffering, and to work toward inclusion… practice in all health professions… For scientific exchange over questions of religion and spirituality concerning matters of health and disease.[5]

Sixteenth, a church's spiritual leadership must de-emphasize hierarchical pursuit and love for wealth and give the Holy Spirit a chance to lead his church. The progressive mission of the local church presbytery must be allowed to blossom into flame. The Holy

---

5. René Hefti and Arndt Büssing, *Integrating Religion and Spirituality into Clinical Practice: Conference Proceedings* (Basel, Switzerland: MDPI AG, 2018), xi.

Spirit must illuminate and lead the church because currently the business of the church is permeated with competition and carnality. This power struggle darkens the Holy Spirit's enlightenment and kills the presbytery's spiritual clarity and ability to function in the spiritual gifts.

To this end, I have been trained as a member of the evangelical clergy. Honestly, some biblical scholars will say that I am out of my mind and my writings are heretical in emphasizing the role of the presbytery ministry. No! I am biblically minded and theological persuaded, calling on the church to teach about James's instruction on healing and practically obey his injunction.

The church's practical obedience will save its members from seeking counterfeit faith healing. The church, especially genuine spiritually circumcised members of the community, must endeavor to teach the distinction that not all faith prayer focuses on the faithful Triune God. The church must understand that it is not wise to train medical professionals who don't even believe in the existence of the divine to offer spiritual and religious care. Neither do some medical professionals acknowledge the authenticity of the Triune God! Instead their practices are based solely on human speculation, philosophy, and teaching about the creature rather than the Creator. These teachings attempt to diminish the power and authority of the sinless Christ, the Lord of lords, King of kings, and Savior of humanity.

And finally, seventeenth, recall that the Great Commission focuses on the preaching, teaching, and healing ministries handed down to the church. There are about ninety-nine Great Commission verses and about ninety-three healing verses in the Bible. Reading them carefully, we will find that Christ has granted his authority and power to born-again believers to do four things: save, heal, deliver, and disciple/teach in righteousness and maturity.

## CHAPTER TWO
# God's Eternal Structuring Plan for Healthy Humanity

*The reason the Son of God appeared was to destroy the devil's work.*
(1 John 3:8)

THIS CHAPTER WILL lay out three fundamental truths about God's divine structuring plan for enjoying a healthy relationship with humanity.

First, his goal has always been to protect humanity's well-being, not only for this life but also for eternity. Second, he not only created man in his glory but also wanted man to be dependent on him for his entire existence. Isaiah wrote:

> *Remember this and consider, recall it to mind, you transgressors, remember the former things of old; for I am God, and there is no other; I am God, and there is none like me, declaring the end from the beginning and from ancient times things not yet done, saying, "My counsel shall stand, and I will accomplish all my purpose," calling a bird of prey from the east, the man of my counsel from a far country. I have spoken, and I will bring it to pass; I have purposed, and I will do it.* (Isaiah, 46:8–11 RSV)

When man's disobedience and sin thwarted God's divine plan, he devised another divine plan to restore the lost relationship and reconcile man to himself (2 Corinthians 5:18). To bring God's plan into fruitfulness, Christ became a redemptive intermediary. Christ has the authority and power to destroy any ungodly thing the devil puts in the way to prevent the fulfillment of God's plan. He has been diligently faithful to bring his plans to pass.

We will describe, first, God's plans for developing a perfectly healthy state for humanity. Second, we will describe God's descriptive plan for man's healthy relationship amid the corruption of this perfect condition. Third, we will explore God's extended plan for restoring man's healthy relationship in the eternal future.

## I. GOD'S PLAN TO DEVELOP A PERFECTLY HEALTHY STATE FOR HUMANITY

Shaw defines God's eternal decree for the community in the Westminster Confession of Faith in these words:

> God from all eternity did by the wisest and holy counsel own will freely and unchangeably ordain whatever comes to pass, yet so, as thereby

neither is God the author of sin, nor is violence offered to the will of the creatures; nor is the liberty or contingency of second causes taken away, but rather established.[6]

God created man in a perfect state for his glory. Thus, man is the only creature endowed with God's characteristics—namely, his image and likeness. As an image and likeness of God (Genesis 1:2), man was created in perfect health and was not subject to death. Therefore, God intends the relationship between himself and this created human being to be perfect and glorious.

The denial of this timeless truth is the bedrock of scientific misery and distortion. It is akin to taking a U-turn from human attention and dependency on the Creator of the heavens and the earth to human self-centeredness and self-dependence. Such a denial tosses God out of the center of human affairs and identifies man's pride and intellectual inadequacy as the solution to human misfortune, affliction, and death.

This denial is the first and most common human fallacy concerning man's destiny. God is relegated to being a kind of remote control while human scientific intelligence is placed at the center. The Bible teaches that *"Christ is the power of God and the wisdom of God. This foolish plan of God is wiser than the wisest of human plans, and God's weakness is stronger than the greatest of human strength"* (1 Corinthians 1:24–25, NLT). If Christ is taken out of the equation, human intellect and knowledge become puffed up.

## GOD PLANS THE ETERNAL FOR HEALTHY HUMANITY

In the divine mind, the Godhead never intended for man to exist in an unhealthy environment or state of mind, functioning in a harmful physical, mental, social, or spiritual lifestyle. There is no seed of imperfection in the character and nature of God.

Instead he intended man to live in a state of absolute perfection. He wanted to have a relationship and fellowship with these perfect and uncorrupted beings, whom he had made to bear his image and like-minded character. He created human beings for his glory (Isaiah 43:7).

His single principal purpose for creating man was for them to worship and fellowship with God. Still, man failed to achieve that purpose because of their disobedience to God's holy standard (Genesis 3).

**God creates man with divine attributes.** The Bible declares, *"And God saw everything that he had made, and behold, it was very good"* (Genesis. 1:31 ESV).

---

6. Robert Shaw, *The Reformed Faith: An Exposition of the Westminster Confession of Faith* (Crossville, TN: Puritan Publications, 2011), 5.

Charles John Ellicott's commentary on Genesis 1 states that the making of man was meant to show that the work of creation had reached its perfection and goal.[7] Although the full understanding of God's perfection, goodness, image, and likeness is beyond complete human comprehension, humans do possess some unique characteristics of God.

The Bible describes man as having been perfect before the fall. However, he did not have a sinless nature, nor was he incapable of committing sin. Man's perfected components include his possession of God's image and likeness; thus, man is a rational being.

Most Bible commentators and Old Testament scholars view humans as also having the ability to rule and possess spirit, the consciousness of reason, the free will of choice, and self-consciousness in functioning and interacting with the physical universe.

In his article, one evangelical theologian describes what it means that God created humans in his own image.[8]

While having God's likeness involves man's external and internal nature, which are moral powers, men also have the ability to self-progress, self-reason, attain holiness, and engage in sin (1 John 3:9). As the God of freedom, he wanted man to have the freedom to make his own decisions. Yes, man was created free from disobedience and sin; he was also free to reject perfection and choose imperfection. Sin and disease are direct products of man's negative choices and imperfect state.

**Man's sinful actions contaminate God's deposited attributes.** Man was not inhabited by imperfection until he misused his own freedom and chose against the imputed image and likeness of God within him.

Robinson helps us to understand that God instituted humanity as a perfect creation. He observes that between Genesis 2 and Revelation 21, the earth became corrupted, broken, out of kilter, and filled with people and forces that worked against God's perfect purposes for humanity.[9]

Genesis 1–2 demonstrate that creation, according to biblical records, was at that time excellent. Again, mankind was not unable to sin; rather, they were living out the characteristics of God's image and likeness in the cursed universe.

**God's relationship with man is disconnected.** Genesis 3–12 was a period of complete disconnection of personal relationships between God and man. God's Spirit

---

7. Charles John Ellicott, *Ellicott's Commentary on the Whole Bible, Volume VI* (Eugene, OR: Wipf and Stock, 2015).

8. Wayne Gruden, *Systematic Theology: An Introduction to Biblical Doctrine* (Grand Rapids, MI: Zondervan, 1994), 442–450.

9. J.A.T. Robinson, "Doubts About Doubts: Honest to God Forty Years On." *Journal of Anglican Studies*, 2016, 181–196.

and humanity' spirits were disconnected. There was life and existence in both, but the functional relationship was lifeless.

The Bible teaches that God is Spirit (John 4:24). He is without physical appearance, biological material, or animated form. Nevertheless, his substance is unseen, untouchable, observable, understandable, livable, impactable, and experienceable.

Man has three components—spirit, soul, and body (1 Thessalonians 5:23). God created man (and woman) in God's image and likeness, being immortal, righteous, holy, absolute beautiful and intelligent, pure, and perfect in his spirit, soul, and body (Genesis 1:26, 5:1–2).

However, man's disobedience contaminated his spirit, soul, and body in the church age. Still, a believer shall have their spirit, soul, and body transformed into perfection again before entering the new kingdom of Christ, which is mankind's eternal future state (Revelation 21:1–4).

Seth was born into the fallen world bearing Adam's image and likeness (Genesis 5:3). Since then, every human has borne Adam's image and likeness, as opposed to God's image and likeness. This has resulted in contamination, self-centeredness, self-rule, self-control, a carnal lifestyle, and sinful intellectual delusion (Psalm 51:5). It represented a move from an affliction-free life to an affliction-dominated life.

Adam Clarke's biblical commentary states,

> He (Adam) had now sinned and consequently had lost his moral resemblance to his Maker. He has also become mortal through his breach of the law. Therefore, his Image and Likeness were widely different at this time from what they were before, and his begetting children in this Image imply that they were imperfect like himself, sinful and corrupt.[10]

At the end of this chapter, we will discuss the effects of this personal disconnection with God on the human body, soul, and spirit.

**Man turns to a self-made god to satisfy his thirst for fellowship, relationship, and worship of the supernatural.** God wired in man the desire for fellowship, relationship, and worship with the Creator as a spirit-deposited being. Since the fall of man, however, we read that Adam continued to uphold righteousness while he feared, fellowshipped, and worshipped God. Why did he do this? Because the Spirit of God was still a dominant part of his human existence.

---

10. Adam Clarke, "Clarke's Notes on the Bible, Genesis 5," *Study Light*. Date of access: June 14, 2020 (https://www.studylight.org/commentaries/eng/acc/genesis-5.html).

Although successive generations were born in Adam's image and likeness (Genesis 5:3), the trace of godly righteousness within them continued until the call of Abram in Genesis 12. In this period, we read of holy men like Enoch, Methuselah, and Noah who profoundly lived out the righteousness of God until the explosion of mankind's wickedness in Genesis 6.

At this time, God became disgusted when the sons of God took human wives. He completely removed his abiding, enabling, and protecting spirit from man's affairs: *"My Spirit shall not abide in man forever, for he is flesh: his days shall be 120 years"* (Genesis 6:2–3, ESV). This act of God led to the multiplication of human affliction through Satan and his radical attacks. The blessings inherent to living for hundreds of years upon the earth came to an end.

Therefore, no matter how far modern medicine develops, man's existence in the world is only as good as 120 years. During this lifespan, a man spends his daily life fighting disease, sickness, and pain, seeking to gain health until death parts him from the earth.

After God let go of his abiding spirit in man, man's acts of wickedness became a way through which they related with other creatures: *"The Lord saw that the wickedness of man was great in the earth, and that every intention of the thoughts of his heart was only evil continually"* (Genesis 6:5, ESV).

From this text, we can see that human affliction will only increase until the rapture of the church. Until then, evil, violence, corruption, disease, and destruction will continue to afflict man until he dies.

As men continued to focus on his own independence, he became even more self-centered (Genesis 11:4–5). However, from Seth to Noah, God had been working to restore man to himself and his glory.

Genesis 11 shows that mankind continued to drift further from a relationship with God. Therefore God caused their language to be confused, and from this point seeds of racism, tribalism, and language superiority began to grow.

Since man lost the opportunity to experience the righteousness, fellowship, and worship of God, he turned instead to intermediaries to reach the divine, creating gods to worship and satisfy his spiritual yearning. He also looked unto them for remedy when dealing with affliction and human pain. With God out of the picture, man's ego took prominence.

**With Abram, God revisits his eternal perfect plan for humanity.** Before the call of Abram, humanity had turned its devotion to the worship of spirits (fallen angels), deities, images, and creatures such as the sun, moon, and stars.

Biblical history shows that from Adam to Noah, man's blessings had been declared and made perfect by Yahweh. He blessed man with all creation, multiplication, and fruitfulness. To the human first family, the Bible said:

> *And God blessed them, and God said unto them, Be fruitful, and multiply, and replenish the earth, and subdue it: and have dominion over the fish of the sea, and over the fowl of the air, and over every living thing that moveth upon the earth.* (Genesis 1:28 KJV).

Man lost its understanding of the nature and characteristics of God, the divine connection no longer existing. The only appealing objects to humanity's carnal mind and understanding were the sun, moon, and stars, which in his mental and spiritual view corresponded to Yahweh.

After the fallen man fell into a state of physical, mental, and spiritual disorder, his will, mind, emotions, understanding, and focus became deformed and impaired. These disorders affected his thinking and decision-making about God. As a result, he worshipped creatures in place of the Creator, unable to see and perceive God. He instead embraced what he could see, touch, and refer to. Therefore, he perceived the level of righteousness, worship, and relationship between man and idols, deities, and images based on his own human intellectualism, his scope of knowledge and wisdom limited to the Adamic image and likeness passed down to him. The sun, moon, and stars—and perhaps certain beasts and reptiles—were probably the most appealing creatures he could worship as God's representatives.

In Genesis 12, we read about God's plan to revisit his eternal, perfect relationship with man.[11] Peter J. Fast reveals that during the time of Abram, when he was growing up in his father's house, Mesopotamia made thousands of gods, with each city having its chief or central god.

The city of Ur, which many biblical scholars believe was the birthplace of Abram, was a prosperous city, not only in superior culture and wealth but also in the practice and worship of idols. Claude Mariottini writes that Ur was a renowned city in antiquity, a city with a history of several religious structures and royal mausoleums that provided hordes of artifacts manufactured in gold, silver, and lapis lazuli. He establishes that archaeological excavations have discovered two important religious structures that help us to understand the religious life during the period when Abram was called. The first of these is the temple of Sin, the moon god. Sin was the patron god of the city of Ur. Second is the temple tower of the ziggurat, which had three ramps with steps that led worshipers to the sanctuary on top, where the people offered sacrifices to the gods.[12]

---

11. Peter J. Fast, "Abraham: From Ur to Haran," *Peter J. Fast*. May 14, 2012 (https://peterjfast.wordpress.com/2012/05/14/abraham-from-ur-to-haran).

12. Claude Mariottini, "Ur and Haran: Abraham's Background." *Biblical Illustrator*, Fall 1997, 50–53.

Scripture states that there was idol worship when God called Abram, and his descendants worshipped manufactured images:

> *If there is found among you, within any of your towns that the Lord your God is giving you, a man or woman who does what is evil in the sight of the Lord your God, in transgressing his covenant, and has gone and served other gods and worshiped them, or the sun or the moon… and if it is true and certain that such an abomination has been done in Israel… and you shall stone that man or woman to death with stones.* (Deuteronomy 17:2–5, ESV)

> *Joshua said to all the people, "This is what the Lord, the God of Israel, says: 'Long ago your ancestors, including Terah the father of Abraham and Nahor, lived beyond the Euphrates River and worshiped other gods.'"* (Joshua 24:2, NIV)

Although Abram's father, Terah, served and worshipped other gods, we do not know whether Abram was serving and worshipping other gods when God called him.

However, the Abrahamic call is critical to the monotheistic faith upon which James asks the presbytery to address the problem of afflicted church members. Abram was called out from a polytheistic religious tradition to distinguish Yahweh from man's understanding of God-centric faith to man's knowledge of polycentric religion. God handpicked Abram and placed him among the Canaanites to restore man's monotheistic faith in the Creator.

Abram's faith in God resulted in a statement of God's imputed righteousness, the bedrock of every Christian's faith in Christ and authority and the power of the presbytery's role in healthy church ministry. Faith is the key to creating a relationship with the Creator. Creation exists by faith (Joshua 24:2–3).

The divine call of Abram introduces five types of healing approaches practiced in our world today. These are: traditional/herbal, religious and spiritual, mental health/psychological treatment, modern scientific, and the PCPM. These five healing traditions will be discussed in detail in Chapters Five through Nine.

*Man's body.* The body harbors his spirit and soul and provides for his physical identity—body size, strength, and color. We see, touch, speak, and interact daily through the body, which contains organs and structures through which the spirit and soul carry out their functions. The function of the soul and spirit determines the existence of the body. When the operations of the body cease, it is considered dead.

Writer Timothy Conway has discussed the subject of enlightened spirituality as it relates to religion and spirituality and their functions pertaining to humanity. However, these functions cannot be accurate when considered against Christian faith and biblical teaching. However, Conway's detailed description of a human's physical components is superb. For example, he provides a detail analysis of what the body consists of:

> ...the body is this fleshy, bony "thing" that we awaken to each morning. We wash it and brush its teeth, we walk, drag or drive it around through the day to the various places we need to go, we (hopefully) give it adequate exercise, we shovel (hopefully) healthy food and liquids into it, we let it relieve itself of accumulated wastes. We might allow it various forms of pleasure (ranging from nature walks to ecstatic dancing to massages and other delights, depending on one's fancies). Finally, we lay it down to rest at night in sleep. For too many doctors, the body is coldly viewed as merely a biochemical machine, needing to be fixed when it breaks down (usually by pumping drugs into it or invading it with surgery, chemotherapy, radiation—such interventions often quite helpful, even life-saving, but also far too often an inappropriate way of dealing with the roots of the problems). From a mercenary point of view, the body is just a skinbag of water (comprising two-thirds of the body), plus carbon, calcium and other materials...
>
> But now, from a more "up close" biological viewpoint, the body is this utterly marvelous, living assemblage of exquisite organ systems, whose simultaneous, relatively-smooth functioning is a major miracle. Consider this: what is the fantastic Power that fertilized a pinpoint-sized egg cell in mama's womb and grew it for nine months into a fetus— unfolding 10,000 generations of genetic memory, and differentiating this single little cell into various kinds of cells such as muscle cells, nerve cells, blood cells, and so forth? What is the Intelligent Power that then brought this organism from the womb into the world, since which time it has grown from infancy into childhood into its present adult form of about five or six feet tall, comprised of some 75 trillion cells for the average body (155 pounds)? Incidentally, the configuration of these approximately 75 trillion cells is rather unusual: only about 3.4 trillion cells are tissue cells, and another 31.5 trillion cells are native non-tissue cells, mainly in the form of erythrocyte red blood

cells (~28.5 trillion), plus platelet cells, white blood cells, lymphocytes, macrophages, and other reticuloendothelial cells. Beyond all these native cells, our bodies contain, on average, about 40 trillion foreign cells, mostly bacteria in our colon?[13]

This is an incredibly detailed description of the human body, the aspect of man that modern medicine dominates since most disease, affliction, and pain exists here. No earthly power could have engineered this complex design other than the Creator of the universe. The false power of evolution could not have created such cells. The complexity of the human body is beyond the human mind to understand and points to the Creator, the supernatural God.

It is also important to note that the human body contains trillions of bacteria and colon cells. Because the human body is a broken and fallen system, disease attacks and drives it towards pain and death. Presbytery righteous prayer can reverse an unhealthy situation in the body, cure the sickness, and heal the spiritual condition, if any exists.

*Man's spirit.* This is the immaterial domain which enables man to exercise God's image and likeness. The spirit allows man to relate with God's Spirit. The spirit is life.

There was in the garden a tree of life and knowledge and evil—I call it a tree of the soul—which had the power to break man's relationship with God. It activated the wickedness and evil that has led to disease, sickness, and death.

God has always related with man through his spirit, because the spirit *is* a person. So when man sinned against God's Spirit, the holy personality of God could not relate to the impure spirit of man. As a result, man's spirit lost connection, fellowship, and relationship with God.

On the other hand, the connection between God's Spirit and Adam's spirit made worshipping the Creator possible. The acceptable must be done in spirit and truth:

> *But the time is coming—indeed it's here now—when true worshipers will worship the Father in spirit and in truth. The Father is looking for those who will worship him that way. For God is Spirit…* (John 4:23–24, NLT)

*Man's soul.* This is another immaterial domain. Every aspect of a man centers on his soul.

---

13. Timothy Conway, "What Do We Mean by 'Body-Mind-Soul-Spirit'?" *Enlightened Spirituality*. Date of access: June 13, 2020 (https://www.enlightened-spirituality.org/Body-Mind-Soul-Spirit.html).

An article for *Compelling Truth* writes that the breath of God is the power and life of God through his Spirit.[14] Although man's creation inhibited God's characteristics, man has possessed the life of God in his physical body while he lives. We know that disease, sickness, and pain may hurt man's spirit and soul—stealing joy and happiness and blocking rational decision-making—but they will only kill the body (Jeremiah 38:16).

The soul enables humans to connect with other creations in the universe, connect for eternal existence, and connect with God's Spirit. All the functions of humanity's earthly characteristics operate in the church age within the realm of the soul, making humans fit with the rest of creation. Only the human soul and spirit do not come from creation; they are part of the Creator. God created all things, but the human soul is the transferred part of God. God created the human body, which will suffer and die, but the soul lives forever.

The human soul is the source of every human operation. The knowledge of good and evil exists and functions in the soul's domain (Genesis 2:16–17). Man's soul uses the brain to coordinate and process all our life-given God's gifts, whereas the brain coordinates all the physical components, controlling the function of eyes, ears, hairs, bones, mouth, as well as the sexual organs, all internal organs, the hands and fingers, the legs and toes, the nails and different layers of skin, veins, vessels, etc. They all function by divine connection for the Creator's glory, meeting a person's physical needs. The brain acquires information and processes it so the human can make behavioral choices based on right and wrong.

The human's ability to feel emotions, endure pain, and make decisions is determined by God's breath in the soul. Disease and pain exists because the broken soul is alive. Material disease only harbors within the material body. God created the tree of the knowledge of good and evil to function within the realm of the soul.

All a human's faculties—the heart, the mind, the conscience—are instruments allowing for proper operation of the soul in the universe. The soul also has the power to choose or reject the offer of redemption. A person's acts of obedience or disobedience operate in the chamber of the soul. In other words, it is possible to understand physical, psychological, and spiritual matters because of the power of intellect, awareness, and experience, all of which are stored in the computer of the human soul.

The body is the frame, and the soul is the content. The cup has no value if not for its precious content. A human's living soul—the breath of God—connects them with other living and non-living creations in the universe, as well as with the immaterial God.

---

14. "The Breath of Life: What Is It?" *Compelling Truth*. Date of access: June 23, 2020 (https://www.compellingtruth.org/breath-of-life.html).

The human body is essential and valuable so long as the breath of God exists within it. Humans cease to be human when the breath of God ceases to exist in the human frame. The Bible does not answer the question of how a man will profit if he gains the whole world (bodily matters) and loses his soul (Luke 9:25).

## GOD PLANS THE ORIGIN OF HUMANITY'S LIVING SOUL

**Eternity past.** Secular historians have described the notion of "eternity past" as prehuman history. These non-biblical sources define prehistory as the time before written history, before the beginning of the universe, or before the beginning of living things existing on the earth.[15]

However, biblical scholars do not ask certain types of question. Was there a civilization on the earth before humans? Was there a prehistory before the written human record? Did another advanced species exist on the earth before humans? The Bible reveals that nothing existed outside the creation record before humans. Therefore, there are no prehistorical written records. Genesis 1 unveils the beginning of man's history, and Revelation 21 reveals its end. God alone knows the entirety of history.

Paul clearly identifies believers' blessing in Christ, writing, *"For he chose us in him before the creation of the world to be holy and blameless in his sight"* (Ephesians 3:4, NIV). God created the world, and creation began with Adam and Eve, the first human parents (Genesis 1–2).

**Breath of God.** Man's physical existence begins with God breathing into man's earthly form, a lifeless body. The breath of God is the beginning of man's existence. It is the source of man's life, thoughts, and feelings. God's breath transforms man into a living soul.

The body is untransformed, suffers in this life, and then dies. It experiences suffering and pain because it is earthly and only harbors the soul, which allows for all possible human experience. Without the soul, the human body cannot have a relationship with the universe; therefore, it would have no experience of disease, suffering, or pain—and it would have no need for healing.

We have established that the human soul is eternal because it connects to God. This eternal redemption is not about the sinful human body but the aspect of God that is part of man, the soul. The soul functions in the body through three domains: conscience, heart, and mind. These three components are windows through which disease, suffering, and pain enter the body because the body contacts the cursed universe. Man's experience

---

15. Brian Fagan, *World Prehistory: A Brief Introduction*, Seventh Edition (Hoboken, NJ: Prentice Hall, 2007); and Colin Renfrew, *Prehistory: The Making of the Human Mind* (New York, NY: Modern Library, 2009).

of disease, affliction, and pain exists because of the interaction of the mortal body with the sinful and broken world.

**Human soul domain.** We have also established that man lives in God's image and likeness. These allow a man to assess, coordinate, analyze, and implement experiences with the physical universe. Man relates to the material or physical world through the conscience, heart, and mind.

*Conscience.* Human virtues reside in man's conscience. Habiger believes that the conscience—the virtue that firm attitudes, stable dispositions, and habitual perfections of intellect—will govern an individual's actions, order their passions, and guide their conduct according to reason and faith.[16] It is the human component that controls one's right and wrong choices. It is the seat of man's character. It is the human response to forgiveness, love, patience, honesty, belief, faith, religion, spirituality, diligence, anger, hatred, relationship, selfishness, greed, morality, justice, dependency, perception, and trust in a higher being, the transcendent God.

*Heart.* The heart is the seat of all human emotion, both positively and negatively. It responds to feelings, stress, fear, worry, anxiety, psychosis, substance abuse, depression, disorder, obedience, gratitude, happiness, hope, sadness, confidence, desire, disappointment, appreciation, rebellion, and evil practices. It is the center of emotional control. How a person relates to these behaviors influences their overall health.

*Mind.* The mind is centered in the brain, the analytical center. It assesses, coordinates, analyzes, and implements our experiences, resilience, ability to cope, responses to rules, practice/exercises, cognitive appraisals, judgment, experiential knowledge, accumulation of information, choices, and understanding and interpretation of nature. It provides data, whether positive or negative, to inform our decision-making.

What a human soul does with their cumulative experiences from the domains of the conscience, heart, and mind will influence their well-being. Someone who isn't informed of the Bible may not understand and appreciate the biblical record of the human race, nature, and man's relationship with the Creator, or how this interactive relationship affects human health and existence.

The Bible describes and uses human parts figuratively and metaphorically in the language that helps man to understand his emotions and actions concerning God, the Creator of the universe, as well as fellow human beings. Human parts—like the heart, mind, bowel, and kidney—are used figuratively in the Scriptures (Lamentation 2:11, Psalm 16:7, Mark 12:30, Philippians 2;1).

---

16. Matthew Habiger, "Role of Conscience," *God's Plan for Life*. Date of access: June 3, 2022 (https://www.godsplanforlife.org/teachings/roleofconscience.html).

## GOD ENVISIONED THE DEFEAT OVER AFFLICTION

The period between Genesis 3 and Revelation 21 is a one of human crises and calamities. Revelation 20 reveals that God will, at the world's end, terminate every human affliction, disease, sickness, pain, and deception of the devil.

This period extended to what the Bible describes as the church age.

Then, for a short time, the stressor of human crises and presence of sin shall exist no more (Revelation 20:7–10). God will crown the restoration of the perfect kingdom and remove the saints from the blameworthiness of their nature. There will exist an eternal separation between righteousness and unrighteousness.

John's prophecy reads: *"And the devil, who deceived them, was thrown into the lake of burning sulfur, where the beast and the false prophet had been thrown. They will be tormented day and night for ever and ever"* (Revelation 20:10, NIV).

Revelation 21–22 then describes a return to the state of absolute perfection that was lost.

In Genesis 3, the state of excellence in the world—one in which there was no curse, sickness, or pain—was done away with.

Commentator John Gill writes,

> the first heaven and earth were made chiefly for men, but, on account of the sin of man, the earth was cursed and brought forth thorns and thistles, and both the earth and air, or the heaven, were attended with noxious vapors, and the whole creations were made subject to vanity and corruption.[17]

John revealed,

> *Then I saw "a new heaven and a new earth," for the first heaven and the first earth had passed away, and there was no longer any sea… And I heard a loud voice from the throne saying, "Look! God's dwelling place is now among the people, and he will dwell with them. They will be his people, and God himself will be with them and be their God. 'He will wipe every tear from their eyes. There will be no more death' or mourning or crying or pain, for the old order of things has passed away."* (Revelation 21:1, 3–4, NIV)

---

17. John Gill, "Commentary on Revelation 21," *Study Light*. Date of access: May 1, 2020 (https://www.studylight.org/commentaries/geb/revelation-21.html).

The "old order of things" here clearly references the time of devastation and affliction that took place from the fall of man to the establishment of the New Jerusalem.

*Calvin's Commentary on the Bible* describes the present human condition as "a shadowy life."[18] These biblical texts describe the complete eradication of human bondage—including affliction, sickness, pain, and eventually physical death.

## II. GOD'S EXTENDED PLAN FOR HEALTHY RELATIONSHIP WITH MAN AMIDST THE CORRUPTION OF THE PERFECT CONDITION

### GOD'S HIGHEST CREATION

God created man in his own image and likeness. Man has been given the existential nature of God through God's breath. The five healing approaches mentioned earlier in this chapter are human attempts to solve human problems caused by human disobedience. Human suffering and pain directly result from our first parents' choice. Every godly characteristic imputed to man is affected by that choice. The image and likeness of God is rendered meaningless, functionless, and unproductive without the breath of God in man's lungs, and even the breath of God in human lungs is affected by sin.

Within the breath of God is the life of God in man, the unpolluted and perfect oxygen in human lungs. This God-given oxygen purifies our blood cells and brain, thus allowing us to function.

> *And Jehovah God formed man of the dust of the ground, and breathed into his nostrils the breath of life; and man became a living soul.* (Genesis 2:7, ASV)

If God were to take back his spirit and withdraw his breath, all life would cease and humanity would turn to dust (Job 34:14–15).

All airborne disease results from the effect of sin on God's breath in man's lungs and man's contact with his own cursed physical nature. Examples of breath-related diseases include tuberculosis, COVID-19, and asthma. The church is responsible for reporting any breath-related disease to God. Scientists have said that the best medicine for COVID-19, when no vaccine exists, is "social distancing." Well, the church is responsible for taking everything to God by prayer. He can keep us secure from any virus and heal us of affliction.

We need to appreciate modern medicine, which is a product of our God-given human intelligence. However, nothing should replace trust and prayer in God for healing. Our

---

18. John Calvin, "Commentary on Romans 8," *Study Light*. Date of access: September 8, 2021 (https://www.studylight.org/commentaries/eng/cal/romans-8.html).

world is complicated and many things are happening in it that we need to understand, either theologically or scientifically. The hope and confidence that will keep humanity going can be found when we to the fundamental truth that our world has a Creator, the Controller and Holder of our destiny. Only then can we have a better understanding of pandemics, natural disasters like hurricanes and tornados, war, and hatred. If humanity rejects God, it cannot reject Satan and suffering.

The image of God gives man dominion over all other creatures and qualifies us to spend eternity with the Creator. The spirit and soul of man are extensions of God's Spirit, which enables our communion and fellowship with God. He endowed man with the freedom of self-will to make our own decisions in the cognitive, moral, and social domains.

**Cognitive domain.** The cognitive domain gives man the power of rationalization. He can choose to spend his life in relationship with the Creator and other creatures. Man was created to think, reason and choose a perfected and sinless lifestyle. He also has the freedom to choose an imperfect and sinful lifestyle.

With this freedom, man chose disobedience and disobeyed God's law. He chose wrath and a life of affliction filled with all manner of suffering, and ever since it has served as a legacy passed on to every member of the human race throughout the generations.

Our trust in the authority and power of the Lord Jesus Christ through the PCPM can help us walk through any affliction.

**Moral domain.** Man's moral ability allows him to choose righteousness or unrighteousness, honesty or dishonesty, goodness or wickedness, right or wrong, love or hatred, and to build or destroy. Since creation, this power of choice has been part of humanity. Man can choose life and godly righteousness and live triumphantly in this life and the life to come.

**Social domain.** The social domain gives man the power of entering into relationship with the Creator, humans, and other creatures (Genesis 2:18, 3:8).

MAN'S DISOBEDIENCE THWARTED GOD'S PERFECT PLAN
Why did God the Son come into the world, take human flesh, and become a man? To comprehensively grasp why God took human flesh and lived among humans is to understand the plight of humanity.

In Genesis 3, we find the entrance of humanitarian crises and calamities—sin, suffering, disease, sickness, and death. Man entered into the bondage of sin and death before God the Son became flesh and dwelled among us to free man from that bondage.

> *And the Word became flesh, and dwelt among us (and we beheld his glory, glory as of the only begotten from the Father), full of grace and truth.* (John 1:14, NIV)

Man's sinful nature characterizes human suffering. Afflictions of life and death did not allow him to transform into the image and likeness of God.

Someone spotless needed to provide the antidote for the penalty of sin and death. The blood of Christ is the only antidote good enough and strong enough to transform a man's sinful nature into the new nature and restore fellowship between sinful man and the sinless God.

> *...for this is my blood of the covenant, which is poured out for many for the forgiveness of sins.* (Matthew 26:28 ESV)

One of the classic texts on the suffering of humanity and the divine plan to redeem sinful man is found in Romans 8:18–22:

> *For I consider that the sufferings of this present time are not worthy to be compared with the glory that is to be revealed to us. For the eagerly awaiting creation waits for the revealing of the sons and daughters of God. For the creation was subjected to futility, not willingly, but because of Him who subjected it, in hope that the creation itself also will be set free from its slavery to corruption into the freedom of the glory of the children of God. For we know that the whole creation groans and suffers the pains of childbirth together until now.* (NASB)

This passage lays out humanity's experience living in our corrupted world, as well as the last and absolute redemption from the bondage of corruption and the present affliction in the world. This sets the stage for the revelation and establishment of the functional presbytery prayer, revealed in James 5:13, to minimize the aggression of disease, sickness, and pain in the new covenant dispensation.

Human corruption and affliction were not part of God's original agenda for human well-being (Genesis 1–2, Romans 8:18–22, Revelation 21). Even in the age of affliction, God revealed to James that the PCPM could heal and restore an afflicted individual's health. However, the apostle Peter warned believers to understand that our affliction, whether spiritual, mental, or physical, happen by God's permission, allowing us to experience and share in the suffering of Christ (1 Peter 4:12–16).

In this sense, human affliction is not an act of punishment but an experiential act which is achieved by Christ on the cross. Christ triumphantly came out from his bodily and spiritual affliction and promised us healing and victory in the time of tribulation. God has endowed our spiritual leadership with the ability to judge the power of human ill health.

Interestingly, the earliest literature in the ancient Near East on the subject of treating sickness and ill health shows the practical approach we read in the epistle of James. Ferngren wrote that medical literature in the ancient Near East reveals that sin and evil spirits were the root cause of disease and sickness, and confessions were a critical feature of therapy.[19] The priests, magicians, and exorcists were physicians providing treatment.

James's teachings reveal that the presbytery is healed by the confession of sin, forgiveness, and prayer for healing affliction. Today some Christian mental health practitioners are turning to Buddhist practices such as meditation, yoga, mindfulness, and spiritual awakening instead of turning to the PCPM through the authority and power of healing of living Christ (Philippians 4:9).

## III. GOD'S COMPREHENSIVE PLAN FOR RESTORING MAN'S HEALTHY RELATIONSHIP IN THE IDEAL ETERNAL STATE

### CHRIST'S SUFFERING IS THE MEANS OF RESTORATION

After the corruption of man's perfect state, God came up with another divine plan to restore man's eternal condition for fellowship and glory. He designed a plan to restore his lasting friendship with man by communicating the process through men and women he chose in different generations.

He decided to restore humanity's perfect state through the afflictions of Christ Jesus. The prophetic decorations about the Suffering Servant were the only divine annunciation of his will that could restore man's healthy eternal state. Christ's death has fulfilled the requirement for man's redemption. The prophet Isaiah has summarized Christ's anguish in these words:

> *He was despised and rejected by men, a man of sorrows and acquainted with grief; and as one from whom men hide their faces he was despised, and we esteemed him not.*
>
> *Surely he has borne our griefs and carried our sorrows; yet we esteemed him stricken, smitten by God, and afflicted. But he was*

---

19. Gary B. Ferngren, *Medicine and Religion: A Historical Introduction* (Baltimore, MD: John Hopkins University Press, 2014).

> *pierced for our transgressions; he was crushed for our iniquities; upon him was the chastisement that brought us peace, and with his wounds we are healed.* (Isaiah 53:3–5, ESV)

The Lord Jesus Christ affirms his redemptive mission in Luke 4:18–19:

> *The Spirit of the Lord is upon Me, because He anointed Me to bring good news to the poor. He has sent Me to proclaim release to captives, and recovery of sight to the blind, to set free those who are oppressed...* (NASB)

The Isaiah passage describes Christ as the Suffering Servant who bore all our afflictions on the cross. Isaiah decries the spiritual and physical disease and sickness that is brought into the our lives, including sorrow, grief, pain, wounds, bitterness, bruises, and so forth. Sometimes we are despised and rejected by many due to our ill health. However, the death and resurrection of Christ has provided us with overwhelming victory over the conditions described by Isaiah.

We repeatedly see in Scripture that Christ's mission was the heavenly business of man's freedom from God's wrath. Although the church will not be emancipated from the affliction of sin in this life, the spiritual and physical well-being of the church is an entire heavenly business of freeing man from the works of the devil and restoring man into a perfect eternal relationship with God. He came to set the captives free.

## GOD'S PRESCRIBED PLAN FOR THE RESTORATION OF MAN'S PERFECT ETERNAL STATE

Most of John's writings describe God's plan for restoring man to a perfect and healthy eternal state.

**The plan describes divine prophecy on this perfect eternal state.** Genesis 1–2 explores how God created the world perfect for man. However, Genesis 3 records how these good and perfect things were contaminated, affecting God's relationship with man. Thus, mankind fell into an imperfect and corrupt state dominated by sin and all human affliction.

God has instituted the presbytery to help the church walk through the miseries of life. In the Old Testament, God used the leaders among his chosen people, Israel—including priests, prophets, and rabbis—to handle their afflictions. In the church age, Christ, his disciples, and the presbytery are spiritual instruments used by God to minister to the needs of his afflicted children.

The text of the prophecy is found in Revelation:

> *He who was seated on the throne said, "I am making everything new!" Then he said, "Write this down, for these words are trustworthy and true."*
>
> *…The city does not need the sun or the moon to shine on it, for the glory of God gives it light, and the Lamb is its lamp. The nations will walk by its light, and the kings of the earth will bring their splendor into it. On no day will its gates ever be shut, for there will be no night there. The glory and honor of the nations will be brought into it.* (Revelation 21:5, 23–26, NIV)

**Christ's High Priest ministry will cease.** There is no need for healing prayer in the perfect eternal state. Prayers are channels to carry our worries to God for divine intervention and solution, and the High Priest and our intercessor will be present in the new heaven and a new earth; there will be a complete absence of human affliction (Philippians 4:6–7).

Therefore, there will be no need for fasting and prayer. Jesus said that healthy people do not need a doctor; sick people do. There will be no need to fast and pray in the presence of the most outstanding physician, the Lord Jesus Christ (Luke 5:34).

**The presbytery ministry will be no more.** The presbytery prayer ministry represents the authority and power of Christ in the church age. The Holy Spirit in the presbytery enables the threefold ministries of Christ: preaching for salvation, teaching for spiritual growth and maturity, and healing for the spiritual, mental, and physical well-being of believers. These ministries should be carried out in the church the world is to benefit from Christ's mission.

**Humanity's godly image and likeness will be without sinful nature.** We will have no sinful nature in the perfect eternal state. God will transform his contaminated image and likeness in the resurrected body of Christ. John the Beloved affirmed this perfectly:

> *Beloved, we are God's children now, and what we will be has not yet appeared; but we know that when he appears we shall be like him, because we shall see him as he is.* (1 John 3:2, ESV)

**Our lifestyle will be free of disobedience and the curse because the deceiver of the brethren will no longer have access.** The consequences of sin shall exist no more. The old world and its evils shall be gone forever. Tears of crying, sorrow, pain, and death will be no more (Revelation 21:4). Only the King's fullness of peace, joy, and worship shall dominate the scene.

CHAPTER THREE
# God's Eternal Plan for Implementing Health

*He who did not spare his own Son, but gave him up for us all—how will he not also, along with him, graciously give us all things?* (Romans 8:32, NIV)

## I. GOD'S DIVINE POWER GIVES HUMANITY EVERYTHING PERTAINING TO LIFE AND GODLINESS

WE HAVE ESTABLISHED the fundamental truth about God's positive moral principle in the universe. He planned a divine structure with the sole purpose of the church's total well-being. The implementation of this positive moral principle is summarized in the biblical teaching that *"every good and perfect gift is from above, coming down from the Father of the heavenly lights, who does not change like shifting shadows"* (James 1:17, NIV). This scripture affirms that every intellectual achievement in both scientific medicine and non-scientific healing are perfect gifts from the Creator.

Scientists did not create the world, nor do they thoroughly grasp the human system and how its parts have come together. They are using only a fraction of their God-given intelligence to swim in the ocean of God's indescribable intelligence. Despite a fantastic explosion of knowledge in this generation, intellectuals struggle to wrap their head around discovering the wonders of the earth (Daniel 12:4).

God is the Giver of all good and perfect gifts, from the gift of his only beloved Son for our salvation to the gift of his generosity in the area of human health. One of the best texts about God's excellent character toward his children is found in Matthew 7:11: *"If you, then, though you are evil, know how to give good gifts to your children, how much more will your Father in heaven give good gifts to those who ask him!"* (NIV) All good gifts are God's gifts—physically, mentally, and spiritually.

Scripture establishes that man became a living being or soul when God breathed into his nostril (Genesis 2:27). We have also made it clear that all human disease, affliction, sickness, and pain operates either in the mental or physical domains. Disease exists and torments only within the living soul. The soul coordinates the functions and activities of the human conscience, heart and mind. The soul is also a battleground for living either a healthy or diseased life.

Therefore, human disease and pain will end when a given soul ceases its practice of earthly living. Those who believe in the creation story of Adam and Eve, the first human parents, also believe that the wiring of Adam's soul came with intelligence with the capacity of all human wisdom and intellectual endowment, including every branch of science. Genesis 2:19–20 describes this story about the composition of superior human intelligence.

> *So out of the ground the Lord God formed every animal of the field and every bird of the air and brought them to the man to see what he would call them, and whatever the man called every living creature, that was its name. The man gave names to all cattle and to the birds of the air and to every animal of the field...* (NRSVUE)

Whether the names appear in Hebrew, Greek, Arabic, Aramaic, English, French, Chinese, German, or Jaba, they display God-given superior intelligence. What an incredible divine gift of intelligence God gave humanity! Through this gift, a small percentage of such intelligence, the sciences flourish.

Besides allocating names to all creation, "God created physical beauty, He provided nourishment, not just carbohydrates, fats, proteins, vitamins and minerals but beautiful food, tasty food, 'pleasing to the eye and good for food' (Genesis 2:9)."[20]

All those scientists do is try to discover what God's creation contains, content that Adam, the first human scientist, identified and named. It is interesting to note the way science has been described, which is the intellectual and practical activity of systematically studying the structure and behavior of the physical and natural world through observation and experiment. This system of scientific research can be classified into four major domains: biological science (biology), chemical science (chemistry), physical science (physics), and earthly science (environmental).[21]

Disease is a direct result of biological, chemical, physical, and environmental science. The most influential scientific and medical contributor, Hippocrates, is called the father of medicine. He lived and practiced medicine in the fourth and fifth centuries B.C. and believed that disease occurred naturally and was not due to supernatural influence. He concluded that natural forces within us are the true healers of disease.[22]

## II. BRIEF ANALYSIS OF THE ORIGIN OF SIN, DISEASE, AND TREATMENTS

It is critical to understand that humanity has been overwhelmed with affliction, that the Bible clearly explains how it all began, and why pain lies at the heart of mankind's condition. The historical discussion pits religion and science against each other, but this gets it wrong; religion and science both concern the creation (in the context of biblical

---

20. Harvey A. Elder, *A Biblical Perspective on Disease, Health, and Healing* (Juan Dolio, Dominican Republic: Institute for Christian Teaching, 2000).

21. "The Definition of Science," *Science Made Simple*. Date of access: April 26, 2023 (https://www.sciencemadesimple.com/science-definition.html).

22. Saugat Adhikari, "Top 12 Contributions of Hippocrates," *Ancient History Lists*. September 2, 2022 (https://www.ancienthistorylists.com/people/top-contributions-hippocrates).

records), not the Creator. Religion and science continue to search for an understanding of the universe, including humanity's internal networking and functionality.

The Bible teaches that God hates religious and spiritual exercises that focus on the created universe and manufactured intermediaries—such as deities, images, and idols. James A. Fowler puts it this way: "Religion is often characterized by absolutism, authoritarianism and activism, which do not derive from God Himself."[23] He stresses further what the word *religion* can be defined as "to bind up," saying that religion "binds people up in rules and regulations or ritualistic patterns of devotion."[24] It is, essentially, idolatry (Acts 17:22).

In essence, Christianity was never meant to be a religion, and it will never be a religion in the way that twenty-first-century researchers understand that term.

For example, understand that spirituality is not connected to the soul, as understood in the Islamic faith.[25] Rather, spirituality is the dynamic relationship with the risen and historical Lord Jesus indwelling in man.

Granted, men have attempted to force Christianity into the molds and form of religion.[26] It is not enough to conduct polls of people in church pews or on the street as a research approach to determine who is a Christian or what they may believe.

For example, Harold Koening conducted a Gallup poll which indicated that ninety-six percent of Americans believe in God, more than ninety percent pray, sixty-five percent are church members, and forty-three percent had attended religious services within the past weeks.[27]

Researchers McPhetres and Zuckerman write that the general public in the United States, including scientists, may not believe that science and religion conflict. Some evidence to the contrary exists, given the relative cultural importance of religion in the United States. They used phrases like "greater religiosity," "religious people," "nonreligious," and "religious beliefs, identity, and practice" to define Christianity.[28]

---

23. James A. Fowler, J., "God Hates Religion," *Christ In You Ministries*. Date of access: June 28, 2020 (http://www.christinyou.net/pages/godhatesrel.html).

24. Ibid.

25. Mohammad Ateeq, Shazia Jehan, and Riffat Mehmmod, "Faith Healing: Modern Health Care." *The Professional Medical Journal 21(2)*, 2014, 295–301.

26. Fowler, "God Hates Religion."

27. Harold Koenig, "Religion and Medicine I: Historical Background and Reasons for Separation." *International Journal of Psychiatric Medicine 30(4)*, 2000, 385–398.

28. Jonathon McPhetres and Miron Zuckerman, "Religiosity Predicts Negative Attitudes towards Science and Lower Levels of Science Literacy." *PLOS One 13(11)*, November 27, 2018.

But these terms do not describe the essence of Christianity. Their research also reveals a misunderstanding of the relationship between religion and science.

Christian faith cannot be measured on a research scale. Nevertheless, some non-Christian professionals have attempted to measure Christianity and completely exclude the foundation upon which Christianity has been built and grown.

For example, McPhetres and Zuckerman use several items to measure religious beliefs and behavior in measuring religiosity. Is a person confident in the existence of God? How often does the respondent attend religious services? How often do they pray? How religious is a respondent? They also question the strength of the respondent's religious affiliation.[29]

However, they excluded asking questions about fundamentalism and the frequency of non-religious activities at the church. Others question whether the Bible is the literal Word of God and whether a personal God exists.

This kind of research, often performed by non-Christians who don't understand what the Bible teaches, show no appearance of godliness. And the terms they use in their polls—belief in God, prayer, church member, religious services, spirituality, and Christian gatherings—can have ambiguous meanings.

**Belief in God.** A person does not become a Christian simply because they believe in God. Which God does a person believe in? Different religious affiliations use the English word "God," but this does not necessarily refer to the Creator. The word "God" does not always connote Yahweh in the context of Judeo-Christianity. "God," in major world religions, is significantly different from the Christian Godhead.

Satan also believes that God exists and quotes the Bible in the temptation of Jesus Christ (Matthew 4:1). He does not believe or accept that he is evil, not that he should trust God to save himself. However, he is cursed and will spend eternity in hellfire with all those who reject God's offer of a reconciliatory relationship with Him through Jesus Christ (Matthew 25:41).

**Prayer.** All people pray, but to what do they pray?

**Church member.** A person can be a church member without having a personal relationship with the Author and Founder of the Christian church. The church is made up of people; it is not a structure.

**Religion service.** Someone can attend religious services without having anything to do with the practice of Bible-based Christian faith.

**Spirituality.** Someone could be spiritually mature in the demonic. Their mind may be controlled by an evil spirit and have a super religious lifestyle. Nevertheless, such religiosity may not have anything to do with the God who is worshipped in the Christian faith.

---

29. Ibid.

**Christian gatherings.** Many people attend Christian gatherings on a religious basis, thus weakening the acts of God by their faithlessness. Lives dominated by the Spirit of God and lives dominated by demonic spirits operate on different platforms of a man's heart, coordinated by the soul and body.

The Bible questions, in Isaiah 40:13 and 1 Corinthians 2:16, who can know the Lord's mind or thoughts. Christians have the mind to understand the ideas of the Spirit because the Spirit indwells every professed Christian (John 14:17, 1 Corinthians 6:19–20).

On the other hand, non-Christians have natural spirits. They are spiritually dead to spiritual matters until they are quickened or come alive at the invitation of the Holy Spirit. John declares, *"It is the spirit that quickeneth; the flesh profiteth nothing: the words that I speak unto you, they are spirit, and they are life"* (John 6:63, KJV).

Therefore, it is essential not to sweep the Christian faith under the umbrella of religion and spirituality and disregard its effective contribution to human healing.

Interestingly, mental health and medical professionals research the effectiveness of prayer, religion, spirituality, and religiosity on human healing. But they deny the efficacy of prayer; this is entirely out of step with biblical teaching on the subject.

Do many non-Christian researchers know and understand that the Christian God hates religion and spirituality based on human wisdom, philosophy, and trust in created things rather than the Creator? God, in his message to Isaiah and Amos, denounces religiosity and spirituality in the strongest terms:

> *…I have had enough of burnt offerings of rams and the fat of well-fed beasts; I do not delight in the blood of bulls, or of lambs, or of goats.*
> *When you come to appear before me, who has required of you this trampling of my courts? Bring no more vain offerings; incense is an abomination to me. New moon and Sabbath and the calling of convocations—I cannot endure iniquity and solemn assembly. Your new moons and your appointed feasts my soul hates; they have become a burden to me; I am weary of bearing them. When you spread out your hands, I will hide my eyes from you; even though you make many prayers, I will not listen; your hands are full of blood.* (Isaiah 1:11–15, ESV)

> *I hate, I reject your festivals, nor do I delight in your festive assemblies… Take away from Me the noise of your songs; I will not even listen to the sound of your harps.* (Amos 5:21, 23, NASB)

## A PERFECT WORLD WITHOUT SIN AND DISEASE (GENESIS 1–2)

In Chapter Two, we discussed the fact that our universe is not an accidental occurrence. A Supernatural Being controls the existence of the universe and all its content. That Supernatural Being, according to the Bible, is the Creator.

The Bible establishes that the Creator created everything perfectly, including Adam and Eve. The detailed record of this ideal creation, without sin and disease, can be found in Genesis 1–2, as well as elsewhere in the Bible.

Evolutionists and atheists do not believe in the biblical creation record, which is okay. Their stand does not overrule the truth of the biblical record on the cause of human problems.

## THE PERFECT WORLD IS CURSED, STAINED BY MAN'S DISOBEDIENCE (GENESIS 3:1–11)

We have also discussed that disease directly results from man's disobedience; thus, man's disobedience introduced a curse into the perfect world. Genesis 3:1–11 provides a vivid description of the cause of human misery and pain.

Harold Elder acknowledges that sin is not a broken part of our personhood, distorted behavior, or cognitive disorder; it's another name for a person to go their "own way" (Isaiah 53:6).[30] Sin is all about trusting the self instead of trusting God. It breaks our fellowship with God.

Although sin broke God's fellowship with man, God didn't sever his relationship from humanity or his desire for their love and well-being (2 Corinthians 4:4). Nonetheless, mankind's act of disobedience lifted man's pain- and disease-free state, replacing it with one filled with disease and pain.

Since God declared a curse on his perfect creation, including man, disease and pain have indwelled man on his earthly journey.

## CREATION SUFFUSED WITH REBELLION AND DISEASE, MAKING LIFE HARD (GENESIS 3:12)

Human suffering is a direct consequence of man's rebellion, for every part of creation has been affected by the curse of disobedience. God cut off his supervisory relationship with mankind and drove them out of the city of perfect creation, the Garden of Eden, into the broken world of misery ruled by Satan. God removed his excellent protection over human affairs, and ever since that time the dominance of disease and pain has continued to increase.

---

30. Elder, *A Biblical Perspective on Disease, Health, and Healing*.

Bob Deffinbaugh explains that man's willful disobedience has not only brought disease and discomfort to humanity but also rampant crime, cruelty, corruption, and injustice.[31] This description fits the structure of James's presbytery crisis prayer because it effectively deals with the fallen man's spiritual and physical problems.

Deffinbaugh notes further that pollution, nuclear waste, the disintegration of the ozone layer, acid rain, and a host of other maladies are bringing the earth to the brink of disaster. Continental drift and climate change are increasingly apparent in the twenty-first century.

The scientific world now understands the reality of the prophetic declaration on global warming. The problem of drought, warmer temperatures, lack of rain, and greater suffering are not new phenomena in the biblical record. In Genesis 3, God talked about cursing the original design of creation. The fall of the first human parents ruined the foundation of the pure and perfect universe.

God controls the climate and every other condition of the earth (2 Chronicles 7:13). The ecological composition and function of the universe are God's prerogative. Paul writes,

> *For the creation was subjected to futility, not willingly, but because of him who subjected it, in hope that the creation itself will be set free from its bondage to corruption and obtain the freedom of the glory of the children of God.* (Romans 8:20–21, ESV)

God withdrew from men his plan of perfect existence when man turned to independence to deal with the menace of disease and pain. Throughout the Hebrew Bible, known to us as the Old Testament, human affliction refers to the retribution for sin, especially in the Torah and books of the minor prophets.

However, the reader will find prescriptive conditions for building relationships that abide—if you do this, I will do that; if you do not, I will not allow that, etc. Some legal prescriptive in Deuteronomy 24:8–9 reads:

> *Guard against an outbreak of a defiling skin disease by being very careful; you shall carefully observe whatever the Levitical priests instruct you, just as I have commanded them. Remember what the Lord your God did to Miriam on your journey out of Egypt.* (NRSVUE)

---

31. Bob Deffinbaugh, "God's Perfect Plan," *Bible.org*. May 17, 2004 (https://bible.org/seriespage/god%E2%80%99s-perfect-plan).

Jesus told the man healed at the pool of Bethesda to be careful how he lived his life: *"See, you are well! Sin no more, that nothing worse may happen to you"* (John 5:14, ESV).

The teaching that sin is a cause of disease, sickness, and pain is not taught only in the Christian faith but even in the religion classified as a "life philosophy."[32]

## MAN SEARCHES FOR SOLUTION TO DISEASE AND DEATH IN THE BROKEN CREATION

Since God created man in his image and likeness, he endowed him with intelligence. After man's banishment from the Garden of Eden, cutting off his relationship with the Creator, man began his own search for a perfectly healthy life in the midst of a broken world. This has been the core religious/spiritual pursuit among humans going back as far as the establishment of Hinduism (1500 B.C. to 500 B.C.)[33] and Buddhism (the fifth century B.C.).[34]

## MAN TURNS TO INDEPENDENCE TO REMEDY HUMAN DISOBEDIENCE

Human independence looks down and searches for perfection amidst creation rather than looking up for divine intervention in its brokenness and calamity. Human wisdom has its limited function, however, because man is limited in knowledge. Disease and pain are penalties of disobedience, but God has not abandoned mankind to total despair.

As a result of man's search for a genuine relationship with God, he introduced himself to self-created gods: religiosity/spirituality. He has used natural means and scientific approaches to healing rather than remaining steadfast to God's remedy for sin and disease through presbytery crisis prayer.

## EVERY TRIBE AND CULTURE DEVISES ITS OWN APPROACH TO HEALING

As descendants of Adam and Eve, God deposited in mankind a superior intelligence. Genesis 9 reveals the renewed covenant made between God and man, filled with abundant blessings. He has given man everything needed to enjoy health and well-being.

---

32. Charity Finch, "Religion and Spirituality in the Treatment of Mental Illness," *Theravive*. March 19, 2015 (https://www.theravive.com/today/post/religion-and-spirituality-in-the-treatment-of-mental-illness-0001844.aspx).

33. Velcia Alston, "Hinduism Goals & Importance," *Study.com*. Date of access: August 4, 2022 (https://study.com/academy/lesson/the-four-goals-of-hindu-life-kama-artha-dharma-moksha.html).

34. Tapas Kumar Aich, "Buddha Philosophy and Western Psychology." *Indian Journal of Psychiatry*, January 2013, 165–170.

Genesis 11 shows us how human society developed its tribal, cultural, and linguistic diversity. Since the scattering of humanity abroad (Genesis 11:4–8), every tribe and culture has devised its own approach to healthy living and dealing with disease and sickness, usually resorting to preventive, reactive, and restorative medicine.

God has always used presbytery to restore health to his people. This godly principle has not changed; we are to cry out to him in times of trouble for divine intervention. Throughout the Old Testament, God used priests and prophets to stand in the gap when it came to the afflictions of his children.

Today, the presbytery is authorized by and empowered in the righteousness of Jesus Christ to function in this role.

## MAN'S SEARCH FOR HEALING THROUGH DEITIES AND SPIRITS

Our dependency on creation apart from the Creator has led to mankind developing many different approaches to human health, including traditional/herbal, religious/spiritual, mental healthcare, modern scientific medicine, and the PCPM healing approach.

Traditional medicine is more appreciated today than ever. To this day, traditional, religious/spiritual, and modern scientific medicine have all grown in their quest to improve humanity's condition.

Unfortunately, the church, whose God has given the mandate and formulated a structure on how to deal with sickness, seems to have neglected its responsibility.

Tacey describes healthcare professionals' improper use of spirituality in treating human health. He asserts that in the 1950s, Australians discussed spiritual issues with priests, ministers, and rabbis. In the 1960s and 70s, secularization overtook the old religious structures, which lost their authority. He stresses further that secular society does not consider the spirit and soul, and now those components of man instead fall to the healing and health of scientific professionals.[35]

The problem is that many of these professionals have no training in spiritual matters and are flying blind. As a result, professionals need more training to address important spiritual health issues.

In supporting this critique, several researchers[36] have revealed the severe need for spiritual care by patients and their family members. When a patient has a spiritual need,

---

35. David Tacey, "Spiritual Connectedness and Healing." *Psychotherapy and Counselling Journal of Australia 3(1)*, July 1, 2015.

36. Yanli Hu, Miaorui Jiao, and Fan Li, "Effectiveness of Spiritual Care Training to Enhance Spiritual Health and Spiritual Care Competency Among Oncology Nurses." *BMC Palliative Care 18*, 2019; and Susan Thrane, "Hindu End of Life: Death, Dying, Suffering, and Karma." *Journal of Hospice and Palliative Nursing*, November-December 2010.

medical personnel must show concern for and satisfy those needs, and such issues must receive more attention in the practice of nursing.

The chief obstacle to effective spiritual care in nursing is insufficient preparation for this role because of inadequate education. These practitioners lack an understanding of Christianity and the spiritual wisdom of Christ.

Hu, Jiao, and Li seem to understand spiritual health as

> the state of an individual's affirmation of the meaning of his or her own life; understanding and affirmation of the value of oneself, and others, and the environment; the ability to connect harmoniously with others and the environment; the possession of inner resources and strength; and ability to adapt to adversity.[37]

This description of spiritual well-being may not apply to an atheist healthcare professional or the spiritual well-being of an atheist patient who believes that life is nothing but a mirage with no connection with any transcendent spiritual being.

Another writer, Susan Thrane, stresses that more than one million practicing Hindus live in the United States. To effectively provide healthcare for them, and to provide culturally sensitive care, health workers must have a good knowledge of the tenets of Hinduism. In addition, to the Hindu faith, she acknowledges that family and community interconnectedness, karma, and reincarnation are significant beliefs. Karma combines a cosmic and moral cause-and-effect principle that can apply to a human soul across lifetimes, with lessons being learned to attain spiritual growth. As a Hindu, Thrane emphasizes that the belief in reincarnation lends fantastic comfort to the dying and their families, because they know their loved ones will be reborn into a new life; they are not gone forever.[38]

This is the direct opposite of what the Bible teaches about life after death. Biblical truth reveals that death is nothing to fear but rather something to look forward to with anxious anticipation, as long as one engages in a daily renewal of mindful faith in Christ.

God created us with the desire to live forever and ever. Furthermore, he has opened the way for that desire to be fulfilled (Ecclesiastes 3:11). Christ says that he is the way, the truth, and the life to eternity. He told those who believed not to be troubled, since a human soul doesn't just evaporate or reincarnate into a cow, horse, baboon, or eagle. No! God created for mankind a way to realize his eternal destiny, either in the heavenly

---

37. Hu, Jiao, and Li, "Effectiveness of Spiritual Care Training…" 1.

38. Thrane, "Hindu End of Life: Death, Dying, Suffering, and Karma."

home of righteousness with God or the hell of torment with Satan and all others who have rejected Christ's gift of eternal life (John 14:1–4).

The apostle Paul declares, *"For to me, to live is Christ and to die is gain… I am torn between the two: I desire to depart and be with Christ, which is better by far"* (Philippians 1:21, 23, NIV). Christ reassures those who trust Him, saying, *"I am the resurrection and the life. The one who believes in me will live, even though they die [physical death]; and whoever lives by believing in me will never die [spiritual death or separation from God]"* (John 11:25–26, NIV).

A Hindu or Buddhist priest could not provide this assuring encouragement to a dying Christian patient because he could not offer what he does not have.

Again, medical professionals see spirituality as a concept to be acquired through experience, age, and knowledge. It will be just another cognitive exercise for a Hindu nurse providing the spiritual needs of a Muslim patient, or a Buddha nurse providing the spiritual needs of a Christian patient, or a Dao nurse providing the spiritual needs of a believer in Judaism. No wonder this concept of religiosity and spirituality results in the conclusion that religiosity/spirituality is ineffective in healing sickness. Such practitioners cause more harm to their patients' health.

This concept of religion and spirituality has dominated the western worldview as it pertains to the importance and confirmed efficacy of the presbytery crisis prayer for healing. The presbytery prays, but it is the Lord who heals. For example, some Christian chiropractors who believe in Christ attest to the truth that their job is to move bones, but it is God who heals.

Tacey, who has an Indigenous understanding of spirituality, as opposed to Christian, says this about spiritual healing:

> Healing is ultimately self-healing, although most of us have no way of knowing that. The "self" that heals is not the ordinary self but something mysterious which is part of our interiority (could this be an understanding of a carnal mind about the indwelling presence of the Holy Spirit or demonic possession?). It sounds contradictory, but there is an objective presence at the core of our subjectivity, and whether we call this deep subjectivity soul, Spirit, or "god within" makes little difference. Healing begins when a patient senses the presence of another at the core of their being and attempts to contact that presence. It is the basis of the claim about the healing power of prayer.[39]

---

39. Tacey, "Spiritual Connectedness and Healing," 4.

He further asserts that

> the idea of a spiritual presence at the core of our subjectivity is new to Western medicine, which tends to externalize the healing process, seeing it as the result of one's encounter with the doctor, or the result of medical interventions and pharmaceuticals. In the West, we have downplayed the healing resources of the body-mind-spirit; many of us are at the mercy of external forces of healing, the objective health. So many are heading to the east for inspiration and insight.[40]

This observation showcases how the church of Jesus Christ fails to fulfill its spiritual obligation in meeting the physical, mental, and spiritual disease, sickness, and pain of hurting members.

Every faith organization is operates by teachings that attempt to help the worshiper become a transcendent being. I do not see how an Islamic, Baha'i, Shinto, Buddhist, Hindu, Confucianist, atheist, or Christian nurse could provide religious/spiritual healing support to a patient of a different faith. A Christian nurse provides prayer through the authority and power of the sinless Christ. Can patients of other faiths believe in the authenticity and efficacy of such prayer?

Disbelief is what prevents the efficacy of presbytery crisis prayer. Such an effort would be like using hydroxychloroquine to treat COVID-19 or a tetanus vaccine to treat a patient with pancreatitis.

Medical practitioners are trained in anatomy, physiology, and pathology, not in the abstract spirit relationship between the human and immortality, between the finite and infinite, and between the material and immaterial.

Much confusion exists among those who believe that adherents of all professing faiths worship the same God, or gods. That belief seemingly qualifies any trained healthcare professional to provide spiritual support sick patients of other faith affiliations.

It is stated elsewhere in this book that religious and spiritual issues are not limited to the human mind. The connection between a patient's religious/spiritual state of mind goes beyond the physical. It also has little to do with a laboratory diagnosis or psychological assessment.

Therefore, it may be true that a nurse's religious/spiritual state of mind could influence their attitude and behavior toward a patient. Still, it may not be religiously and spiritually appropriate to believe that "nurses are the chief providers of spiritual care to patients."[41]

---

40. Ibid.

41. Ibid., 3.

## God's Eternal Plan for Implementing Health

### MAN ADOPTS TWO APPROACHES FOR HEALING AND HEALTHY LIVING

After the fall, God revisited humankind and picked Abram to re-establish his purpose and relationship with man. God provided the opportunity of choice to mankind; they could choose between egocentric dependence or theocentric dependence, self-dependence or a complete reliance on God for their well-being.

God handpicked Abram to create physical opportunities to fellowship with man. However, man's egocentrism keeps him from God and creates an antagonistic spirit between the revealed Word and scientific and psychological discoveries.

### JUDAISM: MAN DEPENDS ON THE ABRAHAMIC GOD HEALING (GENESIS 12:1)

Abram was called at a time when the people worshipped artificial gods and depended on them. Nevertheless, when God promised Abram, *"All peoples on earth will be blessed through you"* (Genesis 12:3, NIV). So when God handpicked Abram and called him to a new covenant, he was re-establishing his control over human affairs. From that time forward, God intended to stamp out man's dependency on the creation as a source for healing and turn them towards faith in the Creator.

To establish his divine will over the destiny of humanity, God took Abram out of a pantheistic society and brought him into a monotheistic one. Then God called the monotheistic community his people. He established his chosen representatives of prophets, priests, and kings, ministering healing through them to meet the people's physical, mental, and spiritual needs.

The Old Testament shares detailed records about God's dealings with his chosen people, and he used them to reconcile the world to himself through the Seed of Abraham. Jesus is the Seed of Abraham, whom God used to complete his reconciliatory plan and establish a new covenant. Thereafter, the church continued to renew mankind's relationship with God through Christ, who is the Head and the Savior. When the body is wounded, the Head also feels the pain. Understanding human pain brought tears to flow down Christ's cheek (John 11:35). He experienced human sorrow and pain and paid the price in order for man to receive the blessing of healing and peace.

Nowhere in Scripture does it say that sin, disease, or sickness should be considered blessings. God only goes negative when man decides to go negative. Anyone who seeks him will find him when he is sought with one's heart (Jeremiah 29:13, James 4:2). In all circumstances, God's promises are sure, true, and righteous, more refined than gold; gaining the fulfillment of his promises is sweeter than the drippings of a honeycomb (Psalm 19:7–11).

## III. FAITH IN GOD THROUGH PROPHETIC AND PRIESTLY HEALING PRAYER

Throughout the Old Testament, God used his servants—the prophets, priests, rabbis, and kings—to provide physical, mental, and spiritual healing to the broken-hearted among his people. The call of Abram has been a yardstick for us in terms of relating to God in every aspect of life. Our sinful nature has always been a barrier to getting God to act in human affairs, but our acts of faith move him to respond to our needs.

Therefore, God always looks at the state of the heart—its motive, desire, faithfulness, glory, benefit, truth, and honesty. Genuine prayer demonstrates faith instead of some collection of mere words or beliefs. The strength in which prayer operates is not a forceful yelling at Satan; rather, they are the terms of faith, the power of faith, and the durable force of faith rooted in Christ alone.

Faith is the key to every productive relationship between God and man. God did not accept or answer the prayer of the saints in Old Testament because of their sacrifices. Their gifts were the product of faith and obedience to God's promises.

RELATIONSHIP BETWEEN CHRISTIANITY AND MODERN SCIENTIFIC MEDICINE

History shows us that Christianity gave birth to what we call modern scientific medicine. Koenig has amassed impressive research on the historical background of modern medicine and its relationship to religion and spirituality. He acknowledges that religion and medicine have a long, intertwined, tumultuous history going back thousands of years. To be precise, he demonstrates that religion, medicine, and healthcare have been interrelated in one way or another in all population groups since the beginning of recorded history.[42]

In recent decades, scientists have tried to destroy this long relationship in order to separate religion from science, especially in the industrialized nations of the west. Nevertheless, developing countries still acknowledge scientific medicine as a part of the ministry of religion. This historical relationship existed from ancient Egypt and Greece to early Christianity through the Middle Ages, Renaissance, and Age of Enlightenment, when the split between religion and medicine became final and complete.[43]

Koenig's article states that the first hospitals in the west for the general population were built by religious organizations and staffed by religious orders. The clergies were physicians, and the religious institutions issued licenses to practice medicine.[44]

---

42. H.G. Koenig, "Religion and Medicine II: Religion, Mental Health, and Related Behaviors." *The International Journey of Psychiatry in Medicine 31(1)*, 2001, 97–109.

43. Ibid., 97.

44. Ibid.

Koenig's findings show that among the many reasons for the continued effort to water down this long history is the accusation that religion may either be irrelevant to healing and human health or has destructive effects.

Author John William Draper wrote that the struggle between Christianity and science began when Christianity ascended to political power. He believed that as more progressive intellectuals advanced, the number of antagonistic relationships increased.[45]

This dichotomy exists because of the nature of the two forces and their convictions. Christian faith is unchangeable regarding the Creator and the nature of creation. In contrast, science is intellectually progressive in its discoveries. Modern scientific intellectualism therefore tries to sever the relationship between the Christian church and modern medicine, brushing Christianity aside.

Deliberate efforts have been made to separate the fundamental truth that scientific medicine fulfills what the Bible says about God's eternal plan for man's health. Genesis 1 is about God's positive plan, good health, fruitfulness, and the multiplication of blessings for man and all creatures. God's original plan excluded disease, sickness, pain, and death. This was possible because sin did not exist.

In perceiving this fact, the main problem of scientists and medical professionals is their devotion to addressing the symptoms of human affliction without knowing the underlining factor: sin. Until Christ returns and restores the eternal and perfect state in the New Jerusalem, man cannot defeat and eradicate the tyranny of sin, disease, sickness, and death.

Fortunately, research reveals that medical professionals are reversing course on this stance to more fully embrace the role of biblical faith in achieving maximum healing in their patients.

Koenig further acknowledges those scientists who have curtailed their tendency to separate biblical faith and modern scientific medicine. He writes that in 1900, fewer than five medical schools in the United States taught students about religion's role in the lives of sick patients. In recent years, 70 of 126 United States medical schools have required elective courses on religion, spirituality, and medicine. He then questions, "Are we now seeing a rapprochement in the long-divided healing traditions of medicine and religion, and more importantly, is there a scientific basis for such reconciliation?"[46]

God put in place the principle of multiplication for mankind's blessings and fruitfulness, and this includes the benefit of the scientific gift of intelligence and knowledge. Science and modern medicine complement God's plan for the health of humanity through the

---

45. John William Draper, *History of the Conflict Between Religion and Science* (New York, NY: D. Appleton and Co., 1998).

46. Koenig, "Religion and Medicine II: Religion, Mental Health, and Related Behaviors," 98.

Lord Jesus Christ. Therefore, modern medicine is not an adversary to God's revelation about human health.

**Physical, mental, and spiritual healing domains.** The presbytery crisis prayer ministry include the physical, mental, and spiritual domains. Christ, his word, and the presbytery are interconnected components that provide the healing criteria for PCPM. These criteria are made available to the church for supernatural transformation. This healing capacity is possible because the Christian church is Christ's body.

Modern scientific medicine only covers the physical and mental domains. Modern medicine has little to do with spiritual sickness. Rather, it deals entirely with physical illnesses and ill mental health.

## MAN'S DEPENDENCE ON MANUFACTURED GODS FOR HEALING

We have already discussed in this book that God called Abram from a paganistic society, one with pluralist religions practicing the worship of idols, deities, and mysticism. The people depended on manufactured gods and departed spirits to resolve life issues.

**Appeasing and praying to manmade gods for healing.** In that society, religious and spiritual healing came through the appeasement of manmade gods and spirits. The use and worship of these gods and spirits (demons) demonstrate the people's desperation for spiritual recognition and reconciliation with the Creator. The idea of worshipping and serving intermediaries shows man's spiritual death and ignorance on how to reconnect with God and worship him. Such a people believe the things of God to be foolish and meaningless (1 Corinthians 2:14).

**Dependence on religiosity/spirituality for healing.** As mentioned, the healing domains are physical, mental, and spiritual. Healing depends largely on meditations, which center on mental exercises that encompass various techniques of concentration, contemplation, and abstraction which are regarded as being conducive to heightened self-awareness, spiritual enlightenment, and physical and psychological health.[47]

Religion and spirituality operate by a set of rules and practices and aren't necessarily centered on a relationship with the Creator. It is less a matter of faith and more a body of laws, observation, regulation, and training. Yoga and meditation practices, for example, can result in some mental health healing because they involve psychology and exercising the body.

It is a mental exercise to follow a set of rules through intensive practice. However, exercising the body is not a spiritual practice and does not attract spiritual healing. This is philosophical and methodological, focusing on the mindfulness of the physiological self.

---

47. Dan Merkur, "Meditation," *Britaccica*. Date of access: May 28, 2020 (https://www.britannica.com/topic/meditation-mental-exercise).

One does not have to be religious or spiritual to practice yoga or other mindfulness therapies. The healing found in such religious and spiritual exercise is affected because of God's general grace. The practitioner could realize physical and mental healing, but not healing from any spirit of sinful disease.

**Dependence on traditions, nature, and rituals.** The healing domains of traditional medicine also include the physical, mental, and spiritual. This type of healing comes through physical characteristics such as aroma, shape, and color. Attendant rituals can also involve incantations and songs.[48]

## IV. WHAT IS CHRISTIANITY?

Christianity is not just one of the world's major religions. It is different from Islam, Hinduism, Buddhism, or Taoism—and it is wrong to view Christianity and equate it with these religions. Doing so contradicts how Christianity is described in Scripture. Indeed, the Christian faith is not at all like other manufactured religions and spiritualities.

Scripture is about the shedding of Christ's blood. Christianity only derives its efficacy from the Christ; it is a divine plan to restore humanity into an eternal relationship with the Triune God—God the Father, God the Son, and God the Holy Spirit.

Christianity is more than a belief in monotheism. Islam believes in monotheism as well, but the Islamic god is different from the Christian God. Monotheistic Christianity teaches that God is one, and that Christ is the way, the truth, and the life; no one can reconcile a man into his eternal reign with the holy God except through Christ.

It is also greater than any of its denominations, like as Roman Catholicism or the Protestant groups of Evangelicals, Pentecostals, and Charismatics. Someone could be a member of any of these groups yet have no personal relationship with Christ.

Christianity is not about building structures. It is not a collection of traditions, political organizations, occultic associations, or hypothetical assumptions on historical text. It is not local or regional (John 12:44–50). It is not about religiosity, artificial spirituality, or organized religious festivals (Amos 5:21–23). It is not about rituals or the worship of imagery (Daniel 3:1). It is not about the excellency of human knowledge, power, authority, intellect, wisdom, or the humanistic philosophy of men (1 Corinthians 1:17–2:16).

Nor is Christianity about worshipping creatures, ancestors, alien spirits, or any departed humans. The Bible says it is given unto man once to die, and after that he

---

48. Tsiry Rasamiravaka, Kahumba J, Okusa PN, Bakari Amuri, Bizumukama L, Jean-Baptiste Ndoumba Kalonji, Martin Kiendrebeogo, Rabemenantsoa C, Mondher El Jaziri, Elizabeth M. Williamson, and Pierre Duez, "Traditional African Medicine: From Ancestral Knowledge to a Modern Integrated Future." *Science 350*, January 2015, 61–63.

faces God's judgment (Hebrews 9:27). This is why ancestral worship is a form of idolatry, and Yahweh hates the worship of idols.

While religion is a sinful man's effort to reach and have fellowship with God through the fallen creation, Christianity is about a holy God who reaches out to redeem wicked men through the payment made by the Suffering Servant, Jesus Christ, ushering mankind into eternal fellowship with God.

Religion looks up and around in search of a relationship with God in sinful creation through human ideology, philosophy, wisdom, and rituals for freedom, transformation, and forgiveness of sin. Christianity is about God reaching out to free, transform, and forgive man's sins. Christianity takes root in Christ, who fulfills God's plan of reaching towards sinful man for reconciliation, freedom, transformation, and forgiveness of sin. Christ's earthly mission was to restore abundant eternal life to whoever came to him by faith (Matthew 6:33, John 10:10, Hebrews 9:22).

Christianity is about the unconditional love of God through the historical, existential, experiential, and futuristic Jesus (Hebrews 13:8). It is about the acts of God in accepting humanity through the righteousness of God the Son (2 Corinthians 5:21), whose death makes those who come to him alive, a people belonging to God as adopted children. God overlooks human sinfulness through the lens of Christ's righteousness, and man relates to him through faith in that righteousness.

Christianity is about the unconditional love of God over humanity's rebellion. It is a community of men whose sin and guilt God in Christ has been forgiven through trust and belief that the shedding of Christ's blood pays for sin and acquires God's righteousness.

Christianity is composed of followers of the Way, for Jesus declares that he is the Way that leads sinful men back into a relationship with God. Luke 24:1 teaches us that all the Hebrew prophets' ministries pointed to Christ as the Way for humanity to reconcile with God. In this way, all the regenerated followers of Christ are called followers of the Way (Acts 92, 19:9, 23, 22:4, 24:14, 22). His righteousness provides us access to petition God with our burdens. Christianity exists as a means for us to worship the living God in the person of Jesus Christ.

THE PRESBYTERY CRISIS PRAYER MINISTRY

The essence and purpose of the blood of Jesus Christ is the authoritative and influential foundation among which is built the presbytery crisis prayer ministry. The PCPM shows that:

> 1. Christ is our only authentic access into the presence of the holy and sovereign God (Ephesians 2:18, 3:12, Hebrews 6:19–20, 10:19–22).

2. Christ is the only divine requirement able to meet God's religious demand to remove guilt or sickness (Romans 8:32, Philippians 4:12–13, Colossian 3:13).
3. Faith in Christ places all the redeemed in right standing with God (1 Peter 3:18).
4. All good conversation and healing with God is channeled through the blood of Christ (Galatians 3:13, 1 Peter 3:18).
5. It is the only provision for believers to triumph over Satan and his demons in the believer's healing ministry (Luke 22:31, 1 John 4:4).
6. Satan is unable to successfully accuse believers if their requests are presented through the shed blood of Christ, because believers have overcome through the blood of the Lamb (Revelation 12:11).
7. The blood of Jesus Christ is superior to human and animal blood. It is blameless, untainted, and has extraordinary power for spiritual and physical purification (Romans 5:9, Hebrews 9:13–14). All blood types are symbolistic and tainted in the eyes of God and worthy only for cleansing the flesh; they are unworthy to heal man's conscience and heart.

*Not with the blood of goats and calves, but with His own blood He entered the Most Holy Place once for all, having obtained eternal redemption For if the blood of bulls and goats and the ashes of a heifer, sprinkling the unclean, sanctifies for the purifying of the flesh, how much more shall the blood of Christ, who through the eternal Spirit offered Himself without spot to God, cleanse your conscience from dead works to serve the living God?* (Hebrews 9:12–14, NKJV).

The presbytery can heal diseases and sicknesses because they have been given power and authority through the shed, innocent blood of Christ (Ephesians 1:7).

What does it mean when the Bible says that Jesus *"called His twelve disciples together and gave them power and authority over all demons, and to cure diseases"* (Luke 9:1)? The power of the innocent blood of Jesus has provided everything the presbytery needs for people to lives of victory, including redemption, fellowship, healing, protection, and claiming authority over the works of Satan.

Our spiritual and physical healing connects us through the innocent blood of Jesus Christ. He is the instrument for our saving and healing grace through the prayer of the presbytery. One can boldly say that the role of Christ's saving and healing blood is a critical component of achieving a presbytery crisis prayer breakthrough.

# Part Two

## God's Divine Plan for Healthy Living in the Church

CHAPTER FOUR
# The Five Approaches to Healing Sickness

> Pharmaceutical companies sponsor disease and promote them to prescribers and consumers. The social construction of illness is being replaced by the corporate construction of disease. The influence of the pharmaceutical industry, in which it expressed concern about the effects of "medicalization of our society—the pill for every problem."[49]
> —Howard Wolinsky

IN THE PREVIOUS chapter, we presented an overview of disease treatment. We discussed the entrance of disease and sickness into the universe and its effect on all living and non-living things. This helps us to understand that the Creator of the universe never left us unsupported to deal with the curse of sin in our earthly journeys.

## GOD'S GOOD AND PERFECT GIFTS

God's good and perfect gifts are given to humanity, Christians and non-Christians alike. These gifts include wisdom, intelligence, the power to make sound decisions, and our quest for progression. All God's given gifts are delightful, and we can receive them in full through God's grace, which demonstrates his loving care for his creation.

> ...so that you may prove yourselves to be sons of your Father who is in heaven; for He causes His sun to rise on the evil and the good, and sends rain on the righteous and the unrighteous. (Matthew 5:45, NASB)

Whether a person is atheist, agnostic, or an adherent of another religion, he or she can choose to acknowledge and embrace this aspect of God's character—or not. One cannot deny the ability to participate in God's grace.

Everything God does in his relationship with his creation is based on our attitude of faith in his promises. He began this relationship when he spoke the living word (rhema) and the word came into being. The Lord Jesus Christ completed the path to this relationship through his death on the cross and resurrection for our reconciliation. God will restore our final perfect state in the New Jerusalem, the city of God.

When God gives a gift, it does not add sorrow, because whatever God does, he does it for his glory. We know very well that grief will not bring glory to his name (Isaiah

---

49. Howard Wolinsky, "Disease Mongering and Drug Marketing: Does the Pharmaceutical Industry Manufacture Diseases as Well as Drugs?" *EMBO Reports 6(7)*, July 2005, 612–614.

42:8, Colossians 1:16). Although Job appreciated God's goodness in times of both abundance and affliction, he never took his nemesis for a blessing. Disease and sickness are not among God's pleasing and honoring gifts. If he allows suffering, he provides a remedy for it. Afflictions bring sorrow, not blessing. So the existence of God's good and perfect gifts is a living witness in our daily lives.

Since human beings live in this sinful, broken, dysfunctional world, our daily experience naturally include disease, suffering, and pain. The Giver of good gifts, however, has invited us to turn to him for solutions to every curse of sin. Such afflictions are moments of brokenness, darkness, and pain—and throughout these afflictions, the victim seems to view God through evil lenses, seeing him as someone who doesn't care, love, or protect them.

But does that view of God depict his holy and faithful character? Of course not. God did not leave us without coping remedies for our ill health. The Bible teaches that God heals us in times of crisis (Exodus 15:26, Psalm 147:3). He uses wisdom, intelligence, and prayer in the faith of Jesus Christ through the presbytery crisis prayer to provide us with remedies.

In acknowledging God's given wisdom, the ancient Greek philosopher Democritus is said to have believed that wisdom is the sister of medicine; one rescues the soul from passions and the other alleviates the disease of the body. He believed that the mind benefits from health, whereas ill health dampens the desire for virtue, with illness binding the soul.[50]

Therefore, to maintain godly perfection in life and health, practitioners of modern medicine and mental healthcare work around the clock to defeat disease, eliminate sickness, and heal all forms of ill health. Scientific discoveries and advancements in medicine have already reached significant heights, yet new diseases and disorders are still on the rise—and they are deadly, including conditions such as HIV/AIDS, SARS, COVID-19, and many cancers.

Our redemptive healing in Christ is about earning a healthy eternal life and caring for our physical, mental, emotional, and spiritual well-being. Healthy eternal life (salvation) is not a life free of imperfection, sickness, sorrow, pains, impurity, and death; that is a condition believers will not enjoy until they are ushered into the New Jerusalem (Revelation 21:4–5).

In this book, we have also noted that it is not in the plan of God to create a normal human and then turn around and attack his system with disease to destroy it. He does not send turmoil into our bodies. Ill health exists as a result of man's disobedience and

---

50. Democritus, "Medicine heals diseases of the body…" AZ Quotes. Date of access: December 21, 2022 (https://www.azquotes.com/quote/658166).

sin. Our human problems took root because of man's rebellion against the righteousness of God. But God, through Christ, works diligently to reach out and provide healing when a righteous prayer reaches his throne of grace.

The bottom line is that God does not inflict anyone with disease and sickness. Illness is a penalty for sin, poor choices, and the attacks of Satan. Rather, God demonstrated his love by bearing our sorrow and pain, delivering us from the terror of affliction. God's love heals us. There can be no doubt that Isaiah got it right when he wrote, *"But he was pierced for our transgressions, he was crushed for our iniquities; the punishment that brought us peace was on him, and by his wounds we are healed"* (Isaiah 53:5, NIV).

However, some theologians believe that Isaiah was referring only to spiritual healing, not mental and physical healing. And yet no one denies that the PCPM is God's instituted remedy for sick members of the church, nor do they deny that God's miraculous healings are proven experiences in the life of the church.

Readers should be reminded here that the efficacy of Christ's wounds has spiritual, physiological, and psychological impacts on believers. No wonder Jeremiah wrote that God's perfect plan is not for harm but goodwill, prosperity, and a promising future (Jeremiah 29:11). He established a divine program after the fall of man and the corruption of his perfect creation. Through James, God has conveyed to the clergy and afflicted believers may carry to him every needless pain in prayer, and he has promised to prevail. God inspired James with this revelation knowledge of what he intends for his church to know and do.

The psalmist also underscores that God does not desert his children in hardship. He is present to salvage our conditions during unprecedented and unpleasant times.

Because God is with us amidst affliction, he gave James a road map on how to deal with such a moment. He instructed James that a crisis member should summon the righteous leaders of the church who have been given the authority and power to call down divine healing through prayer in the faith of Jesus Christ.

It is imperative to restate here that the PCPM is not in any way in conflict with the role of traditional/herbal or modern scientific medicine in addressing the challenges of ill health. These other approaches are complementary to God's divine plan to provide a source of remedy for human suffering. Therefore, we must acknowledge that human intelligence and knowledge are part of the Creator's good and perfect gifts for us; they should not conflict with the biblical approach to presbytery healing prayer. The church must applaud the advancement of modern medicine and mental healthcare and their contributions to human health. God will act when the church complies with his written word.

No act of human effort can replace the resilient power of the righteous prayer of the clergy. However, this resilience seems to face an uphill journey in the church today. The power of the righteous is an antidote to every affliction because God says so. Prayers and petitions are presented to God in everything (Philippians 4:6). Traditional/herbal and scientific medicines may fail, and when this happens we may wonder as to the cause of our illness. Therefore, any act of obedience in line with God's will shall result in the glory of God.

Peter's leadership charge in Matthew 16:18–19 shows Christ's ordination to be a perfect example that the mantle of leadership has the "binding" task and "loosing" responsibility of implementing God's will on the earth, just as his will is done in heaven.

Of course, this binding and the loosing refers to spiritual matters. Nevertheless, it will make sense that the authority and power given to the church consists of the spiritual, physical, and mental well-being of the church.

To understand God's plan for the well-being of humanity, we shall discuss five methods of treating human sickness.

## THE FIVE APPROACHES FOR TREATING HUMAN SICKNESS

| FIGURE 1: FIVE APPROACHES OF TREATING HUMAN SICKNESS | | | | | |
|---|---|---|---|---|---|
| | Practitioner | Healing Source | Method of Diagnosis | Treatment | Healing Capability |
| 1. Traditional/ Herbal Medicine | Traditional healers, herbalists, | Natural herbs and spiritual rituals. | Personal interaction with patients and consultation with intermediaries. | Natural herbs, touching, recitation, or the invocation of spirits. | Heals some mental and physical sickness. |
| 2. Modern Scientific Medicine | Doctors, nurses, lab technicians, and other medical professionals | Preventive drugs and therapeutic medicines. | All tests and diagnoses are ascertained and obtained for the best treatment to occur. Most diagnoses are physiological in nature. | Treatment is determined by the prescription. Random treatment does not occur. | Heals the majority of illness with lab results, drugs, and surgery. Where lab certainty fails, the healing capability is significantly limited. |

The Five Approaches to Healing Sickness

| | | | | | |
|---|---|---|---|---|---|
| 3. Mental Healthcare | Psychiatrists, psychologists, psychotherapists therapists, and counselors. | Antidepressants and counselling. | Questionnaires to learn symptoms and provide analysis. Laboratory assessments are limited in their ability to diagnose mental health issues. | Antidepressants, counselling and therapy. | Heals many mental health issues. |
| 4. Religion and Spirituality | Spiritualists, religionists, mystics, and diviners. | The observance of religious teachings, laws, and rules through which one adheres to religious beliefs and practices. | Most diagnoses here are related to mental health issues. | Treatments are conducted with or without medication. Treatments are psychotherapeutic, obeying religious norms. Counselling also occurs. | Some results are attained through the strict observance of religious and moral codes. |
| 5. The Presbytery Crisis Prayer Ministry (PCPM) | The redeemed presbytery through Christ. | The Holy Spirit, promises in God's word, prayer, and counselling. | Prayer, spiritual assessment questioning, and Scripture. | Confession of sin, forgiveness of sin, scripture, the laying on of hands/ touch therapy, anointing oil, meditation, prayer, talk therapy, and faith in Christ's righteousness. | Miraculous interventions occur for all sicknesses, through faith in the authority and power of Christ. |

The purpose of this section is not to engage in detailed discussions, critiques, and analyses of the different healing options available but to briefly acknowledge the five options that exist: traditional/herbal, modern scientific medicine, mental healthcare, religiosity/spirituality, and the Presbytery Crisis Prayer Ministry; the PCPM needs to be more publicly emphasized.

In discussing these approaches to human wellness, I do not claim expertise in the dispensation of them, except for the PCPM.

Each of these options attempts to practice a holistic approach—embracing the body, mind, spirit, and emotions—to dealing with human health. The philosophy of holistic medicine rests on the belief that the whole person is composed of interdependent parts. Therefore, if one part isn't working correctly, all the others will be affected, harming one's overall health.

This suggests that man's dependence on any single approach to healing isn't enough. We must pursue wellness holistically to bring about complete healing.

In Christianity, we believe that when one believer falls ill, the whole body suffers. This is the biblical perspective on interconnectedness. However, our bodies follow the same principle. If the eye is sick, it affects the function of the entire body.

## INCLUDING SPIRITUAL CARE IN THE HEALING PROCESS

Modern scientific medicine struggles to accept the reality that a person's interconnectedness is not limited to physiological components; spirituality must also be considered. Thus, a person must be cared for physically, spiritually, and mentally to attain holistic healing.

The Bible paints the picture in these words: *"For just as the body is one and has many members, and all the members of the body, though many, are one body, so it is with Christ"* (1 Corinthians 12:12, NRSVUE).

While other approaches deal with certain aspects of human health, both physical and mental, the PCPM is capable of producing positive effects on the whole person, but only if the church obeys the leading of the Jesus Christ, the Master Healer.

Some Christian theologians may argue that 1 Corinthians 12 presents a spiritual illustration relating to the believers' spiritual gifts. Of course it does. However, the benefits continue beyond that point.

In this section, I will discuss the interconnectedness of a believer's spiritual gifts in meeting their needs. There are significant lessons to be learned about the interconnectedness of our physical, mental, and spiritual health in order to function optimally.

It is not a surprise to say that modern scientific medicine aggressively encourages the inclusion of religion/spirituality in treating disease. However, the problem with using religion and spirituality as part of healing needs to be explored and clarified, because being religious or spiritual doesn't guarantee recovery.

Earlier, we discussed the reality that God hates religiosity and spirituality, because these terms describe the human effort to find help in nature—herbs, vegetation, the sun, moon, stars, etc. Therefore, religion and spirituality are rooted in man's own wisdom, philosophy, and ideology.

In the following chapters, we will briefly examine each of the five healing approaches. Not all of them can produce holistic healing, but the PCPM can heal physical, mental, psychological, and spiritual sicknesses. This is possible because the Creator has assured it (Psalm 103:3, Matthew 12:15, 14:14–17, James 5:14–15).

CHAPTER FIVE
# Traditional and Herbal Methods of Healing

Patient use of herbal/natural remedies to reveal likely side effects and avoid potential conflict with prescribed medications. Patients may not know that "natural" does not necessarily mean "better" or "safe."[51]
—Fred Friedberg

We are here to add what we can to life, not to get what we can from life.[52] —William Osler

HERBAL MEDICINES ARE a combination of herbs, herbal materials, herbal preparations, and finished herbal products that contain parts of plants as active ingredients. Practitioners believe that herbal medicine is powerful and can heal an array of illnesses and boost overall health.[53]

The use of traditional and herbal medicine in the ancient Near East has been linked to the Magis, the wise men of biblical fame. The Magis directed rituals and religious rites as healers of the soul. However, healing prayers and the reading of sacred texts were considered superior recovery methods.[54]

Nayernouri explains further that the essence of herbal healing is the prevention of mental and physical illness achieved through religious observance of moral purity and physical hygiene. He seems to suggest what modern scientific medicine calls "preventive medicine";[55] the Bible refers to it as the transformation, not conformation, of what the world offers (Romans 12:1–2)

This shows that even traditional and herbal healers link the efficacy and consistency of their healing power to reading, applying, and obeying the tenants of Scripture.

---

51. Fred Friedberg, "Fred Friedberg," *Goodreads*. Date of access: June 2, 2023 (https://www.goodreads.com/author/show/483383.Fred_Friedberg).

52. William Osler, "We are here to add…" *Goodreads*. Date of access: May 20, 2023 (https://www.brainyquote.com/quotes/william_osler_384242).

53. Anestis Dougkas, Marine Vannereux, and Agnès Giboreau, "The Impact of Herbs and Spices on Increasing the Appreciation and Intake of Low-Salt Legume-Based Meals." *Nutrients 11(12)*, December 2019.

54. Chittaranjan Andrade and Rajiv Radhakrishnan, "Prayer and Healing: A Medical and Scientific Perspective on Randomized Controlled Trials." *The Indian Journal of Psychiatry 51(4)*, October-December 2009, 247–253.

55. Touraj Nayernouri, "A Brief History of Ancient Iranian Medicine." *Archives of Iranian Medicine 18(8)*, 2016, 549–551.

## I. HEALING SOURCE

Traditional and herbal healers believe that conventional and herbal medicine has been divinely established, especially as it pertains to herbs and ancestral spirits, whereas the healing domains of conventional and naturistic medicine are physical, mental, and spiritual. These practitioners heal through physical characteristics such as aroma, shape, and color; attendant rituals can involve incantations and songs.[56]

Definitions of traditional and herbal medicine can take time to arrive in written secular documents. Traditional medicine has been defined as

> the total of knowledge, skill, and practices based on theories, beliefs, and experiences in indigenous to different cultures, whether explicable or not, used in the maintenance of health as well as in the prevention, diagnosis, improvement or treatment of physical and mental illness.[57]

Traditional and herbal practices are considered as old as human existence. These healers believe that before humans existed on the planet, plants covered the face of the earth. This is a typical affirmation of the biblical record about the relationship between the third-day and sixth-day creation stories, at which time vegetation and plants existed for the benefit of humanity (Genesis 1:10–13, 26–29).

This is what God had said about creation and nature:

> *God blessed them and said to them, "Be fruitful and increase in number; fill the earth and subdue it. Rule over the fish in the sea and the birds in the sky and over every living creature that moves on the ground."*
>
> *Then God said, "I give you every seed-bearing plant on the face of the whole earth and every tree that has fruit with seed in it. They will be yours for food. And to all the beasts of the earth and all the birds in the sky and all the creatures that move along the ground—everything that has the breath of life in it—I give every green plant for food." And it was so.* (Genesis 1:28–30, NIV)

Professional researchers in the field of traditional and herbal medicine believe that this approach to maintaining human health has a long history. As a result, we have a long record of its theoretical concepts and practical skills.

---

56. Rasamiravaka et al, "Traditional African Medicine," 62.

57. C. Che, V. George, T. Iijinu, P. Pushpangadan, and K. Andrae-Marobela, "Chapter 2—Traditional Medicine." *Medicine*, 2017, 1.

Although the World Health Organization does not ascribe one definition for traditional medicine, it has diverse health practices, approaches, knowledge, and beliefs. Traditional medicine incorporates plants, animals, and minerals. It combines spiritual therapies, manual techniques, and exercises to maintain well-being and treat, diagnose, or prevent illness.[58]

This traditional practice is passed down from generation to generation through verbal teachings.[59]

An article for *Alive* records that the use of medicinal herbs is probably as old as humankind. When humans first appeared on this earth, the planet was covered by an infinite variety of plant life. This article further states that plants were not only eaten for food but used as a source of medicine.[60]

Today, traditional and herbal medicines are essential to healthcare in many countries. However, how they are used varies extensively. The usage factors include culture, history, personal attitudes, social values, and philosophy.[61]

## II. METHOD OF DIAGNOSIS

Research on the method of diagnosis in traditional and herbal healing reveals concerns about consistency, validity, and accuracy of its procedures. For example, while diagnosing a patient some herbalists will want to know everything about their patient and their state of health. Some will take a detailed medical history and perform a physical examination.[62]

Other experienced herbal healers will identify the safety of plants by observing their effects on animals. Instead of scientific trial-and-errors tests, these healers will observe whether plants are consumed or are not consumed by animals.

---

58. Karunamoorthi Kaliyaperumal, Kaliyaperumal Jegajeevanram, Jegajeevanram Vijayalakshmi, and Embialle Mengistie Beyene, "Traditional Medicinal Plants: A Source of Phytotherapeutic Modality in Resource-Constrained Health Care Settings." *Journal of Evidence-Based Complementary and Alternative Medicine 18(1)*, December 2013, 67–74.

59. Che, George, Iijinu, Pushpangadan, and Andrae-Marobela, "Chapter 2—Traditional Medicine," 1.

60. "History and Traditionals in Herbal Healing," *Alive*. April 24, 2015 (https://www.alive.com/health/history-and-traditions-in-herbal-healing).

61. Pierre-Louis Lezotte, "State of Play and Review of Major Cooperation Initiatives," *International Cooperation, Convergence and Harmonization of Pharmaceutical Regulations*, January 17, 2014, 7–170.

62. David Peters, Leon Chaitow, Gerry Harris, and Sue Morrison, *Integrating Complementary Therapies in Primary Care: A Primary Guide for Health Professionals* (Edinburgh, NY: Churchill Livingstone, 2001).

The efficacy of traditional and herbal treatments are often determined by word of mouth passed from generation to generation.[63]

Traditional and herbal medicine claims to treat mental and physical sicknesses, as well as offering various treatments for social and spiritual issues. However, this approach to healing and alleviating human suffering faces fundamental challenges. The challenges are safety, efficacy, quality control, the transfer of oral knowledge, standardization, and a clean environment.[64]

Today, traditional and herbal medicine still struggles with the problems of thorough diagnosis, efficacy, and acceptability in some religious circles, as well as the pharmaceutical field.[65]

## III. TREATMENT

We identify three main aspects to healing and treatment through the practice of traditional and herbal medicine.

1. Nature (plants and vegetation).
2. Blended traditional/herbal, psychological engineering, and scientific medicine.
3. Spiritual world (ancestral spirits, rituals, deities).
4. Departed spirits.

**Natural providential (natural plants and vegetation).** Traditional and herbal medicine practitioners believe that plants are the best means of healing disease and sickness. They think that herbal treatments are natural, plant-based materials with healing properties. Such medicines are powerful and can heal various illnesses and boost overall human health. As a natural medicine, traditional healers believe in a wide range of healing approaches.

The traditional methods of treating sickness are the direct use of God-given materials found our world. History reveals that in the ancient Near East, traditional healing was

---

63. Karunamoorthi Kaliyaperumal, Kaliyaperumal Jegajeevanram, Jegajeevanram Vijayalakshmi, and Embialle Mengistie Beyene, "Traditional Medicinal Plants: A Source of Phytotherapeutic Modality in Resource-Constrained Health Care Settings." *Journal of Evidence-Based Complementary and Alternative Medicine 18(1)*, December 2013, 67–74.

64. Ibid., 70–72.

65. Jon Merrills and Jonathan Fisher, *Pharmacy Law and Practice*, Fifth Edition (Southport, UK: Elsevier Science, 2013); and Namrita Lall, *Medicinal Plants for Holistic Health and Well-Being* (Southport, UK: Elsevier, 2017).

linked with the biblical record, wherein priests used religious rites and the reading of sacred texts as the superior method of healing the soul.[66]

Other researchers reveal that traditional and herbal medicine operates on six fundamental principles to attain and maintain human health. These include a healthy climate, adequate movement and stillness, proper sleep, wakefulness' appropriate excretion process, and proper control of the psychological state of mind. The healing sources are natural herbs, spiritual rituals, and cultural beliefs.[67]

Historical records show that an individual's health and wellness rely on the integrated effects of the mind, body, and spirit. For decades, scholastic researchers in the United States have revealed that the health of the human body, mind, and spirit is linked to the product of our earthly environment.[68]

Again, Scripture teaches that God has given every plant for the benefit of man (Genesis 1:11–12). Therefore, natural herbs are among God's sacred vegetation. These plants are meant to provide and food and medicine for humanity.

> *God said, "See, I have given you every plant yielding seed that is upon the face of all the earth and every tree with seed in its fruit; you shall have them for food. (Genesis 1:29, NRSVUE)*

Much is written in the Bible about God's plan for the planet's vegetation serving as sources of food and medicine. However, traditional and herbal healers might need to learn about the origin, history, and divine establishment of this vegetation. The church, on the other hand, is not ignorant on these matters.

The writers of the Bible received revelation on God's intention for vegetation. God instructed Moses on this very subject:

> *Then God said, "I give you every seed-bearing plant on the face of the whole earth and every tree that has fruit with seed in it. They will be yours for food. 30 And to all the beasts of the earth and all the birds in the sky and all the creatures that move along the ground—everything that has the breath of life in it—I give every green plant for food." And it was so. (Genesis 1:29–30, NIV)*

---

66. Nayernouri, "A Brief History of Ancient Iranian Medicine," 549.

67. Leila Hashemi Chelavi, F. Ghaffari, and S. Sadeghi, "An Introduction to Traditional Iranian Medicine." *Journal of Traditional Medicine and Clinical Naturopathy*, December 30, 2020, 295.

68. Todd Pesek, Lonnie R. Helton, and Murali Nair, "Healing Across Cultures: Learning from Traditions." *EcoHealth 3(2)*, June 2006, 114–118.

To King Solomon, God declared,

> *Your shoots are an orchard of pomegranates with all choicest fruits, henna with nard, nard and saffron, calamus and cinnamon, with all trees of frankincense, myrrh and aloes, with all choice spices…* (Song of Solomon 4:13–14, ESV)

To Ezekiel, the Lord said,

> *And by the river upon the bank thereof, on this side and on that side, shall grow all trees for meat, whose leaf shall not fade, neither shall the fruit thereof be consumed: it shall bring forth new fruit according to his months, because their waters they issued out of the sanctuary: and the fruit thereof shall be for meat, and the leaf thereof for medicine.* (Ezekiel 47:12, KJV)

Also, to Isaiah, the Lord revealed,

> *For Isaiah had said, Let them take a lump of figs, and lay it for a plaister upon the boil, and he shall recover.* (Isaiah 38:21, KJV)

In a nutshell, our environment is the umbrella through which man attracts healing to the body, soul, and spirit. We are connected to the natural world in terms of health. In fact, we depend on and are interconnected with ourselves and everything around us.[69]

**Blended traditional/herbal, psychological engineering, and scientific medicine.** This approach to human health dives deep into the prices of psychological engineering and modern medicine. In addition, it has embraced some clinical methods.

Yet data shows that traditional and herbal healers in the twenty-first century criticize modern scientific medicine for killing thousands, if not hundreds of thousands, of patients due to human error and pharmacological side effects. These errors, they claim, occur at multiple levels of care. Preventable medication errors are believed to impact more than seven million patients.[70]

---

69. Ibid., 114.

70. Brianna A. da Silva and Mahesh Krishnamurthy, "The Alarming Reality of Medication Error: A Patient Case and Review of Pennsylvania and National Data." *Journal Community Hospital Internal Medicine Perspective 6(4)*, September 6, 2016.

Another researcher, Roman Jaeschke, states that "prescription drugs are taken as directed kill 106,000 American a year."[71] A report from Mark Hagland indicates that a Johns Hopkins study showed that more than 250,000 people die yearly from medical errors. The record revealed that as many as 400,000 people die a year.[72]

Another report has noted that 14,000 to 98,000 people die yearly in the United States from drug complications.[73]

**Spiritual world (ancestral spirits, rituals, deities).** As we continue the discussion on traditional medicine, we will briefly discuss the mystical belief in Mother Earth as a means of natural healing.

*The mystical belief in Mother Earth.* Since God drove the first human family out of the first paradise, forcing them out into the broken world, mankind has turned to nature as a source of health. Hence, Mother Earth. Who is Mother Earth? It is the spirit that controls the world and its activities.

Goldman and Baginski understood Mother Earth to be mystical and delusional. They described Mother Earth as a "priest-born monster":

> Man issued from the womb of Mother Earth, but he knew it not, nor recognized her, to whom he owed his life. In his egotism he sought an explanation of himself in the infinite, and out of his efforts there arose the dreary doctrine that he was not related to the Earth, that she was but a temporary resting place for his scornful feet and that she held nothing for him but temptation to degrade himself. Interpreters and prophets of the infinite sprang into being, creating the "Great Beyond" and proclaiming Heaven and Hell, between which stood the poor, trembling human being, tormented by that priest-born monster, Conscience.[74]

Many people believe that Mother Earth is the controller of the universe, including man's existence.

---

71. Peter C. Gøtzsche, "Our Prescription Drugs Kill Us in Large Numbers." *Polskie Archiwum Medycyny Wewnetrznej*, 2015, 105–106. Quoting Roman Jaeschke.

72. Mark Hagland, "John Hopkins Research Finds Medical Errors Third Leading Cause of Death in U.S.," *Healthcare Innovation*. May 6, 2016 (https://www.hcinnovationgroup.com/policy-value-based-care/news/13026728/johns-hopkins-research-finds-medical-errors-third-leading-cause-of-death-in-us).

73. F. Charatan, "Medical Errors Kill Almost 100,000 American a Year." *BMJ*, December 11, 1999.

74. Emma Goldman and Max Baginski, "Mother Earth," *The Anarchist Library*. Date of access: April 28, 2023 (https://theanarchistlibrary.org/library/emma-goldman-max-baginski-mother-earth).

*Collins English Dictionary* describes the idea that Mother Earth came from the earth because the earth is considered a living being and the provider of all. As a result, plants often need time to grow as nature intended and enrich themselves properly with the goodness of nutrients.[75]

*The Editors Encyclopedia Britannica* (1998) describe the Earth Mother as a timeless provider of everything. She is, according to "ancient and modern nonliterature religions... an eternally fruitful source of everything.[76]

Again, this is a humanistic perspective of the cosmos and a denial that our universe came to be through the work of the Creator.

Some believe that Mother Earth is not about earthly plants but rather mother goddesses who must undergo periodic sexual intercourse for the fertility of specific healings. They would say that all things come from her, return to her, and are her. According to this belief, Mother Earth both causes and heals physical, mental, and spiritual sickness.

Doesn't this description of Mother Earth sound like she has taken the Creator's place? Only some of these definitions refer to religious and spiritual practices. For such believers, the earth becomes the natural remedy for all of humanity's needs.

The traditional medicine practitioner believes that the power of disease and healing belongs to the Earth Mother. Therefore, he will turn to the universe for help and healing in times to affliction. Believers in every tribe, culture, and people—both ancient and current—have turned to the Earth Mother to solve every human predicament. They believe that she transcends all and controls terrestrial creation. Man has installed the Earth Mother in the position of God, the Creator, who oversees all human affairs.

An article for *Angel Messenger* views disasters as a bitter response from Mother Earth. The author believes that when she becomes unable to bear the pain within her, she has no choice but to allow earthquakes, tsunamis, and other natural disasters to be unleashed. Such disasters result from man's overzealousness in controlling and manipulating nature.[77]

Dinesh Trivedi believes that the COVID-19 pandemic was sent by the almighty Mother Nature to teach humanity a lesson about life. He writes that religious bodies have tried to capture Mother Nature through the closed doors of edifices they call temples, churches, gurdwaras, and mosques.[78]

---

75. "Mother Earth," *Collins English Dictionary* (New York, NY: Harper Collins, 2019).

76. "Earth Mother," *Britannica*. July 20, 1998 (https://www.britannica.com/topic/Earth-Mother).

77. "Mother Earth, the Divine Feminine, and Woman," *Angel Messenger*. September 16, 2019 (https://www.angelmessenger.net/mother-earth-the-divine-feminine-and-woman).

78. Dinesh Trivedi, "Coronavirus Lockdown: Dear World, Mother Nature Has a Message," *The Quint*. March 30, 2020 (https://www.thequint.com/voices/blogs/dinesh-trivedi-on-coronavirus-covid-19-pandemic-holy-scriptures-mother-nature-silent-message).

Does the earth have a mother who causes and then heals human calamities? According to this belief, humanity somehow needs to depend on Mother Earth to flee them from disease and sickness.

The position of Trivedi and the *Angel Messenger* article demonstrates a gross ignorance of who God is and his relationship to our world. The idea that the universe is the product of Mother Earth is nothing but an attempt to erase God. If God, as Creator of heaven and earth, doesn't play a central role in all things, it is easy to fool men into accepting his nonexistence.

We must emphasize that God has created everything that exists for the benefit of humanity. Nowhere in creation does a being like Mother Nature exist to exert control, and she certainly doesn't have the power to cause or heal sickness.

In an attempt to be faithful to the Bible, one online writer declares,

> We believe that God upholds and governs all things—from galaxies to subatomic particles, from the forces of nature to the movements of nations, and from the public plans of politicians to the secret acts of solitary persons—all in accord with His eternal, all-wise purposes to glorify Himself, yet in such a way that He never sins, nor ever condemns a person unjustly; but that His ordaining and governing all things is compatible with the moral accountability of all persons created in His image.[79]

Scripture attests that the Creator, the all-powerful, all-knowing sustainer of the universe, is nothing like a nonexistent, ideological Mother Earth. In establishing the sovereignty, foreknowledge, and purpose of God in the world, the Bible testifies,

> *Then the Lord said to him, "Who has made man's mouth? Who makes him mute, or deaf, or seeing, or blind? Is it not I, the Lord?* (Exodus 4:11, ESV)

> *He commands the sun not to shine and seals off the stars.* (Job 9:7, HCSB)

> *Remember this and stand firm, recall it to mind, you transgressors, remember the former things of old; for I am God, and there is no other; I*

---

79. "The Desiring God Affirmation of Faith," *Desiring God*. Date of access: April 29, 2023 (https://www.desiringgod.org/affirmation-of-faith).

> am God, and there is none like me, declaring the end from the beginning and from ancient times things not yet done, saying, "My counsel shall stand, and I will accomplish all my purpose..." (Isaiah 46:8–10, ESV)
>
> For his invisible attributes, namely, his eternal power and divine nature, have been clearly perceived, ever since the creation of the world, in the things that have been made. So they are without excuse. (Romans 1:20, ESV)
>
> He [Christ] is the image of the invisible God, the firstborn of all creation [including the presumptuous Mother Earth]. For by him all things were created, in heaven and on earth, visible and invisible, whether thrones or dominions or rulers or authorities—all things were created through him and for him. And he is before all things, and in him all things hold together. (Colossians 1:15–17, ESV)

These discoveries have led to a growing interest in spirituality as a valuable source for exploring the body-mind-spirit philosophies of health and wellness.[80]

*The growing impact of traditional medicine.* An article in *Cultural Survival* acknowledges the claims that traditional medicine has been gradually forced underground in many societies due to pressure from missionaries and governments who perceive such practices to be witchcraft. Nonetheless, traditional medicine persists and is respected in some part of the world.[81] It is encouraged especially in eastern Asia (China, Japan, and Korea), southeast Asia (Thailand, Vietnam, and India), eastern Europe (Russia and Poland), the Middle East, and Africa. Furthermore, it is believed that traditional medicine has proven to be quite effective in treating both chronic diseases and psychological problems such as stress, anxiety, and low self-esteem.

Today, traditional medicine is receiving high recognition among practitioners of modern medicine to the detriment of the presbytery healing ministry.

Researchers in India have revealed that traditional medicine is making solid inroads in modern medicine there, specially in the areas of heart disease, diabetes, hepatitis, hypertension, and mental health. They reiterate that medicinal plants are the oldest known

---

80. Todd Pesek, Lonnie R. Helton, and Murali Nair, "Healing Across Cultures: Learning from Traditions." *EcoHealth 3(2)*, June 2006, 114–118.

81. David Young, Ingram Grant, Swartz Ingelise, "The Perspective of Traditional Medicine in the Modern World," *Cultural Survival*. February 22, 2010 (https://www.culturalsurvival.org/publications/cultural-survival-quarterly/persistence-traditional-medicine-modern-world).

# Traditional and Herbal Methods of Healing

healthcare products used around the world. Furthermore, they stress that research on Indian medicinal plants has resulted in the publication of thirteen volumes of high quality. As a result, people are turning to herbalists, diviners, future-tellers, mystical healers, and spiritualistic experts for remedies and spiritual satisfaction.[82]

Many Christians, too, have turned to these traditional services in rejection of biblical truth because the church seems to have little to demonstrate in the way of God's promises and the power of Jesus Christ as it pertains to healing.

Amulets and potions made of ritually sacrificed body parts seemingly make people invincible, protecting them from illness, accidents, economic failure, or attacks from evil spirits.[83]

Today, Christianity in Nigeria, and Africa in general, still struggles with witchcraft, ritualistic activity, occultism, demon passion, divination, mysticism, and secret societies. Some researchers support the belief in the supernatural cause of illness, divination as a diagnostic tool, and ritualized use of a wide variety of plants and animal-derived agents in the treatment of sickness.[84]

*Cultural Survival* reports that traditional medicine tends to thrive in conjunction with westernization, modernization, and urbanization in African countries like Ghana and Nigeria. This study reveals that traditional practitioners adapt their practices to attract a large clientele from a more diverse population.[85]

For example, for practitioners in urban settings of Africa, such as Ghana and Nigeria, their treatments include native religious rituals, meditation, and consultation with the departed spirits. African traditional healers call this "consultation with the ancestral spirits."[86]

---

82. Neeraj Yandon, Satyapal Singh Yadav, "Contributions of Indian Council of Medical Research (ICMR) in the Area of Medicinal Plants/Traditional Medicine." *Journal of Ethnopharmacology*, February 2, 2017, 39–45.

83. Ben Adebayo, "Ritual Human Sacrifice Uncovered in Africa," *Christian Aid*. Date of access: July 2, 2020 (https://www.christianaid.org/missions-insider/2019-ritual-human-sacrifice-uncovered-in-africa).

84. Tsiry Rasamiravaka, Kahumba J, Okusa PN, Bakari Amuri, Bizumukama L, Jean-Baptiste Ndoumba Kalonji, Martin Kiendrebeogo, Rabemenantsoa C, Mondher El Jaziri, Elizabeth M. Williamson, and Pierre Duez, "Traditional African Medicine: From Ancestral Knowledge to a Modern Integrated Future." *Science 350*, January 2015, 61–63.

85. David Young, Ingram Grant, Swartz Ingelise, "The Perspective of Traditional Medicine in the Modern World," *Cultural Survival*. February 22, 2010 (https://www.culturalsurvival.org/publications/cultural-survival-quarterly/persistence-traditional-medicine-modern-world).

86. Tsiry Rasamiravaka, Kahumba J, Okusa PN, Bakari Amuri, Bizumukama L, Jean-Baptiste Ndoumba Kalonji, Martin Kendrebeogo, Rabemenantsoa C, Mondher El Jaziri, Elizabeth M. Williamson, and Pierre Duez, "Traditional African Medicine: From Ancestral Knowledge to a Modern Integrated Future." *Science 350*, January 2015, 61–63.

**Departed spirits.** Traditional and herbal healers believe that other methods of treating sicknesses involve consultation with departed human spirits, otherwise known as the spirits of the dead, or ancestral spirits.

The term ancestor is difficult to define. Generally, it is viewed in connection to people or things of the past. For example, "Ancestors are the individuals from whom you biologically descended."[87] In other words, an ancestor is anyone from whom a person has descended.

Although this book's discourse isn't focused on African theology and its controversial relationship to western theology, it is crucial to discuss healing from a traditional African perspective. Traditional and herbal healers attach a unique role to ancestral spirits as a source of healing power, even when plants and vegetation are used. Some of these healers believe that they possess healing power through an ancestral calling. However, that calling has no fixation, design criteria, or means of ascertaining which ancestral spirit made the call. African traditional and herbal medicine practitioners believe that they receive their calling through dreams or visions and undergo informal training by a living practitioner.[88]

Phiri explains that a deceased ancestor calls them to be diviners who can interpret the messages and will of the ancestor to heal living descendants. African traditional healers believe that to experience good health, prosperity, and success, overcoming danger and misfortune, the descendants need to be subordinate to their ancestral spirits. The diviners help to explain that an incidence of sickness reveals an imbalance between the metaphysical and the physical, disturbing the expected flow of relationships.[89]

Some African societies believe that ancestral spirits protect them from the dangers of disease, drought, famine, and infertility and even facilitate family harmony. Also, their ancestors supposedly protect them from witchcraft and guarantee the survival of the human species, punishing those who err in their practice of moral norms.[90]

If one were to have grown up in a village called Ryome in Nigeria, one would have experienced the annual harvest festival among the Jaba people. This harvest festival occurred at the beginning of the farming season. Sacrifices were made to gods or spirits through the shedding of chicken blood at the four corners of every plot of land. People

---

87. Iain Mathieson and Aylwyn Scally, "What Is Ancestry?" *PLoS Genetics 16(3)*, March 9, 2020.

88. M.G. Mokogobi, "Understanding Traditional African Healing." *African Journal for Physical Education, Recreation, and Dance*, September 2014, 24–34.

89. Jason Kelvin Phiri, *African Pentecostal Spirituality: A Study of the Emerging African Pentecostal Churches in Zambia*, University of Pretoria. October 2009 (https://repository.up.ac.za/bitstream/handle/2263/28976/Complete.pdf?sequence=6).

90. Ibid.

prayed to the gods for a good harvest to bring rain and to protect their crops from locusts and other insects.

In the case of my own ancestors, their prosperity or failure would have depended on the gods' decision on how great the crops' yield should be. The community's fate was determined by how happy and pleasant the gods were. If the gods were happy because of how they were treated, there would be a good harvest, less death, and no pestilence. If the gods are angry because of their maltreatment, the community would experience calamity, sickness, a poor harvest, and many deaths.

Again, Christians know that all blessings are made sufficient through God's grace.

Traditional and herbal healers have specified practices for effectively dispensing their medicine. Some duties include providing protection to individuals, groups, and families and administering healing medication. Also, they purge witches and wizards, destroy sorcery, remove curses, control the spirits of the dead, and access the forces of nature.[91]

This view of the duties of ancestors is contrary to the biblical view of disease and healing. The idea of one ancestral spirit fighting against another does not speak of the unity of the dead or express their common goal in building families or producing good sustenance. Instead it reveals the wickedness of the human heart and the fruitless efforts of man attempting to have a genuine relationship with the Creator through the channel of departed spirits.

Those who promote African traditional medicine have compared such healing practices with the Old and New Testaments of Scripture. They teach that there are healing commonalities. Such practitioners should not forget that the Bible does not take a stand against the use of herbs for food and medicine.[92]

However, the men of the Old Testament did not consult with departed spirits. Biblical teachings reject the traditional African belief that our health and wellness can be attained through the ancestors. Ancestral spirit do not determine the health and wellness of Africans.

The false belief of equating the Holy Spirit to an ancestral spirit is similar to the event that provoked God's anger in 1 Samuel 5. In that instance, the Philistines had equated their idol god, Dagon, with the Ark of God of Israel in the city of Ashdod.

How can some Bible-believing Christians, who know the Holy Spirit as a third member of the Godhead, water down the transcendent sovereignty of the Holy Spirit by putting him on an equal footing with African ancestors? Every falsehood will result in God's divine judgment.

---

91. Ibid.

92. Willem Berends, "African Traditional Healing Practices and the Christian Community." *Missiology: An International Review 21(3)*, July 1993.

When the presbytery takes an affliction to the Lord in prayer, all they need to attain healing is faith in Christ's authority and power.

Without a shadow of a doubt, these unbiblical teachings must be thrown out of the window. The Bible teaches that only God Almighty is to be revered (Psalm 11:19). We also read, in Hebrews 9:27, *"And as it is appointed unto men once to die, but after this the judgment…"* (KJV)

Therefore, no ancestor returns to earthly life once it is dead. And based on God's special grace and revelation, only prayer in the name of the Lord Jesus has the authority and power to redeem ugly human circumstances.

> *Some became fools through their rebellious ways and suffered affliction because of their iniquities… Then they cried out to the Lord in their trouble… He sent out his word and healed them; he rescued them from the grave.* (Psalm 107:17, 19–20, NIV)

Again, it is an act of idolatry to pray for healing and health in the name of a mortal person, an inanimate and animated object, or any demonic invocation. Only an immortal being could deal effectively with our health needs.

To this end, Jesus Christ, an immortal being, heals all disease and sickness. Matthew 10:8 tells us that he healed the sick, raised the dead, cured those with leprosy, and cast out demons. God's grace and generosity are sufficient to help us deal with any thorn in the flesh. Also, he promised that the church, in his name, would carry out even more extraordinary miracles, including healing.

The Bible commands us to pray and make our requests alone to God the Father through Christ Jesus, not to any departed spirit.

> *Be anxious for nothing, but in everything by prayer and supplication, with thanksgiving, let your requests be made known to God; and the peace of God, which surpasses all understanding, will guard your hearts and minds through Christ Jesus.* (Philippians 4:6–7, NKJV)

Jesus commanded, *"Stretch out your hand to heal and perform signs and wonders through the name of your holy servant Jesus"* (Acts 4:30, NIV). And John wrote, *"Very truly I tell you, whoever believes in me will do the works I have been doing, and they will do even greater things than these, because I am going to the Father"* (John 14:12, NIV).

The church has been given the power of excellent miraculous works in Christ Jesus through the Holy Spirit. This miraculous healing power has nothing to do with our mortal ancestors who are dead and await God's final judgment.

## IV. HEALING CAPABILITY

**Side effects of traditional and herbal healing.** The use of unregulated herbs has the potential to cause terrible side effects. The most prominent such practitioners practice in Asia and Africa.

For example, traditional Chinese herbal medicine affects human parts and organs. These treatments can affect the kidneys and liver, accelerate disease, and cause high blood pressure and hepatitis. Worrisomely, they sometimes use formulas consisting of five, ten, or thirty different herbs. This approach makes it difficult to get an accurate picture of the risk of the treatment—at least if the practitioner does not keep systematic records of adverse effects.

These factors may explain why Chinese herbal medicine traditionally uses therapies that are recognized for being dangerous, including substances such as mercury, arsenic, lead, licorice, coltsfoot, and aristolochic.[93]

**Herbal conceptual methodology.** The methodological concepts used in religious/spiritual healings can make it difficult to interpret facts. This includes defining religion and spirituality, assessing the pertinent issues, and identifying specific components such as social dimension, cognitive schemas that influence perception, and meditating behavior of such prayers.[94]

---

93. Xin Ma, Jing-Hua Peng, and Yi-Yang Hu, "Chinese Herbal Medicine-Induced Liver Injury." *Journal of Clinical and Translational Hepatology 2(3)*, September 2014, 170–175.

94. C. Kornreich and H.-J. Aubin, "Religion and Brain Functioning (Part 2): Does Religion Positively Impact Mental Health?" *Revue Medicale de Bruxelles 33(2)*, March-April 2012, 87–96.

CHAPTER SIX
# Modern Scientific Medicine

> The person who takes medicine must recover twice, once from the disease and once from the medicine.[95] —William Osler

SINCE I AM not an expert in modern scientific medicine specifically, or science in general, the information discussed in this chapter largely comes from the review of other literature.

The Merriam-Webster Dictionary defines the word *medicine* as "the science and art dealing with the maintenance of health and the prevention, alleviation, or cure of disease."[96]

Practitioners of modern scientific medicine include doctors, nurses, laboratory technicians, and various other specialties. Their tasks cover diagnosis, treatment, the prevention of disease, and medical research.[97]

The *Encyclopedia Britannica* states, "The medicine depends on a mythology of how the body works and how its inner organs are connected."[98] An organ, in biology, is a group of tissues in a living organism that have adapted to perform a specific function.

## I. HEALING SOURCE

The primary sources of healing in modern scientific medicine derive from surgical procedures, pharmaceuticals and medicines, therapy, and counselling. Medical professionals use approved drugs to treat specific diseases and sicknesses, provide treatment for various conditions, and administer preventive medicine where such an approach is needed. Sometimes surgical procedures—or in the case of many cancers, radiation—are performed to effect healing.

---

95. William Osler, "The person who takes…" *Goodreads*. Date of access: June 2, 2023 (https://www.goodreads.com/quotes/758943-the-person-who-takes-medicine-must-recover-twice-once-from-the).

96. "Medicine," *Merriam-Webster*. Date of access: April 29, 2023 (https://www.merriam-webster.com/dictionary/medicine).

97. "What Is Medicine?" *Medical News Today*. Date of access: May 20, 2020 (https://www.medicalnewstoday.com/articles/323679).

98. Wesley D. Smith, "Hippocrates," *Britannica*. Date of access: March 14, 2023 (https://www.britannica.com/biography/Hippocrates).

## II. METHOD OF DIAGNOSIS

All tests and diagnoses take place in laboratories to ascertain the best means of treatment. Most diagnoses are physiological, although sometimes they are psychological.

Laboratory assessments are limited in their ability to diagnose mental health issues. Although evidence regarding a patient's prognosis is useful, the clinical process remains focused on identifying the disease.

A group of researchers have reiterated that diagnosis provides clinicians with the means to organize and interpret a range of information supplied by patients. Symptoms, signs, tests, and investigations form the basis for decision-making.[99]

## III. TREATMENT

Practitioners of modern scientific medicine do not ever pray as part of their approach to healing or offering therapy and counselling. Instead the integrity of the recovery approach depends on the accuracy of laboratory examinations and test results.

## IV. HEALING CAPABILITY

In modern scientific medicine, the treatment is determined by laboratory tests. This description determines the prescription.

Malpractice is not allowed in medical practice and culture, since those in medical practice always aim for the highest precision in their techniques. The word *precision* is defined as

> the tailoring of medical treatment to the individual characteristics of each patient... to classify individuals into subpopulations that differ in their susceptibility to a particular disease or their response to a specific treatment. Preventive or therapeutic interventions can then be concentrated on those who will benefit, sparing expense and side effects for those who will not.[100]

However, it is essential to note that one of the deceptions of modern scientific medicine is the use of a placebo. Placebo is a sugar pill known which is administered

---

99. Peter Croft, Douglas G Altman, Jonathan J Deeks, Kate M Dunn, Alastair D Hay, Harry Hemingway, Linda LeResche, George Peat, Pablo Perel, Steffen E Petersen, Richard D Riley, Ian Roberts, Michael Sharpe, Richard J Stevens, Danielle A Van Der Windt, Michael Von Korff, and Adam Timmis, "The Science of Clinical Practice: Disease Diagnosis or Patient Prognosis? Evidence About "What Is Likely to Happen" Should Shape Clinical Practice." *BMC Medicine*, January 30, 2015, 1–2.

100. Geoffrey S. Ginsburg and Kathryn A. Phillips, "Precision Medicine: From Science to Value." *Health Affairs (Millwood)* 37(5), May 2018, 696.

by doctors; this gives patients a false sense of hope, as they think they will be cured. However, doctors often cannot find an explanation concerning why these medication-free pills sometimes provide relief from symptoms.[101]

The term *placebo* is described as a "harmless pill, medicine, or procedure prescribed more for the psychological benefit to the patient than for physiological effect."[102] In other words, this is a substance without an appreciable therapeutic effect.

Bishop, Aizlewood, and Adams explain that, psychologically, a placebo enhances patients' expectations. Furthermore, it invokes the power of mind-body interactions.[103]

An article on *WebMD* calls this type of episode "the power of the imagination," explaining that this is

> what occurs when patients think they're getting a fancy new drug, but what they're really getting is just a sugar pill. Then, in a case of 'mind over medicine,' they start to recover from their ailment as though they'd been taking the real deal."[104]

Yet another article claims that the "dummy pill is an insert (inactive) substance, typically a tablet, capsule or other dose form that does not contain an active drug ingredient… Physical placebos, or 'sham' treatments, have also been used, such as inactive acupuncture devices."[105]

This author continues by writing that combining an active drug with a placebo may be effective in treating diseases that involve the mental state and immune system, including asthma and multiple sclerosis. In addition, placebos have been used to treat sleep, anxiety, gastrointestinal disorder, chronic pain, and other disorders. However, it has adverse side effects due to psychological nocebo effects.[106]

---

101. "What Is the Placebo Effect?" *Drugs.com*. May 26, 2022 (https://www.drugs.com/article/placebo-effect.html).

102. Kenneth Gilbert, "Acknowledging the Place of Placebo," *Psychiatric Times*. October 15, 2020 (https://www.psychiatrictimes.com/view/acknowledging-place-placebo).

103. Felicity L. Bishop, Lizzi Azlewood, and Alison E. M. Adams, "When and Why Placebo-Prescribing Is Acceptable and Unacceptable: A Focus Group Study of Patients' Views." *PLoS One 9(7)*, July 9, 2014.

104. Serusha Govender, "Is the Nocebo effect Hurting Your Health?" *WebMD*. Date of access: March 14, 2022 (https://www.webmd.com/balance/features/is-the-nocebo-effect-hurting-your-health).

105. "What Is the Placebo Effect?" *Drugs.com*. May 26, 2022 (https://www.crugs.com/article/placebo-effect.html).

106. Ibid.

An article for *CBS News* cites a study that looked at 679 doctors in the United States, especially rheumatologists. This study shows that about eighty percent of doctors have prescribed fake drugs, placebos, in their clinical practice. However, fifty-six percent of the doctors interviewed recommended a placebo to their patients.[107]

In 2012, a study conducted among German doctors revealed that eighty-eight percent had used placebos with their patients at least once, most often active placebos like antibiotics. A U.K. study in 2013 found that ninety-seven percent of doctors had prescribed active placebos at least once in their careers. It has been estimated that for every one hundred patients treated, on average 8.33, or one in eleven, are given an active placebo.[108]

Some medical professionals have argued that prescribing placebos is unacceptable, on the basis that the prescribers are deceiving patients. By doing so, it is argued, doctors compromise patient autonomy, which could result in medical harm.

Other stories of medical and mental health in the literature show how deception is increasing. A group of researchers have observed,

> There's a lot of money to be made from telling healthy people they're sick: Some forms of medicalising ordinary life may now be better described as disease mongering: widening the boundaries of treatable illness in order to expand markets for those who sell and deliver treatments.[109]

The pharmaceutical industry continues to insist on "marketing diseases"[110] because the marketing strategy behind disease-mongering is to link a disease with a drug.

Michael Walsh reiterates this view: "Studies show that pharmaceutical industry 'normal' business is characterized by persistent deceit, ranging from subtle image manipulation to outright and frequent research fraud."[111] Pertaining to the fear of disease,

---

107. Daniel DeNoon, "50% of Doctors Prescribe Placebos," *CBS News*. October 24, 2008 (https://www.cbsnews.com/news/50-of-doctors-prescribe-placebos/).

108. Ed Cara, "You'd Be Surprised How Often Doctors Prescribe Placebos," *Gizmodo*. December 2, 2019 (https://gizmodo.com/youd-be-surprised-how-often-doctors-prescribe-placebos-1840155857).

109. Ray Moynihan, Iona Heath, and David Henry, "Selling Sickness: The Pharmaceutical Industry and Disease Mongering." *BMJ*, April 2002, 886–891.

110. Ibid.

111. Michael Walsh, "Malady Mongers: How Drug Companies Sell Treatment by Inventing Diseases," *Huffington Post*. June 8, 2018 (https://www.huffpost.com/entry/malady-mongers-how-drug-companies-sell-treatments-by-inventing-diseases_n_5b1ab5e4e4b0adfb8268c762).

Walsh references a statement made sexologist and psychologist Leonore Tiefer: "I feel that we're still in the ascendent in terms of people expecting more from medicine and therefore being gullible to disease-mongering claims."[112]

This appears to be the reason behind people's vulnerability and receptiveness to the medications doctors throw at them without question. It could also account for the prevalence of placebo use in treating many mild to serious diseases.

An article on *Medical News Today* claims that some patients with health challenges such as pain, anxiety, depression, epilepsy, erectile dysfunction, Parkinson's disease, cough, and fatigue received placebo prescriptions because it was expected to have a psychological effect on healing between the brain and body.[113]

If you suffered from one of these conditions and your doctor prescribed a placebo, and subsequently explained that to you, would you believe in the pill's efficacy and take it? Of course not. Pharmacists and doctors know that these colorful pills only have the ability to affect one's psychology. What a world of deception we live in!

As a theologian, I would suggest that the power of God's common grace is the true source of healing in such a case. Medical professionals know that a placebo cannot effect a cure, whereas God heals every illness, physiologically and psychologically, without the need for scientific medicine. t is accomplished through the work of Jesus on the cross.

Therefore, when a placebo is administered, the body produces God's grace for healing, and a patient is made whole.

Having noted the effect of a placebo, I do not in any way or form suggest that one shouldn't seek modern medical attention for illnesses. But I want to stress that the church has the sacred responsibility to seek God's face for our well-being, especially during times of crisis.

Medical professionals are affluent in God's unrestricted gift of intellectual knowledge, which they have acquired through intensive study. As a result, they have mastered a great deal of the function and interconnectedness of human physiology.

There are medical doctors who occasionally seek prayer support for wisdom as they undergo their own critical surgeries and illnesses. These Christian doctors know that complete healing comes from the Creator. Therefore, the church must always pray for God to give medical professionals the wisdom, understanding, patience, and courage to deal with the mystery of disease and sickness. This happens because of the belief that righteous prayer from a righteous presbytery can work supernatural outcomes.

---

112. Ibid.

113. "Is the Placebo Effect Real?" *Medical News Today*. Date of access: May 22, 2021 (https://www.medicalnewstoday.com/articles/306437).

Again, if the church looks inward, its members will be reassured that the pathogenesis of disease and sickness is rebellion and sin. Also, medical pathogenesis has its roots in the church. The PCPM has given the church healing power through the authority of Christ Jesus.

I believe that God's gift of intelligence has been used to study nature and human misery; the discovered solutions are intended to complement the presbytery healing ministry, not replace it. But since there have been substantial advancements in modern scientific medicine, the church has wholly neglected this divine charge to meet humanity's physiological, mental, and spiritual needs. If crisis members have faith and trust in the power of the Bible's promises concerning healing, their faith would stimulate their spirits to manifest healing physiologically. This is an affirmation of faith in the promises of Yahweh.

The church preaches, teaches, sings, and describes God's wonder-working character and deeds. Yet the church remains faithless in the testimony of divine healing. No wonder we are yet to understand the miraculous working of God in our bodies.

The task of the church is to obey God's instructions to James and have faith in his promises. God is waiting to set crisis members free from the captivity of sickness, but the church is not yet ready to witness the magical arts of God. God has instructed the board of elders in every local congregation to be instrumental in meeting the healing needs of crisis members.

CHAPTER SEVEN
# Mental Healthcare

Always laugh when you can. It is cheap medicine.[114] —Lord Byron

The greatest medicine of all is teaching people how not to need it.[115]
—Hippocrates

MENTAL HEALTHCARE EXISTS to provide treatment for mental illnesses. The World Health Organization describes menta health as "a state of well-being in which individuals realize their abilities, cope with the everyday stress of life, works productively and fruitfully, and contribute to their communities.[116]

The Canadian Chronic Disease Surveillance System (CCDSS): Mental Illness in Canada 2015 states,

> Mental illnesses are characterized by alterations in thinking; mood or behaviour associated with significant distress and impaired functioning. They result from complex interactions of biological, psychosocial, economic and genetic factors. Mental illnesses can affect individuals of any age; however, they often appear by adolescence or early adulthood. There are many different types of mental illnesses, and they can range from single, short-lived episodes to chronic disorders.[117]

Mental illness could also be defined as "changes in emotion, thinking, or behavior, or interaction with of these factors.[118]

---

114. Lord Byron, "Lord Byron Quotes," *Goodreads*. Date of access: June 2, 2023 (https://www.goodreads.com/author/quotes/44407.Lord_Byron).

115. Hippocrates, "The greatest medicine of all…" *Anderson Family Chiropractic*. June 2, 2020 (https://universitycharlottechiro.com/blog/200735-the-greatest-medicine-of-all-is-teaching-people-how-not-to-need-it-hippocrates).

116. Silvana Galderisi, Andreas Heinz, Marianne Kastrup, Julian Beezhold, and Norman Sartorius, "Toward a New Definition of Mental Health." *World Psychiatry 14(2)*, June 2015, 231–233.

117. "Report from the Canadian Chronic Disease Surveillance System: Mental Illness in Canada, 2015," *Public Health Agency of Canada*. May 2015 (https://healthycanadians.gc.ca/publications/diseases-conditions-maladies-affections/mental-illness-2015-maladies-mentales/alt/mental-illness-2015-maladies-mentales-eng.pdf)

118. "What Is Mental Illness?" *American Psychiatric Association*. Date of access: April 29, 2023 (https://www.psychiatry.org/patients-families/what-is-mental-illness).

One word that perhaps best explains the concept of mental illness is *abnormality*. When an individual doesn't function normally, they are assessed as having a form of mental illness, or mental ill health.

But what causes mental abnormalities? Sin. Sin causes the whole human system to malfunction, including the brain. No human's mental state has been normal since mankind's disobedience in Genesis 3.

Practitioners in mental healthcare include psychiatrists, psychologists, psychotherapists, therapists, counselors, traditional healers, physicians, nurses, social workers, and spiritualists. The presbytery's role in healing mental sickness is usually absent from the list, even though all these professionals enjoy God's grace in the healing process and none of them adequately understand the root cause of mental illness and the perfect source of healing—that is, unless they have a divine connection to the Creator through Jesus Christ.

## I. HEALING SOURCE

The source of healing in mental healthcare comes from multiple directions, including psychotherapy, counselling, medication, education, and community support programs.

But again, Bible-based faith healing prayer is typically not welcome. Instead religionists and spiritualists promote methods such as yoga, meditation, and mindfulness based on Buddhist and Hindus practices.

## II. METHOD OF DIAGNOSIS

Mental healthcare professionals do not fully understand mental illness. The diagnostic approaches in mental health take different forms. Most diagnoses are more effectively made through standardized psychological evaluations, observations, medical tests, and interviews, which mental health professionals use to assess an individual's mental health status. These tests help practitioners to evaluate, define, and identify the symptom associated with the disorder.

The Canadian Chronic Disease Surveillance System (CCDSS) recognizes individuals who do not meet all standard diagnostic criteria for a mental illness and assign a diagnostic code based on clinical assessment.[119]

The diagnosis of spiritual misery sin is missing from the diagnostic criteria for mental illness, even though all mental illness results from man's physical, mental, emotional, and spiritual imperfection. Our sinful nature causes ill health in our hearts and minds.

---

119. "Report from the Canadian Chronic Disease Surveillance System: Mental Illness in Canada, 2015," *Public Health Agency of Canada*. May 2015 (https://healthycanadians.gc.ca/publications/diseases-conditions-maladies-affections/mental-illness-2015-maladies-mentales/alt/mental-illness-2015-maladies-mentales-eng.pdf).

Some professionals may diagnose mental health problems by approaching the spirit world, natural energy, or other available powers—for example, the spirit of animals or ancestral spirits.

However, James 5:8–13 lays out the presbytery diagnostic approach that non-Christian professionals don't recognize or use in their diagnoses. It seems that the spiritual diagnosis criteria of the American Psychological Association takes its cue from Buddhist and Hinduist perspectives.

## III. TREATMENT

The treatment of mental illness ranges from preventive to proactive and reactive. Aside from medication, such as antidepressants, other approaches can include a balanced diet, exercise, and counselling.

However, no treatment approach suits every mental health issue, because the curse of sin has affected every aspect of man's biology, causing philosophical and mental diseases that we do not understand.

For some patients in mental health settings, religion and spirituality—not necessarily Christian faith and spirituality—are emerging as relevant factors in research and clinical care.[120]

For example, a survey by Lindgren & Coursey (1995) of twenty-eight "seriously ill" psychiatric patients from a rehabilitation center with diagnoses including schizophrenia, bipolar disorder, unipolar depression, schizoaffective disorder, and personality disorder found that sixty percent reported religion/spirituality as having a great deal of beneficial impact on their illness through the feelings of fostered of being cared for and of not being alone. In addition, seventy-six percent thought daily about God or spiritual matters.[121]

## IV. HEALING CAPABILITY

The process of treating mental illness does not heal every instance of it, nor could any specialist make that claim. Types of healing may include medication, counselling, therapy, stimulation techniques, physical exercises, and dietary changes. The spiritual dimension of therapy is often ignored.

The real essence of a human is his spiritual aspect, and we must paying attention to this when treating mental illness.

We are moving beyond positivism, which limits knowledge to observable facts, and empiricism, which regards nothing as accurate save what can be sensed, towards

---

120. Koenig, "Religion and Medicine II: Religion, Mental Health, and Related Behaviors," 97–109.

121. Karen N. Lindgren and Robert D. Coursey, "Spirituality and Serious Mental Illness: A Two-Part Study." *Psychosocial Rehabilitation Journal 18(3)*, January 1995, 93–111.

a participant-observer type of approach.[122] This approach is relevant to the PCPM in healing mental sickness.

In the PCPM, the crisis member (participant) and the presbytery have the same sources for effective healing, the Holy Spirit and God's word. An active experience of the PCPM faith prayer is vital. Through participant observation, a professional can gain access to a patient they would not otherwise be able to treat.

One cannot provide spiritual healing while one is spiritually deficient. Religionists and spiritualists who seek to provide spiritual healing must first wrestling with their own spiritual needs—and win—before attempting to heal others.[123]

A mental health professional who does not have Christian values and skills cannot provide spiritual healing to a believer's mental health issue from the living God's perspective.

Earlier, we explained that a mental illness is akin to an abnormality. But what causes such an abnormality? An article from *WebMD* writes,

> Although the exact cause of most mental illnesses is not known, it is becoming clear through research that many of these conditions are caused by a combination of biological, psychological, and environmental factors.[124]

Of course, sin is the root cause of every human predicament. Individual mental health problems today may not be linked to sinful acts, however. A victim should seek both divine treatments and humanistic remedies.

Mental health experts should understand that mankind's relationship with the Creator is our greatest resource for dealing with psychological crises. We are living souls endowed with spirit, and the spirit connects us to God's Spirit. Nevertheless, the human spirit and soul are wounded and imperfect due to sin. Our hearts and minds are polluted with weakness and wickedness; we need God's daily renewal to function (Jeremiah 17:9, Acts 17:28, Romans 12:2).

---

122. Larry Culliford, "Spiritual Care and Psychiatric Treatment: An Introduction." *Advances in Psychiatric Treatment 8(4)*, 2002, 249–258.

123. Peter Nolan and Paul Crawford, "Towards a Rhetoric of Spirituality in Mental Health Care." *Journal of Advanced Nursing*, June 28, 2008, 289–294; and Larry Culliford, *Spiritual Care and Psychiatric Treatment: An Introduction* (New York, NY: Cambridge University Press, 2018), 249–258.

124. "Causes of Mental Illness," *WebMD*. Date of access: April 29, 2023 (https://www.webmd.com/mental-health/mental-health-causes-mental-illness).

Physical dysfunction and mental illness have much to do with our brain abnormalities and hormonal imbalances.[125] These are indicators that something is wrong with the human mental system.

The Bible teaches that human and environmental abnormalities and imbalances result from sin, lack of knowledge of God's righteousness, and lack of genuine fear of God. The Bible reveals, *"The fear of the Lord is the beginning of knowledge, but fools despise wisdom and instruction"* (Proverbs 1:7 NIV).

The absence of the word of God in the human heart can cause mental illness (Psalm 119:9–16). These conditions give space to fear, stress, anxiety, loneliness, worry, bitterness, anger, unforgiveness, greed, selfishness, depression, and a host of other mental health problems (Deuteronomy 28:28, 2 Corinthians 2:10–11, Philippians 4:6–7, Hebrews 12:15).

The Bible testifies that such conditions cause all of our issues, including mental illness. Just as there are many diseases in our world, the crises of mental illness will continue to increase because more and more people, especially the young, are rejecting God and adopting the vanities of life. Our generation thinks that peace, success, happiness, education, and money are the true means of gaining satisfaction and excellence. However, only godly righteousness, knowledge, and fear can transform the rising problem of mental health.

As we read in Proverbs 14:34, *"Righteousness exalts a nation, but sin is a reproach to any people"* (NRSV). Proverbs 3:7–8 tells us, *"Do not be wise in your own eyes; fear the Lord and shun evil. This will bring health to your body and nourishment to your bones"* (NIV).

---

125. Margaret Altemus, "Hormone-Specific Psychiatric Disorders: Do They Exist?" *Arch Women Mental Health 13(1)*, February 2010, 25–26.

## CHAPTER EIGHT
# Religion and Spirituality

> Gratitude is the best medicine. It heals your mind, body and soul, increasing its vibration. Once you are vibrating at a higher frequency, you are aligning to the universe to attract more things to be grateful for.[126] — Asma Bushra Anwar

UNDERSTANDING THE ROLES of religion and spirituality in healing medicine, in this chapter we shall define the terms religion and spirituality.

## WHAT IS RELIGION?

Religion began with Satan, whose goal has been to take the place of God, the Creator. God created angelic beings, including Lucifer, Satan, who invented religion as a substitute for God's way.

All religions have a substitute god. In a sermon, Fred R. Coulter says that religion means taking one's eyes off the fact that God is God. When we get your eyes off the facts and get into feelings and suppositions, we start to self-deceive.[127]

When we engage in religion without the Creator's ruling, God's light is snuffed out in our hearts and substituted with darkness. Jesus said, *"But if your eyes are unhealthy, your whole body will be full of darkness. If then the light within you is darkness, how great is that darkness!"* (Matthew 6:33. NIV)

This description of religion explains why the Bible teaches that God hates religion. Being religious is about searching for an unknown supreme Being and not living in a relationship with the known supreme Being. It's about searching for an unknown supreme Being while rejecting the revealed way, truth, and life about the known supreme Being.

In religion, as well as manufactured spirituality, there is a gap of darkness in the relationship between the mortal man and immortal Being, the finite and infinite, the unrighteous and righteous, and creatures and the Creator. Since the gap of darkness exists, man loses the ability to relate with the immortal Father.

In that state of bewilderment, mankind looks for a substitute to satisfy his spiritual yearning. What will man do to meet the desire implanted within him for a relationship

---

126. Asma Bushra Anwar, "Gratitude is the best medicine..." *Goodreads*. Date of access: June 2, 2023 (https://www.goodreads.com/author/quotes/20548156.Asma_Bushra_Anwar).

127. Fred R. Coulter, "Who God Hates Religion #3: Who Started Religion?" July 31, 1999 (https://www.cbcg.org/series/religion/god-hates-religion-05.html).

and fellowship with God the Father? He encounters aspects of creation like the sun and moon, wild beasts and flying birds, and deems them good enough to take the place of the Creator. He sets them up as objects of worship to help him attain spirituality.

All of the world's major religions have erected crafted gods to worship in the place of the Creator. This is at the heart of the practice of spirituality throughout human history. Thus, all religions have representatives, created intermediaries.

In my opinion, without apology, religion and spirituality is nothing more than an ideological, philosophical, and intellectual pursuit. When religious people pray, they pray to anything perceived to be higher than themselves. These prayers may or may not be addressed to the supreme Being. Buddhism, for instance, is not a theistic religion, so they pray to the universe.[128]

Scripture states that religion is connected with iniquity (Ezekiel 28:13–15). Religion is Satan's continuous effort to dethrone God, and it becomes the object of man's worship. Religion and spirituality are constructed out of cultural and social resources, and the same processes are involved in creating non-religious belief systems as religious ones.[129] Religion is developed from human thought, experience, social structure, and cultural beliefs, which Satan initiated and controlled.

The fact that there are hundreds of religions, each with its tangible statues, should demonstrate that religion is about human relationships with its own creations. These religious and spiritual practices have all kinds of crafted images to represent their mindset and portray the spiritual concept of the supreme Being.

Many researchers distinguish between religiosity and spirituality, indicating that spirituality rejects religious dogma. Instead it ties in to religious concepts such as God, Scripture, and creationism.[130] David Tacey sees religion as involving a private experience of soul and spirit through culture, dreams, and conversational experiences with humans and non-humans.[131]

---

128. Larry Dossey, "Spirituality, Prayer, and Medicine: What Is the Fuss Really About?" *AMA Journal of Ethics*. May 2005 (https://journalofethics.ama-assn.org/article/spirituality-prayer-and-medicine-what-fuss-really-about/2005-05).

129. James Murphy, "Beyond 'Religion' and 'Spirituality': The Consequences of a 'Meaning Systems' Understanding for the Study of 'Religion' and 'Non-Religion.'" *Canterbury Christ Church University*, September 5–7, 2016, 1.

130. Jonathon McPhetres and Miron Zuckerman, "Religiosity Predicts Negative Attitudes towards Science and Lower Levels of Science Literacy." *PLOS One 13(11)*, November 27, 2018.

131. Tacey, "Spiritual Connectedness and Healing," 4.

## WHAT IS SPIRITUALITY?

The biggest dilemma in human healthcare and wellness rests in a broad understanding of what spirituality is. According to researcher Christina Maria Puchalski, it is rather unfortunate that only in the early 1990s did academic centers, medical and nursing schools, residency programs, and hospitals begin to recognize the role of spiritual care as a dimension of palliative care.[132]

Our poor understanding of the role of the Christian faith in addressing problems of suffering and pain in human history, and the development of scientific medicine, have influenced the negative view of faith prayer. Sarah Whitman writes, "We are at the initial stages of our scientific understanding of how their (majority of religions) tenets and practice affect health."[133]

This assertion reveals that Puchalski has forgotten the pathogenesis of modern medicine and the role of faith prayer for healing among different human groups. She believes that the dilemma of accepting the spiritual role of the church in healthcare and wellness only began in the 1990s.

It perplexes the mind to read that many homes for long-term care (LTC) in Ontario, Canada increasingly struggle over how spiritual care fits, who should take responsibility for it, and how funding dollars should best be allocated.[134] In comparison, history submits to us that what is called medical and mental health today was started by the church to share the soteriology of Christ's mission to the dying world.

It is understood that scientists have tried to destroy the pathogenesis relationship and separate religion from science, especially in the industrialized nations of the west. But developing countries still see modern scientific medicine as part of the healing ministry of the church of Jesus Christ. This historical relationship existed in ancient Egypt, Greece, and early Christianity through the Middle Ages, the Renaissance, and the Age of Enlightenment, when the split between religion and medicine became final and complete.[135] Harold Koenig states that the first western hospital for the care of the sick amidst the general population was built by religious organizations and staffed by religious

---

132. Christina Maria Puchalski, "Religion, Medicine and Spirituality: What We Know, What We Don't Know, and What We Do." *Asian Pacific Journal of Cancer Prevention*, 2010.

133. Sarah M. Whitman, "Pain and Suffering as Viewed by the Hindu Religion." *The Journal of Pain 8(8)*, August 2007), 607–613.

134. Thomas St. James O'Connor and Elizabeth Meakes, "Three Emerging Spiritual Practices in the Canadian Association for Spiritual Care (CASC): From Pastoral Care and Counselling to Multi-Faith, Evidence-Based Spiritual Care and Psycho-Spiritual Therapy." *The Journal of Pastoral Care and Counselling 75(4)*, August 27, 2021.

135. Koenig, "Religion and Medicine II: Religion, Mental Health, and Related Behaviors," 97.

orders. Physicians were members of the clergy and their licenses to practice medicine was issued by the church.

It must be stated that from the beginning of the church's physical healing ministry, its primary mission has been evangelization and physical healing. Today, the codes of conduct that exist among hospital chaplains prohibit evangelization and heavy-handedness.[136]

The act of not sharing with a person how to remedy their condition defeats the very purpose of the healing mission of Jesus Christ. When the light of the gospel transforms a person, they are plucked out of their hospital beds. Thus, the role of faith prayer for physical and spiritual healing in the power and authority of Jesus Christ is in jeopardy.

Scientists have tried to destroy this fundamental aspect of the history of modern scientific medicine. Why do scientists and non-Christian medical professionals disbelieve the efficacy of faith healing prayer when they have not proved the existence of God, who answers healing prayers? No study can prove whether God answers prayer, or even whether God exists.

How could a non-Christian experience healing because of prayer in the name of Jesus Christ when they believe that consciousness is derived from the human brain and not faith in the healing power and authority of Christ? It is an article of faith in most scientific circles that consciousness is derived from the brain, and its effects are confined to the brain and body. It is also an assumption that conscious intentions cannot act remotely in space and time.[137]

When we believe that human consciousness resides within the brain, we lose the reality of something much higher than the human brain. It shows that we don't acknowledge the existence of the Creator of that human brain, the supreme Being in the person of Jesus Christ. Neither does the non-Christian believe in the healing authority and power in the blood of the sinless Christ.

The church's role in the history of modern scientific medicine cannot be erased, no matter how hard intellectuals try to brush it aside. Christianity is the root of modern scientific medicine.

The local presbytery must resume its primary function of caring for the total needs of crisis members. The preaching of God's word quickens, empowers, and convicts sinners into embracing the gift of Christ's righteousness (John 16:8–11, Hebrews 4:12). He takes care and heals the broken soul, providing access into the presence of God for the healing of afflictions.

---

136. Dossey, "Spirituality, Prayer, and Medicine: What Is the Fuss Really About?"

137. Ibid.

Christ uses the teaching of the word to develop the redeemed soul into spiritual maturity and his likeness (2 Corinthians 5:17, Galatians 3:26). The process of spiritual maturation gives each believer a daily sanctification experience. These sanctified experiences cause us to know how to handle the arrows of Satan and how to correctly apply principles from the word to our daily struggles against the world and the devil.

Christ uses healing to meet the mental and physical needs of afflicted members of the church. Through the presbytery, the ministry of the Holy Spirit aims to redeem the psychological and physical challenges of the devil's works.

Modern medical scientists must recognize and genuinely pursue the reality of the interconnectivity of the body, mind, and spirit to achieve total healing. The holistic treatment of a person cannot occur by focusing on merely their physiobiological components, neglecting the central spiritual part. Medical professionals must recognize that spirituality is a particular need that affects healthcare decision-making, and spirituality also affects healthcare outcomes, including quality of life.[138] In an attempt to define spirituality, Puchalski et al. understand that

> spirituality is an aspect of humanity that refers to the way individuals seek and express meaning and purpose, and the way they experience their connectedness to the moment, to self, to others, to nature, and to the significant or sacred.[139]

Health professionals are finally putting it together that every human being has a spiritual dimension, a quality that goes beyond religious affiliation, that strives for inspiration, reverence, meaning, and purpose, even in those who do not believe in the existence of God. The spiritual dimension tries to be in harmony with the universe, strives for answers about the infinite, and comes into focus when the person faces emotional stress, physical illness, or death.[140]

---

138. Christina Puchalski, Betty Ferrell, Rose Virani, Shirley Otis-Green, Pamela Baird, Janet Bull, Harvey Chochinov, George Handzo, Holly Nelson-Becker, Maryjo Prince-Paul, Karen Pugliese, and Daniel Sulmasy, "Improving the Quality of Spiritual Care as a Dimension of Palliative Care: The Report of the Consensus Conference." *Journal of Palliative Medicine 12(10)*, October 2009, 885–904.

139. Ibid., 885

140. Ruth Beckmann Murray and Judith Proctor Zentner, *Nursing Concepts for Health Promotion* (London, UK: Prentice Hall, 1989).

The universe is composed entirely of a divine loving consciousness. Some may refer to this as "God," while others may understand it as simply the living spirit of the universe itself.[141]

Based on this colossal dilemma, spirituality can be described in different ways by different people and faith groups for various reasons, applications, and practices based on values, ultimate beliefs, and a sense of purpose.

> Spirituality is intimately connected to the supernatural, the mystical, and to organized religion, although also extends beyond organized religion (and begins before it). Spirituality includes both a search for the transcendent and the discovery of the transcendent and so involves traveling along the path that leads from nonconsideration to questioning to either staunch nonbelief or belief, and if belief, then ultimately to devotion and finally, surrender.[142]

On the other hand, Tacey describes spirituality as "wholeness."[143] He further notes that when researchers report whether religion/spirituality heals physical, mental, and even spiritual afflictions, they present all religious/spiritual healing approaches on the same level.

One of the definitions of spirituality, from Giovanni Dienstmann, and the one that reveals the confusion at to what spirituality is all about, goes like this:

> spirituality is a worldview and the way of life based on the belief that there is more to life than what meets the senses, more to the universe than just purposeless mechanics, more to consciousness than just electrical impulses in the brain, and more to our existence than the body and its needs.[144]

Dienstmann explains further that spirituality usually involves believing in a higher form of intelligence or consciousness that runs the universe as well as life after death.

---

141. Gary Zukav, *The Seat of the Soul* (New York, NY: Simon & Schuster, 2014).

142. Harold G. Koenig, D.E. King, V.B. Carson, *Handbook of Religion and Health, Second Edition* (New York, NY: Oxford University Press, 2012), 3.

143. Tacey, "Spiritual Connectedness and Healing," 1.

144. Giovanni Dienstmann, "What Is Spirituality? A Guide to Spiritual Paths and Practices," *Live & Dare*. Date of access: April 29, 2023 (https://liveanddare.com/what-is-spirituality).

Dienstmann's definition explains some professionals' dilemma in understanding the true essence of spirituality, especially as it pertains to spiritual and scientific medical healing. Spirituality is not simply a worldview, a way of life based on belief. It is not limited to superhuman intelligence, wisdom, philosophy, or an unknown consciousness that runs the universe. One can believe that the longest reptile in the world is an anaconda; that does not make the snake spiritual, nor does it make the snake's worshiper spiritual. The spirit of lions and other wild cats, as powerful, brave, and violent as they are, cannot constitute the characteristic of spirituality attributed to man. Lower mammals such as reptiles, birds, water creatures, trees, and rocks do not have spirits and souls that bring physical, mental, and spiritual healing to man's crises. Neither does man share or have the exact source of spirit and soul as other mortal creatures.

Only an immortal spiritual Being is capable of inducing, inducting, and transforming the evil spirit of a mortal being and causing it to be spiritual. The evil spirit of a mortal being cannot change another evil spirit of a mortal being into a spiritual state. Even King Solomon was hyperbolic in Ecclesiastes 3:20, stating that all living and breathing creations would die and return to dust, including man. And then there is Genesis 7:21–22, which states that all flesh shall fail and return to dust.

The human spirit source came from God's breath of life (Genesis 2:7), not from other creatures. Therefore, creatures cannot be spiritual sources for humans. Man is more than a higher animal, as the evolutionist thinks. The Bible says of believers: *"I have said, 'You are "gods"; you are all sons of the Most High'"* (Psalm 82:6, NIV).

The Bible describes animals' lives as mortal and perishable. The human spirit and soul return to God through whom they came into existence. The creation of man and woman in the image of Yahweh makes them the pinnacle of creation.

In contrast, the spirits and souls of all other created living things go back to the earth at the termination of their earthly existence.

The human race is not just another branch in the evolutionary tree of living life (Genesis 1:20–25). Neither does man share the same spirit, soul, breath, flesh, and blood as all other living creature, as Charles Darwin and promoters of evolution would like us to believe.

Technological advancement and the development of God-given intelligence presently link human DNA to the Adam of the Bible. Scientific reports involving the analysis of DNA sequences point back to the first man and the first woman from which all humans descended. One researcher, Abner Chou, notes that science has revealed a commonality in human cells, the proof of which can be found in mitochondria.[145]

---

145. Abner Chou, *What Happened in the Garden: The Reality and Ramifications of the Creation and Fall of Man* (Michigan, MI: Kregel Academic & Professional, 2016).

All other creatures were created for the benefit of man. Man was created for God's glory.

> Therefore **God has highly exalted him and bestowed on him the name that is above every name, so that at the name of Jesus every knee should bow, in heaven and on earth and under the earth,** and every tongue confess that Jesus Christ is Lord, to the glory of God the Father. (Philippians 2:9–11, ESV)

Islamic ethics surrounding the treatment of animals teaches that "Allah made all living creatures." Another writer asserts that

> the Qur'an explicitly states that animals can be used for human benefit. "It is God who provided for you all livestock, that you may ride on some of them and from some, you may derive your food. And other uses in them for you to satisfy your heart's desires. On them, as on ships, you make journeys" (Qur'an 40:79–80).[146]

It is a misunderstanding that man shares the same spirit, soul, and purpose of existence with the rest of creation. This misunderstanding has led to the development of many religions and types of spirituality around the world. Some people derive their spirituality from the spirits and souls of animals, relying on them as a medium of worship and using them as a spiritual source of health and healing.

Today, religion and spirituality—at least, the forms not derived from faith in Christ—are increasingly included in healthcare policies.[147] For example, Puchalski started the first formal spirituality course for medical students in the United States in 1991 at George Washington Medical School.[148] In 2012, a survey about teaching spirituality in medical schools showed that ninety percent of United States medical schools taught some form of spirituality, and fifty-nine percent of British medical schools had courses on spirituality.[149]

---

146. Sarra Tlili, "Animal Ethics in Islam: A Review Article," *Religions 9(9)*, September 10, 2018, 269.

147. Larry Culliford, *Spiritual Care and Psychiatric Treatment: An Introduction*.

148. Christina Maria Puchalski, "Religion, Medicine and Spirituality: What We Know, What We Don't Know, and What We Do," 45–49.

149. Giancarlo Lucchetti, Alessandra Lamas Granero Lucchetti, Daniele Corcioli Mendes Espinha, Leandro Romani de Oliveira, José Roberto Leite, and Harold G. Koenig, "Spirituality and Health in the Curricula of Medical Schools in Brazil." *BMC Med Education*, August 18, 2012.

# Religion and Spirituality

This asserts the undeniable role of yearning patients to connect to what they believe to be the Creator of their physiological and spiritual beings. Addressing spirituality with patients has been shown to positively impact a range of health outcomes, including improved quality of life, increased ability to cope, increased self-esteem, a greater sense of hope, and a more extraordinary ability to find meaning.[150]

The latent sensitivities of this topic provide a reason to include teaching about spirituality in the curriculums of many medical schools. If spirituality is a sensitive topic that needs to be addressed, it would be better for doctors to do it in an informed fashion.

But the question remains: which spirituality is taught in medical schools? What are the sources for such spirituality? What or who is behind such spirituality? The fact that the word *spirituality* sounds pleasing to the ears, looks attractive to the eyes, and appeals to the mind and imagination does not guarantee that humans should look unto creation as the means for physiological and spiritual healings. Almost all the practices associated with yoga, except mindfulness and connection, are exercise practiced by man since time immemorial. These exercises have now become channels for healing.

When I was growing up in a typical village in central Nigeria, the people were engaged in all kinds of exercises that are practiced in yoga today. Besides the robust work on the farm, we participated in sporting activities, local wrestling, and gymnastics. We ended up chasing animals into their designated abodes. What we call yoga today in the scientific world is nothing to compare with the acrobatic exercises in my village. In the scientific world, however, such a lifestyle is considered to be primitive.

This effort of teaching spirituality in medical schools is likely to be an uphill climb because of the tenets of other world religions being taught in medical schools as well. One group of researchers explains from a scientific perspective that religion's effect on health is an important one yet to be fully answered.[151]

It is partly due to the preponderance of studies being in the United States, Europe, Israel, and China, that research from Muslims, Hindus, and Buddhists is relatively rare, difficult to access, and hard to interpret. Medical schools will encounter a similar situation in applying spirituality to traditional and herbal healings.

---

150. Kenneth Calmar, "Spiritual and Medical Edicuation." *Medical Education 42(2)*, March 2008), 123–125; Richard Egan and Fiona Timmins, "Spirituality as a Public Health Issue: The Potential Role of Spirituality in Promoting Health," *Spirituality in Healthcare: Perspectives for Innovative Practice* (New York, NY: Springer International Publishing, 2019), 55–66; and Paul A. Swinton, Arthur Stewart, Ioannis Agouris, Justin W.K. Keough, and Ray Lloyd, "A Biomechanical Analysis of Straight and Hexagonal Barbell Deadlifts Using Submaximal Loads." *Journal of Strength and Conditioning Research*, July 2011, 2000–2009.

151. Koenig, "Religion and Medicine II: Religion, Mental Health, and Related Behaviors."

The quest to train medical professionals about religion and spirituality based on the full variety of world religions and spiritualities is uncharted territory; only time will showcase the efficacy of such efforts. The fact that there are hundreds of different views, beliefs, and practices of spirituality should inform the reader that there needs to be more clarity about what spirituality is. Hundreds of blogs and websites on spirituality try to satisfy the human ego and search for truth.

But one who clearly understands spirituality knows that it is an abstract word and doesn't necessarily take a source from the material world or metaphysics. As many different perspectives exist, so are the different understandings of spirituality and its application in people's daily lives.

The concept of spirituality is misunderstood and misused because of limited knowledge and too little acceptance of the Creator. This is one of the most complex human endeavors.

Peter la Cour and Povl Götke have concluded that the term *spirituality* is of little use unless it is followed by one or two notions or cue words that frame what is meant by the word in the specific context, because spirituality could mean "an inner striving," "lived belief," "contacting invisible world and energies," or another unexplained mental phenomenon.[152]

## GOD'S GRACE OF HEALING

Any spiritual healing outside the healing power and authority of Jesus Christ happens due to God's common grace, which enables recovery to occur to all creatures. Even wild beasts get sick and are healed. Reptiles and all other creeping creatures also enjoy healing through God's mercy. The Bible testifies that all of creation enjoys healing as a product of God's unconditional love. The understanding and love of God enable him to administer his grace of healing to all.

The Lord Jesus and apostle Paul explain how God uses his common grace to heal every human condition:

> *But I tell you, love your enemies and pray for those who persecute you, that you may be children of your Father in heaven. He causes his sun to rise on the evil and the good, and sends rain on the righteous and the unrighteous.* (Matthew 5:44–45, NIV)

---

152. Peter la Cour & Povl Götke, "Understanding the Word 'Spirituality' by Theologians Compared to Lay People: An Empirical Study from a Secular Region." Journal of Health Care Chaplaincy, 18(3–4), July 2012, 97–109.

> *In the past, he let all nations go their own way. Yet he has not left himself without testimony: He has shown kindness by giving you rain from heaven and crops in their seasons; he provides you with plenty of food and fills your hearts with joy.* (Acts 14:16–17, NIV)

So people of every race, generation, religion, spirituality, and belief can enjoy the rain, sunshine, and air through the Creator. These benefits are not derived from humanity or any departed spirits or created objects. Instead they receive these blessings as gifts from God.

## I. HEALING SOURCE

The source of healing from a religious and spiritual perspective dwells on preventive medicine. Such healing is possible through observance of religious teachings and behavioral responses to a set of laws, rules, or regulations. Most recoveries in this arena take place in psychological or mental healthcare.

Let us now look at some essential concepts related to religion and spirituality.

PRINCIPLES IN THE PRACTICE OF RELIGIOUS/SPIRITUAL HEALINGS

Because religious/spiritual healing is based on the relationship between humans and other creatures, the use of terms like soul, spirit, transcendence, higher Being, and higher power do not refer to the Creator of the universe. For religious/spiritual healers, the use of "God" or "transcendence" doesn't always refer to the holy, sinless, immortal Creator of all things. When they use words like spirit, spiritual, or spirituality, they aren't referring to the infinite, infallible, and incorruptible Holy Spirit but rather the finite, fallible, and corruptible spirit of man.

In this section, we will present amazing yet confusing truths about man's ignorance and efforts to count out the Creator in order focus on his own delusions.

Responding to the following questions will help us gain an understanding of religious/spiritual healing that excludes the Creator of the universe.

- Who are religious/spiritual healers?
- What is religious/spiritual healing?
- How do religious/spiritual healers describe the sources of religion/spirituality?
- Where do religious/spiritual healers get their healing powers?
- What hinders the true efficacy of religious/spiritual healing?

**Who are religious/spiritual healers?** Religious/spiritual healers claim to be sacred beings who possess divine powers to navigate natural or supernatural energies to effect healing. They have an affinity with spiritual beings and facilitate relationships between humans and spiritual entities. These spiritual healers see themselves as sacred helpers for the spirit world, and they carry a heavy responsibility to help humans living on the earth to facilitate prayer and communicate with the human spirit to recognize problems and promote healing. know which problems are there and how to promote healing.[153]

According to Malcolm Tatum,

> Spiritual healing is a collective term for various types of alternative practices related to restoring wholeness of body, mind and spirit by calling on energies or forces beyond the human condition. While the specific process varies from one tradition to another, all forms of spiritual healing have to do with connecting with supernatural resources that are capable of bringing about healing, assuming that a restoration to wholeness is within the Divine or Universal will. It is not unusual for this kind of alternative healing to make use of common elements such as oil or water, coupled with chanting or prayer as part of the process.[154]

These healers have skills that focus on treating a person's soul so they can lead a happier, healthier, and more fulfilling life. It is said that they can sense spirits and pass spiritual healing energy to themselves and others.[155]

**What is religious/spiritual healing?** There are many descriptions of the meaning of spiritual healing. However, the writings of Aletheia Luna and Malcolm Tatum are some of the most sophisticated—and delusional. They propagate falsehoods of the highest order. Their instructions about religious/spiritual healing take a cue from Buddhism. Below are some quotes from their teachings.

According to Luna, spiritual healing is

---

153. "Who Are Spiritual Healers, and What Do They Do?" *My Amazing Blog*. May 19, 2021 (https://myamazingblog2021.blogspot.com).

154. Malcolm Tatum, "What Is Spiritual Healing?" *The Health Board*. March 29, 2023 (https://www.thehealthboard.com/what-is-spiritual-healing.htm).

155. Su Mason, "Spiritual Healing: What Is It? Does It Work and Does It Have a Place in Modern Healthcare?" *Royal College of Psychiatrists*. Date of access: June 2, 2023 (https://www.rcpsych.ac.uk/docs/default-source/members/sigs/spirituality-spsig/su-mason-spiritual-healing-in-modern-healthcare-x.pdf?sfvrsn=4fc21449_2).

…a practice (and experience) of restoring, harmonizing our spirit or soul. It seems as a transcendental experience of reconnecting with our true nature.[156]

Perhaps a better question is "what isn't my True Nature?"

There are innumerable names from endless traditions that point to what our True Nature is. It has been called Brahman, Tao, Buddha-nature, Christ Consciousness, Self, Allah, the Absolute, Non-Dual Awareness, the Holy Spirit, Spirit, God, Goddess, Satchitananda, Oneness—just to name a few.

Our True Nature is often described as infinite, boundless, pure, all-pervading, serene, silent, and unconditionally loving. It is the space from which everything arises and returns, and has no beginning or end. We call it the Sacred Wild as it manifests as both form and formlessness, and is ultimately indefinable and unknowable to the mind which tries to limit it through mental constructs. It is the very essence of inner peace and freedom.[157]

Luna believes that pursuing spiritual enlightenment is a delusional and non-existential spiritual treadmill. It is a life cycle of garbage in and garbage out. Her explanation of chasing after "enlightenment" is meaningless and fruitless.

The following lengthy quote summarizes her confusion about spiritual enlightenment:

Enlightenment is a big juicy carrot dangled in front of the ravenous mind that believes itself to be broken and missing something. In other words, enlightenment is a story created by the ego that feels separate from the Divine. It doesn't exist…

…It's a spiritual treadmill.

The more we seek, the more we reinforce the separate self, the ego. The more the ego is reinforced, the more we seek. And so continues the cycle of unhappiness and desperation…

Enlightenment doesn't exist because there is no "me" to become enlightened.

---

156. Aletheia Luna, "5 Types of Spiritual Healing (& What to Be Careful Of)," *Loner Wolf*. March 31, 2023 (https://lonerwolf.com/spiritual-healing).

157. Aletheia Luna, "7 Ways to Awaken to Your True Nature" (THE END)," *Loner Wolf*. November 18, 2022 (https://lonerwolf.com/true-nature).

> How can "I" become enlightened when the "I" is just a mental story to begin with – the very story the entire spiritual journey is set out to dismantle!?
>
> The whole point of the spiritual journey isn't to reinforce this small and separate ego, but to untangle this contracted "me" energy, make space in the mind, and allow us to taste the Truth of Who We Really Are: Our True Nature.[158]

Luna cites Scott Kiloby, a teacher in spiritual enlightenment, to illustrate her concept of the spiritual journey:

> There are many spiritual methods and belief systems that promise future fulfillment, happiness, money or other success. If you look closely, the whole idea that you can gain something from spirituality is based on a false premise, which is that there is a separate "you" that lacks something… As long as you seek enlightenment, enlightenment is unavailable. In seeking, you act from the false concept that you are a separate self that lacks something. It is that very concept that creates the need for a search. Enlightenment is the realization that there is no separate "you" to gain anything personally from life. There is only life and you are THAT. No separation. In that realization, your entire resistance to what is vanishes and the deepest truth of spirituality is revealed.[159]

Religious/spiritual healers like Aletheia Luna believe that "spiritual healing occurs as we begin to consciously reconnect with our essential being—the wise, loving, powerful, creative entity that we are at our core."[160]

Luna wants those searching for spiritual healing not to know that the search is an endless journey. This summarizes the code of falsehood and taboo of the religious/spiritual healing campaign today in our dying world.

Suppose religious/spiritual attainment and healing were based on false premises and error. In that case, teaching it in medical schools would be a fraudulent campaign producing fruitless results in our hospitals and medical centers.

---

158. Ibid.

159 Ibid., quoting Scott Kiloby (www.kiloby.com).

160. Shakti Gawain, "Spiritual healing occurs…" *QuoteFancy*. Date of access: April 30, 2023 (https://quotefancy.com/quote/907823/Shakti-Gawain-Spiritual-healing-occurs-as-we-begin-to-consciously-reconnect-with-our).

Because genuine spirituality does not exist, it is self-spiritual deceit and self-delusion. It is a mirage of vanity and falsehoods. It is the pursuit of something that does not have a spiritual basis.

Medical schools must answer several questions. What is the content of spirituality that should be taught to medical professionals? Can such schools adequately and objectively teach nonexistent spirituality?

*A challenge to Christian medical professionals.* The church should rise to the challenge and separate genuine spiritual healing of the Lord Jesus Christ, the true source of healing, from the endless search for spiritual healing from false perspectives like those espoused by Luna, Tatum, and others.

This challenge is more compelling for believers in Christ who have been called to medical ministries in our hospitals and clinics. Religious/spiritual healers throughout human history have trusted the wisdom of religious founders such as Brahman, Tao, Buddha, the Goddess, Achuthanandan, etc. All these names are finite and sinful. They are non-omniscient, non-sovereign, and non-omnipotent. They, too, must experience a personal relationship with the Savior to attain true healing of the soul and body.

As we read in the gospel of Jesus Christ, *"Do not be afraid of those who kill the body but cannot kill the soul. Rather, be afraid of the One who can destroy both soul and body in hell"* (Matthew 10:28, NIV). In Christ, there is no endless search for true physiological and spiritual healing for those who diligently seek him.

**How do religious/spiritual healers describe the sources of religion/spirituality?** Some religious/spiritual healers believe that spirituality can be transferred during childbirth.

Mark, a Buddhist professor, teaches that Buddhist spirituality concerns the end of suffering through the enlightened understanding of reality. Spiritual practices are oriented toward ultimate freedom from suffering and cultivating wisdom and compassion.[161]

According to the Buddhist faith, a person's level of spirituality can transfer at the time of birth. The acquisition of spirituality and its level is assigned when an individual is born. The story of spirituality is determined as an individual grows and matures.

> We are all born at a certain spiritual level. This is based on the spiritual level achieved in the previous life time. So suppose a person does spiritual practice and grows to the 50% spiritual level, then in the next lifetime he will be born at the 50% spiritual level. Basically

---

161. Mark W. Muesse, "What Does It Mean to Lead a Spiritual Life? A Buddhist Perspect," *Explorefaith.org*. Date of access: April 5, 2022 (http://explorefaith.org/steppingstones_SpiritualLife_Buddhist.htm).

in Spirituality we take off from where we left, in a previous birth or lifetime.[162]

*A challenge to Christian medical professionals.* This teaching contradicts the testimony of Scripture. Sin and fallible human nature do not allow for the belief that a living being has undergone birth and rebirth. We read in Hebrews 9:27, *"And as it is appointed unto men once to die, but after this the judgment…"* (Hebrews 9:27, KJV)

**Where do religious/spiritual healers get their healing powers?** There are various ways to obtain healing powers. These include the following.

*Universal energy.* Numerous articles have been written on the subject of universal energy, how our existence depends on it, and how all human minds are interconnected. For our purpose, I want to highlight article by Valerie Soleil.

Soleil describes universal energy as the universal mind, an intelligent energy force that human beings can tap into to develop consciousness. She stresses that the universe is made up of nothing but energy. Therefore, the human brain is created of molecules and atoms. The same movement of molecules and atoms began with trees, cars, animals, and humans.

> The entire world of matter, everything we know with our 5 senses, including our brains and that table we sit at for a meal, is really just energy. That energy has formed molecules and atoms that have gathered in numbers and patterns of movement to create that brain and that table. And the same is true for trees, cars, animals, and humans.
>
> Physicists also tell us that energy can neither be created nor destroyed—it can only be re-arranged. Thus, ice turns into water and water into steam. We take the energy that has been turned into matter and rearrange it all the time. Thus, we have our physical world.[163]

Soleil believes that everything is energy and that pure energy could be called God. She says that some understand God as someone who sets all things in motion and either stays involved by hearing our prayers and responding, although some religious groups believe that such a God created the universe and remains a detached observer.

---

162. "What Is Spiritual Level?" *Spiritual Science Research Foundation*. Date of access: April 30, 2023 (https://www.spiritualresearchfoundation.org/spiritual-practice/spiritual-growth/spiritual-level).

163. Valerie Soleil, "How to Connect with the Universal Mind and Raise Your Consciousness," *Learning Mind*. March 26, 2016 (https://www.learning-mind.com/connect-with-the-universal-mind).

# Religion and Spirituality

Nevertheless, she prefers to use the term "Universal Mind," an intelligent energy force into which we can tap if we develop consciousness.

She understands the material world from the Hindu doctrine of Brahman's relationship to the cosmos or the physical world:

> Verily, this whole world is Brahman. Therefore, tranquil, let one worship it as that from which he came forth, that into which he will dissolve, and that in which he breathes. It consists of the mind, whose body is light, whose conception is Truth, whose soul is space, containing all works, containing all desires, containing all odors, containing taste, encompassing this whole world, the unspeaking, the unconcerned, that it the soul of mine within the heart, that is Brahman. Chindogya 3:14.[164] (Woodbourne, 1925, p. 55).

*A challenge to Christian medical professionals.* The Bible teaches that man has been created in the image and likeness of God. God's breath is the source of our existence; we are not a collection of molecules and atoms. Energy does not produce flesh, blood, and life and power does not get sick, because it has no life or soul. What enables human existence is the breath of the Almighty God and the life we receive from him (Genesis 1:26, 2:7).

The seat of the human soul is God himself. It did not develop and diversify from living organisms; it came from God, exists for God, and will return to God after its earthly existence.

Luna also has this to say about the subject of spirit animals:

> Spirit Animals are powerful allies on our spiritual awakening journeys as they help us to reconnect with our Souls. As the essence of an animal is raw, pure, and untainted by the issues that human beings undergo, they can help us tune into our authentic, untamed nature.[165]

*A challenge to Christian medical professionals.* All of creation, including animals, has been created for the benefit of man. Animals are not raw (undeveloped) or pure (without defect). They are selfish, fighting and destroying one another. Animals have instincts, not intelligence. They can be attacked by disease, get sick, suffer, and die.

---

164. A.S. Woodbourne, "The Idea of God in Hinduism," *The Journal of Religion 5(1)*, 1925, 52–66.

165. Aletheia Luna, "7 Ways to Connect with Your Spirit Animal," *Loner Wolf*. December 8, 2021 (https://lonerwolf.com/spirit-animal).

Mankind takes care of animals, not the other way around. Animals have a mortal destiny whereas man's destiny is eternal (Genesis 1:26, 2:20, 9:2).

Man has spirit and intellect. Religious/spiritual healers use this intellect to heal mental and physical illnesses. In his blog, Dale Wilbanks writes that he believes in a single universal consciousness that pervades the universe. He stresses that this universal mind is present everywhere simultaneously, at every point, in its entirety. It follows, therefore, that it must also be present within every person—in your mind; indeed, in you.[166]

Is there anything pure in an animal's nature? None. Zero. They are perishable and dusty. They have life but not souls. Animals are not sacred, for mankind has derived his spirit through the breath of God. Man's spirit is eternal, reflecting the image and likeness of God, and does not depend on the spirit of any animal for its existence or and wellness (Genesis 2:26, Colossians 1:15).

Healing does not come from animal spirits, trees, or any form of universal mind or energy. Therefore, we do not pray to such creations. We pray to the Creator through the authority and power of the resurrected Lord Jesus Christ. By his name, every knee must bow and every tongue confess his lordship over all created things (Philippians 2:10–11).

As a Christian physician, nurse, psychiatrist, psychologist, chaplain, or other medical or mental health practitioner, how will you respond should a professor or colleague say that your soul is equal to that of an animal or other created thing? You must defend what you believe and keep faith in the biblical truth about the human soul.

**What hinders the true efficacy of religious/spiritual healing?** The main factor that hinders the efficacy of religious/spirituality healing is the reality that such healing is based on falsehoods rather than God's common grace. If you assume that the power of human existence depends on the formation of molecules and other physical processes, you have no choice but to rely on the spirit of the air, the beast, the heart of fantastic sea monsters, or the limits of human intellect.

*A challenge to Christian medical professionals.* If spiritual healing were about the practice of restoring, harmonizing, and balancing one's spirit or soul, as Luna claims, then any Christian medical professional ought to be informed that there is no absolute authenticity in man, because the entirety of man exists in the realm of imperfection. No wonder the Lord Jesus Christ says, *"If a kingdom is divided against itself, that kingdom cannot stand. If a house is divided against itself, that house cannot stand. And if Satan opposes himself and is divided, he cannot stand; his end has come"* (Mark 3:24–26, NIV).

The PCPM should encourage the church to operate in the authority and power of Jesus Christ in dealing with any crisis.

---

166. Dale Wilbanks, "The One Universal Mind," *Mind Your Reality*. June 8, 2021 (https://www.mind-your-reality.com/universal-mind.html).

## REFLECTION OF GOD IN OTHER SPIRITUAL PERSPECTIVES

The word "God" presents a problem. It is not necessarily synonymous with Allah, Hashem, Brahman, Buddha, Tao, or Dao. Although Judeo-Christianity and Muslims claim Abraham as the father of their various faith traditions, the condition and construct of these traditions differ significantly from each other.

Some Islamic apologists in the west currently argue that there is no difference between the Judeo-Christian God and the Islamic God. Some accuse biblical writers of distorting God's messages to them. In their view, the Bible has many errors and its content should not be trusted as God's ultimately revealed divine message.

Let me briefly comment on why some non-Christian scholars and critics believe Scripture to be unreliable.

With the most vital force, assert the authenticity and trustworthiness of the Bible. Critics who argue that Scripture contains errors probably have never seen the biblical text as inspired by God the Holy Spirit at the time of its revelation. The Spirit-inspired word of God does not contain errors. Its inspired content is accurate and trustworthy.

These arguments have pointed to the process of copying and translating the Bible. Also, portions of the Bible may appear to contradict facts, make false statements against the revealed message of God, or proffer inaccurate interpretations. Other factors include poor translations, typographical errors, and incompetency in language.

Therefore, it must be said that not all statements in the Bible represent the revealed truth of the Godhead. Nonetheless, such statements are statements of facts. For example:

- Satan told Adam and Eve that God's instruction prohibiting them from eating from the tree of the knowledge of good and evil is a statement of fact, but it is not the revealed truth from God the Father to Adam and Eve (Genesis 3:2–4).
- God instructed that their disobedience would result in death, but Satan told them that they wouldn't die and instead have their eyes opened to good and evil.
- What Satan said to the Christ at the time of his temptations in Matthew 4 are contradictions to the revealed truth of the word of God about whom we should worship, what we should depend on for our physical needs, and where our protection should come from. The Bible records the statements of facts on what Satan said to Christ, but the revealed truth tell us otherwise.
- The three friends of Job accused him of sin, determining that his suffering resulted from his own sins. The record of what they

said is factual. However, what they said is contrary to the divine revelation relating to the reason behind Job's pain and suffering (Job 1:1–10).

Therefore, every inspired word in Scripture is accurate, complete, and trustworthy.

Despite strong arguments that the Bible contains errors and is untrustworthy, no Christian scholar vigorously defends the concept of oneness between Allah (the God in Islam) and Yahweh (the God of Judeo-Christianity). Not one true Bible-based theologian presents such an argument.

It is interesting to note the depth of energy and time that has gone towards singularizing the story of Ishmael and Isaac into a single monotheistic faith, with Abraham at the foundation of both. The promoters of this erroneous proposition should stop their discourse and instead address the doctrines, teachings, and theologies that differ between the two. There are many differences on the subjects of love and forgiveness, the treatment of women, the theology of life after death, and the path by which sinful humanity is adopted and reconciled to God.

Therefore, Allah is not the same as Yahweh. Despite this, Randa Amer and Mona Kayyali write that

> both Christians and Muslims Arab Americans believe in one and same God. "Allah" is the Arabic word for God (in English) used in Christianity, Islam, and in other religions, and it is therefore not the God of Muslims only.[167]

Many scholars teach this erroneous representation of the Lord Jesus Christ, saying that Christians worship the same universal God as other religions.

Saying that all religions present different ways of worship that lead to the same omnipresent God, Dr. Zakir Naik teaches that "if we study the commonalities of beliefs of major world religious scriptures, we will find that the concept of God is the same."[168] He further asserts that "a common feature of all major religions is the belief in a Universal divine authority that is Omnipotent and Omniscient. Followers of all

---

167. Mona M. Amer and Randa A. Kayyali, "Religion and Religiosity: Christian and Muslim Faiths, Diverse Practices, and Psychological Correlates," *Handbook of Arab American Psychology* (New York, NY: Routledge, 2016), 50.

168. Zakir Naik, "Concept of God in Major Religions." *Islamic Research Foundation*. Date of access: May 30, 2021 (https://d1.islamhouse.com/data/en/ih_books/single/en_Concept_of_God_in_Major_Religions.pdf).

major religions believe that the God (gods) they worship is the same God for them and others."[169]

With the same intent to prove that Christians worship the same God as other world religions and spirituality, it has been claimed that biblical writers distorted God's oneness, making Jesus Christ the Son of God.[170]

To further solidify the oneness between these two Middle East faiths, I have Muslim friends who call a mosque a church, and some of them bear biblical names such as John, David, and Joseph. The effort is a deception that causes confusion, delusion, and falsification of the truth.

I call on religious scholars, theologians, and academicians to stop engaging in this debate over whether Allah and Yahweh reveal the same message from the same God. If it is the same God, we would have to turn our attention to the teachings and doctrines that God has given to the leaders of all religions and spiritualities. I want to re-emphasize that it is not possible for the same true God to reveal distinct teachings and doctrines to various religious leaders.

It has been observed elsewhere in this book that significant distinctions exist between the doctrines of the various religions. The idea that all religions worship the same God is an all-time fallacy and one of the biggest deceptions of Satan.

An article for *GainPeace* reads,

> The unique usage of Allah as a personal name of God is a reflection of Islam's emphasis on the purity of the belief in God that is the essence of the message of all God's messengers. Because of this, Islam considers associating any deity or personality with God as a deadly sin that God will never forgive, despite the fact that He may forgive all other sins.[171]

One fundamental truth exists about the founders of all the world's religions and spiritualities. Their founders were sinners. This is true for all, except for Christianity, which has the sinless Jesus Christ. In other words, only God is sinless, and Christ fulfilled a life of sinlessness. There is no sin so grievous that couldn't be atoned for by the death and resurrection of Christ. He is the resurrection and the life; no sinful human can be

---

169. Ibid.

170. "Have Christians Corrupted the Bible?" *Compelling Truth*. Date of access: March 25, 2023 (https://www.compellingtruth.org/Christians-corrupted-Bible.html).

171. "The Concept of God in Islam," *GainPeace*. Date of access: April 30, 2023 (https://www.gainpeace.com/what-is-islam/the-concept-of-god-in-islam).

reconciled with God except through him (Colossians 1:11–14, Hebrews 5:15, 1 Peter 2:22, 1 John 1:8–10, 3:5).

Some scholars maintain that God is not a person, not a spirit disconnected from creation, transcendent but not imminent. Everything in the universe happens through him.

Ken Silva writes,

> Everything that happens in the universe, whether good or bad, is foreordained by the unchangeable decrees of Allah. Muslims believe all our thoughts, words, and deeds (good or evil) were foreseen, foreordained, determined, and decreed from all eternity. Everything is irrevocably and fatefully written (Hadith 8:611).[172]

He goes on to quote a Muslim theologian, Risaleh-i-Barkhawi:

> Not only can he (God) do anything, he actually is the only one who does anything. When a man writes, it is Allah who has created in his mind the will to write. Allah at the same time gives power to write, then brings about the motion of the hand and the pen and the appearance upon paper. All other things are passive, Allah alone is active.[173]

The tenets of the two faiths are significantly different, including the stories of Ishmael and Isaac. These religions deliver different messages about the Creator and how to access him. Christians have access to God by having faith in what Christ did on the cross to bridge the relationship between a sinful man and sinless God. This relationship is not accessed by man's wisdom, intelligence, good works, religion, or spirituality.[174]

Jesus Christ is the only sinless man who ever existed in human history. No other religion, founder, or religious text can divinely assert a claim of sinlessness and declare any authority to forgive the sins of humanity. Does any scholar, theologian, anthropologist, scientist, or religious historian have proof of the existence of some other spiritual leader or founder who lived a sinless earthly life?

---

172. Ken Silva, "Allah: The God of Islam," *Apprising Ministries*. July 10, 2011 (https://www.apprising.org/2011/07/10/allah-the-god-of-islam).

173. Gerhard Nehls, *Christians Ask Muslims* (Colorado Springs, CO: Global Mapping International, 2000). Quoting Risaleh-i-Barkhawi.

174. Stephen Blanton, "Compare Islam to Christianity," *Stephen Blanton*. Date of access: May 2, 2021 (https://stephenblanton.com/compare-christianity).

This book does not focus on a comprehensive study of these monotheistic faiths, or other faiths, to showcase their differences and similarities. But it is essential to understand that Allah of Islam, Lord Brahma of Hinduism, and Gautam Buddha of Buddhism cannot be conflict with Yahweh of Christianity.

When Christians pray for healing, they do not depend on self-righteousness or good deeds to attract God's favor. Christ's threefold earthly mission was to free humanity from sin's bondage, teach the people how to be free from evil, and heal their afflictions. In Christianity, God brought salvation and established relationships by faith through Christ alone.

One giant pillar of encouragement in the Christian faith is authentic hope. This hope is not only about the assurance of eternal life; it also causes believers to confidently face afflictions due to the healing power and authority of Jesus Christ.

Christ's mission and divine identity cannot be comprehended through mere human wisdom or intellectualism. The Bible must be divinely understood through the ministry of the Holy Spirit, who reveals to believers the mind of God. Christ says,

> *These things I have spoken to you while I am still with you. But the Helper, the Holy Spirit, whom the Father will send in my name, he will teach you all things and bring to your remembrance all that I have said to you. Peace I leave with you; my peace I give to you. Not as the world gives do I give to you.* (John 14:25–27, ESV)

The natural mind does not understand the spiritual things of God or have the understanding to teach it. On the opposite, the natural mind is in enmity against God. The Scripture records:

> *The mind governed by the flesh is death, but the mind governed by the Spirit is life and peace. The mind governed by the flesh is hostile to God; it does not submit to God's law, nor can it do so.* (Romans 8:6–8, NIV)

> *Do not let anyone who delights in false humility and the worship of angels disqualify you. Such a person also goes into great detail about what they have seen; they are puffed up with idle notions by their unspiritual mind.* (Colossians 2:18, NIV)

To properly grasp healing through the practice of religion/spirituality, we will next discuss some selected words used from Koeing's descriptions of religion and spirituality.

Do words like "God," "prayer," "spirituality," or "religiosity" mean the same thing among the adherents of different faiths?

It is evident here that "God" and "prayer" do not mean the same thing according to all religious beliefs and practices. Who is God? To whom do believers in other religions recognize as God, and to whom do they pray? Do they pray to the same entity behind English word "God"?

CONCEPT OF GOD AND HEALING PRAYER

It cannot be that all religions merely represent different ways to reach the same God. The concepts of God and prayer differ significantly between them.

**Christianity (founder: Jesus Christ).** Bible-based believers understand that God is holy, absolutely knowledgeable in all things, all-powerful, and the Creator of all that exists in heaven and on earth (Genesis 1:1–31, Colossians 1:16, John 1:1–3). So when Christians pray to God, they don't ask for an answer based on any religious or spiritual activities or achievement. Instead all responses to prayer are made possible by faith in the authority and power of Christ alone, who has reconciled the sinful man to the holy God (John 16:23–24, Romans 5:18–19).

Monica Polonyi, Richard Henriksen, Sheryl Serres describe the Evangelical Christian faith as a "component" of spirituality and religiosity. Their article stresses that an individual's belief, identity, purpose, healing, and well-being are connected to their faith.[175]

Therefore, faith remains a fundamental construct in the Christian journey. For Evangelical Christians, the word "spirituality" refers to communication with God through prayer and worship of God and his word, obedience to the true tenets of the Bible, and servanthood to God and humanity.[176]

On the other hand, "religiosity" is considered to refer to trusting in God and believing that the Bible is the ultimate and authoritative source for one's beliefs, practices, and personal relationship with God. Meditations and incantations do not determine Christian religion/spirituality, nor do the number of prayers said per day. Christian religiosity/spirituality is not focused on individual efforts and personal achievements but rather the blessing of God's grace, mercy, and favor through faith in the accomplished work of Christ on the cross and the ministry of the Holy Spirit. Faith is encouraged for seeking

---

175. Monica A. Polonyi, Richard C. Henriksen Jr., and Sheryl A. Serres, "A Matter of Faith: A Qualitative Study with Evangelical Christians," *American Counseling Association*. Date of access: August 4, 2020 (https://www.counseling.org/resources/library/vistas/2011-v-online/article_102.pdf).

176. Leanne Lewis Newman, "Faith, Spirituality, and Religion: A Model for Understanding the Differences," *The College Student Affairs Journal 23(2)*, April 1, 2004, 102.

God, but fasting is not a criterion for having one's prayer answered prayer. You do not have to make a pilgrimage to Israel to be a mature Christian. You do not have to labor or engage in an intense meditation to earn God's favor. In short, no specific good works are necessary in order to earn God's favor.

One thing that stands out about prayer is that you can pray to any god you want, but there is only one emissary between man and Jesus Christ. The flaw of every other religion is that they cannot promise eternal life or answered prayer. Christ died to save humanity from the wrath of God and offer the gift of eternal life to whoever believes in him.

**Islam (founder: the prophet Muhammed).** For our discussion, we will use Merriam-Webster's definition of Islam: "the religious faith of Muslims including belief in Allah as the sole deity and Muhammed as his prophet"; it is a "submission (to the will of God)."[177] Islam further teaches that Allah's word was conveyed to Muhammed through the angel Gabriel.

When Muslims pray to Allah, do they pray to the same God as Christians? Do they use the same criteria? I do not know the requirements for prayer in Islam. However, I know that to be a devoted Muslim, you must accomplish some good works to attract Allah's response in prayer.

In Islam, it is believed that one's relationship with Allah depends on good works. Thus, in a good relationship, answered prayer depends on what man can do to appease Allah.

In an attempt to explain the relationship between prayer and sickness in Islam, one article notes that Muslims see illness not as a punishment from Allah but rather as a test and purification of one's sin. The author posits that a victim of illness in Islam should ask, "Will you see your illness as a cause of despair or as an opportunity to turn to Allah for mercy and healing?"[178]

The author further states that reciting certain prayers from the Quran or Sunnah can result in healing. He gives an example from the prophet Ayyub—who is known as Job in the Old Testament: "Truly distress has seized me, but You are Most Merciful of those that are merciful" (Quran 21:83–84).[179]

He also stresses that there are four prayers in the Sunnah that the prophet Muhammad himself recited when someone fell ill:

---

177. "Islam," *Merriam-Webster*. Date of access: April 30, 2023 (https://www.merriam-webster.com/dictionary/Islam).

178. Huda, "Du'a: Muslim Prayers for Healing Sickness," *Learn Religions*. April 8, 2020 (https://www.learnreligions.com/prayers-for-healing-sickness-2004521).

179. Ibid.

It is recommended to touch the area of pain with the right hand while reciting this supplication: "Allahuma rabbi-nas adhhabal ba'sa, ashfi wa entashafi, la shifa' illa shifa'uka shifa' la yughadiru saqama." (Oh Allah! The Sustainer of Mankind! Remove the illness, cure the disease. You are the One Who cures. There is no cure except Your cure. Grant us a cure that leaves no illness.)[180]

Christianity does not teach that Jesus Christ answers the prayer of only "those that are merciful." On the contrary, Christian prayers are answered by faith in the redemptive work of Christ; they aren't based on any merciful act of goodness one may have done.

**Hinduism (founder: Brahman).** The available literature on Buddhism, Hinduism, Bahaism, Shintoism, and Daoism reveals a different story about the supreme Being and his prayer for healing. Some of these groups don't call themselves religious, nor do they worship a supreme Being; instead they revere teachings, ideologies, philosophies, patterns of life, and ritualistic practices.

Nevertheless, much research has revealed what these ideological and philosophical groups believe, worship, and practice to satisfy their religious/spiritual yearning.

Because of similarities in the beliefs and practices of their spiritualities, we will briefly look at Hinduism and Buddhism only.

Although Hinduism does not appear to have a founder, it is a fusion of various beliefs, including the Vedas, Brahman, and the worship of many gods and goddesses.[181] Many believe that Brahman is the ultimate God, a non-deity force, and an unknown mystery.[182] Woodbourne states that the Hindus scripture reveals the non-dualistic nature of Brahman: the Upanishads, known as the "end of the Veda." Brahman defined it as "all in all."[183]

The existing literature on the Hindu religion reveals it to be a complex religion with no dogma or specific revealed scripture. Instead it embraces an eclectic range of doctrines and practices from pantheism to agnosticism, reincarnation, and a caste system.[184]

---

180. Ibid.

181. Hnin Mar Khin, "A Study of Hindu Concepts About Gods and Goddess." *Dagon University Research Journal 11*, 2020, 60–62.

182. Sarah M. Whitman, "Pain and Suffering as Viewed by the Hindu Religion." *The Journal of Pain 8(8)*, August 2007, 607–613.

183. Woodbourne, "The Idea of God in Hinduism," 52.

184. Shashi Tharoor, *Unity, Diversity, and Other Contradictions* (Dlf Cyber City, Delhi: Penguin Random House India, 2018), 5; and Khin, "A Study of Hindu Concepts About Gods and Goddess," 60.

Woodbourne further states that polytheism, henotheism, pantheism, and monotheism are all found within Hinduism. According to him, most educated Hindus are adherents of the Advaita Vedanta, which means "the non-dualistic Vedanta as interpreted by Sankara, which is the continuous cycle of individual life, death, and reincarnation."[185]

Modern Hindus believe that Hinduism is not polytheistic but pluralistic. Rahul Dudhane writes that there are 330 million gods, but in practice Hindus do not worship or even know the names of them all. He makes an interesting assertion:

> Hinduism believes in only one God but (it) allows its followers to worship the God in many forms such as nature (including trees, sun, idols, animals, etc.). Regarding animals, Rahul reveals that in Hindu temples in India, you will find pictures of monkeys, dogs, rats, cows, elephants, and otters are part of Hindu mythology.[186]

The Hindu God appears to be detached, indifferent, and disinterested in the created world. It seems equal to Lord Brahma, Lord Vishnu, and Lord Shiva.

> Brahman is the genesis of life in all living beings, the principle of unity in all apparent multiplicity. He is essential to the world's existence, yet not in the relation of cause to effect or Creator to creation. He exists in the world and should not be identified with it since that would reduce him to its limits and rob him of transcendence.[187]

The world is preserved for the sake of Dharma, which makes the Ultimate/God respond to human needs by them worshiping millions of idols, deities, and spirits.

Dudhane, a Hindu by birth, teaches that Hinduism continues to develop and change its teachings. As a result, the religion has no single founder—because it was not founded as a religion. He writes that according to the Shiva Purana, the Brahma created Lord Shiva, who created Lord Vishnu, and Lord Brahma was born from lotus originating from the navel of Lord Vishnu.

The Hindu faith teaches that these three gods are assigned three jobs to run the universe systematically:

---

185. Tharoor, *Unity, Diversity, and Other Contradictions,* 53.

186. Rahul Dudhane, *What Exactly Is a Shiva Lingam* (United States: Independently Published, 2021).

187. Woodbourne, "The Idea of God in Hinduism," 55.

- Satvik form: Lord Brahma. It is a creator.
- Rajasik form: Lord Vishnu. It is a protector.
- Tamasik form: Lord Shiva. It is a destroyer.[188]

Hinduism teaches that Lord Brahma "created this universe and set the rules that are the bases of Sanatan Dharma, and Hinduism is the modern name of it."[189] Dudhane describes Hinduism as a way of life, which helps a worshiper to be liberated from the cycle of birth and rebirth, eventually setting his soul free from the domination of suffering.

The Absolute is the Dharmakaya, the essence of the universe and unity of all things and beings, unmanifested, beyond the existence of non-existence and concept.[190] The reality of man is consciousness, Brahman is the reality of consciousness, and reaching the reality of consciousness is to become one with Brahman.

Regarding prayer, it is believed that Hinduism is a religion of sounds and prayer.

> To begin with, it was the spoken hymn or magical formula, from which it came to signify the power inherent in the hymn or prayer.[191]

The Vedas are prayer books filled with the power of specific sounds. A worshiper can unlock the sounds through speech to invoke gods, fulfill desires, and manifest objects.[192] Hindus offer prayers to various personal and family deities and divine beings daily. Hindus do not have a single religious book or look elsewhere to find God; they look for God within themselves, their consciousness, through symbols and images such as a fruit or a flower. Imagery is the driving force behind mindfulness therapy.

Prayer may not necessarily be addressed to a supreme Being. Buddhism, for instance, is not a theistic religion such as Islam or Christianity, yet prayer addressed to the universe is a vital part of the Buddhist tradition.[193]

---

188. Rahul Dudhane, *What Exactly Is a Shiva Lingam*, 2.

189. Ibid., 1.

190. Barbara O'Brien, "What Does Dharmakaya Mean?" *Learn Religions*. February 8, 2021 (www.learningreligions.com/dharmakaya-449805).

191. Woodbourne, "The Idea of God in Hinduism," 55.

192. Rahul Dudhane, "Concept of God in Hinduism," *Hinduism Facts*. August 12, 2021 (https://www.hinduismfacts.org/concept-of-god-in-hinduism).

193. Dossey, "Spirituality, Prayer, and Medicine: What Is the Fuss Really About?"

Therefore, in the words of anthropologist Stephan A. Schwartz, "The intent to heal, either oneself or another, whether expressed as God, a force, energy, or one of many gods, has consistently been believed to be capable of producing a therapeutic result."[194]

The more pain a Hindu worshiper undergoes before a god, the happier it is, thus the outcome of prayer.

> "The more pain you have before god, the happier he is." This belief compels many Hindus to crawl on their hands and knees or pull themselves on their bellies through the temple, or to walk barefoot for hours or days to try to please their gods.[195]

Hindus achieve healing not through prayer but through pain. They attain happiness and freedom by pleasing their idols through hardship.

In helping a Hindu patient heal, a medical professional would probably identify a deity associated with the family. But how could such a nurse help minister healing to that patient, who may relate to a god through a fruit, a flower, the sunrise, the sunset, or any medium of worship?

**Buddhism (founder: Gautama or Shakyamuni Buddha).** A historical review of Buddhism reveals that Gautama Buddha is the seventh Buddha, but the religion's followers believe that there will be an infinite number of Buddhas.

There are two main traditions of Buddhism. On one hand, there is **Theravada Buddhism**; on the other, there is Mahayana Buddhism. Theravada Buddhism focuses on individual enlightenment and experience and a monastic lifestyle. Mahayana Buddhism dwells on collective freedom from suffering and teaching the ways to enlightenment.[196]

Mahayana Buddhism can be translated as "the way of thinking." According to a Buddhist scholar, the primary ideal of Buddhism is

> attaining liberation from suffering and the cycle of life and rebirth by achieving a state called nirvana. You can achieve nirvana through

---

194. Stephan A. Schwartz, "Therapeutic Intent and the Art of Observation," *Subtle Energies and Energy Medicine Journal*, 1990, i–viii.

195. Madison Strauder, "The Posture of Prayer: A Look at How Hindus Pray," *Church Leaders*. July 5, 2019 (https://churchleaders.com/outreach-missions/outreach-missions-articles/354878-the-posture-of-prayer-a-look-at-how-hindus-pray.html).

196. Aich, "Buddha Philosophy and Western Psychology."

moral striving, using various meditation techniques and learning the Dharma, which is the Buddha's teachings.[197]

Tapas Kumar Aich writes that an understanding of Buddhism reveals that it is different from other religions. Buddhism is not centered on the relationship between humans and a high god. Buddhists do not believe in a personal Creator. It claims to be more than a religion; it is a tradition that focuses on personal spiritual development.[198] It is more of a philosophy and a humanistic way of life. It can be summed up as striving to lead a moral life, being aware of one's thoughts and actions, and developing wisdom, compassion, and understanding.[199]

Buddhism has four noble truths, as preached by Buddha:

> That the life is full of suffering (Duhkha); that there is a cause of this suffering (Duhkha-samudaya); that it is possible to stop suffering (Duhkha-nirodha); and that there is a way to extinguish suffering (Duhkha-nirodha-marga).[200]

This implies that a thorough knowledge of the four noble truths and their application can eliminate human suffering.

But can it? I believe not.

We will comment briefly on Buddha's four truths. Then I will rearrange the order of how this is perceived in the light of biblical truth about human suffering and the resources available to deal with suffering.

*There is a cause of suffering.* The most crucial truth missing from this list is the biblical truth about man's disobedience, sin, and fallibility. Buddha's philosophical and psychological understanding of man's journey in this sinful and broken world does not include the pathology of sin and the ultimate divine consequences of sin, which is the root cause of all suffering. The climax of every suffering is death.

The Bible calls the root cause of human suffering disobedience and sin. The Creator of mankind, including Buddha and his followers, must journey through the consequences

---

197. Alex Shashkevich, "Stanford Scholar Discusses Buddhism and Its Origins," *Stanford News*. August 20, 2018 (https://news.stanford.edu/2018/08/20/stanford-scholar-discusses-buddhism-origins).

198. "Chinese Religions and Philosophies," *National Geographic*. May 20, 2022 (https://education.nationalgeographic.org/resource/chinese-religions-and-philosophies).

199. Bhikkhu U. Thittila, "The Meaning of Buddhism," *The Atlantic*. February 1958 (https://www.theatlantic.com/magazine/archive/1958/02/the-meaning-of-buddhism/306832).

200. Ibid.

of sin, which God has ordained and declared in Genesis 3:9–19. God's description of the consequences of disobedience and sin reads this way:

> *Then the Lord God said to the woman, "You will suffer terribly when you give birth…"*
>
> *The Lord said to the man, "You listened to your wife and ate the fruit I told you not to eat. And so, the ground will be under a curse because of what you did. As long as you live, you will have to struggle to grow enough food… You will sweat all your life to earn a living; you were made out of soil, and you will once again turn into soil."* (Genesis 3:16–17, 19, CEV)

This scripture reveals both the cause of human suffering and sicknesses as well as where man came from and where his dead body will go. Acknowledging the truth that life is full of suffering without stating the root cause of that suffering is a significant factor in why Buddhists focus on human effort to eliminate suffering. Man's ability to deal with the problem of sin, sickness, and suffering culminates in death. The Bible has revealed to humans the root cause and end of suffering. Sin causes it, and death ends it.

*This is a life of suffering.* The second statement about human suffering in Buddhist belief is an authentic one built on a false premise; therefore, it arrives at the wrong conclusion as to why suffering occurs, how we are to live successfully through it, and what will be its ultimate end.

In responding to the first premise, that life is full of suffering, the Bible echoes that the lives of humans and rest of creation groans because of suffering. Buddhism has not explained how man came about his suffering. The Bible answers this question:

> *For I consider that the sufferings of this present time are not worthy to be compared with the glory which shall be revealed in us. For the earnest expectation of the creation eagerly waits for the revealing of the sons of God. For the creation was subjected to futility, not willingly, but because of Him who subjected it in hope; because the creation itself also will be delivered from the bondage of corruption into the glorious liberty of the children of God. For we know that the whole creation groans and labors with birth pangs together until now. Not only that, but we also who have the firstfruits of the Spirit, even we ourselves groan within ourselves, eagerly waiting for the adoption, the redemption of our body. For we were saved in this hope, but hope that is seen is not hope; for why does one still hope for what he*

> *sees? But if we hope for what we do not see, we eagerly wait for it with perseverance.* (Romans 8:18–25, NKJV)

The ultimate enlightenment that all Buddhists need to know about their suffering is that it is the consequence of sin. Human suffering doesn't just happen; it has a history, a beginning, a root cause, and a consequence. As Romans 8:22 tells us, *"For we know that the whole creation groans and labors with birth pangs together until now"* (NKJV).

The existence of suffering in the life of every person begins at the moment of their birth and continues throughout life and ends at the point of death. God declared this penalty (Genesis 3:16–19) and allows it to survive throughout human history until the ultimate return of the Son of God, Jesus Christ, who alone can take away all sickness, pain, and death (Revelation 21:4).

So life is full of suffering, because suffering is not a cause but a product of human guilt before the righteousness of God. Suffering is a notable consequence of disobedience and sin. The penalty of sin causes suffering for humanity as well as all other creatures.

No truth arrived at my humans could explain suffering or provide a remedy for it in this life without recognizing our fallen state and seeking God's merciful healing in Christ. Our authentic hope is that the return of Jesus Christ to the world will eradicate all suffering and death. The Bible says to those who do not have this authentic hope in Christ Jesus,

> *But as for the cowardly, the faithless, the detestable, as for murderers, the sexually immoral, sorcerers, idolaters, and all liars, their portion will be in the lake that burns with fire and sulfur, which is the second death.* (Revelation 21:8, ESV)

*It is possible to stop suffering.* Since God first declared the penalty for man's disobedience and sin, there has been no manmade remedy. As humans we must appreciate the gift of intelligence by the Creator of the universe and thank God for allowing us to continue tapping into his image and likeness.

I believe that man continues to enjoy God-given wisdom and intelligence because of his church on earth (1 Kings 3:9–12). Man still exhibits high intelligence, morality, and creativity because of God's mercy and grace.

The five methods of healing mentioned in this book have helped curtail human suffering and pain. However, there is no absolute path to eradicate human suffering. Only the power and authority inherent in the name of Jesus Christ can heal our crises.

*There is a way to extinguish suffering.* There is no end to suffering in our physical world; mankind cannot change and redeem himself from his fallen state and brokenness. All men and women are sinners and fall short of the sinless and righteous God.

Because man cannot redeem himself from the penalty of disobedience and sin, he cannot escape and extinguish suffering in this life. Man's nature is weak and he is incapable of redeeming his sinful nature and freeing himself from suffering. No matter how fervently he believes in the delusion of rebirth and reincarnation, suffering and death will continue to permeate his earthly journey until Christ returns to do away with suffering and death.

The penalty of sin is suffering unto death. Buddha didn't save himself from suffering and death, so his premise on conquering suffering and death is meaningless.

Because our wisdom and intelligence are deficient due to sin, we deny the absolute righteousness of God in our decision-making. Our sinful nature cannot produce "right view/right understanding, right thought/right intention, right speech, right action/conduct, right livelihood, right effort, right mindfulness, right concentration," as put forth by Buddha's teachings.[201] No man or woman is perfect, and man's nature is reliable to mistakes and failure.

> *Surely there is not a righteous man on earth who does good and never sins.* (Ecclesiastes 7:20, NIV)

The Buddhist perspective on disease, sickness, and suffering is based on the philosophy of wrong thinking, incorrect knowledge of the human condition, and a false understanding of the material world. Therefore, there is no reason to pray to a higher god for healing disease, sickness, and suffering—because to them, the notion of a Creator does not exist.

The point of offering education on religion and spirituality in medical schools is to equip practitioners in integrating these ideas into their patients' treatment plans. Yet you may find yourself with Buddhist lab technician, nurse, or doctor who doesn't even believe that there is a supreme Being. What would be the value of offering religious/spiritual teachings to such a person? And what kind of training would be relevant to Buddhist patients?

We know that sin permeates every aspect of our human nature, corrupting every function of the mind, will, spirit, and body. Therefore, we cannot think righteously toward God, because man is hostile to him. Instead man can think according to the ways of the world and what the world presents to him. Therefore, Buddhism only presents a humanistic solution to suffering.

---

201. Ibid.

## II. METHOD OF DIAGNOSIS

The literature shows that religion and spirituality emphasize the prognosis of diseases, such as patient diet and lifestyle.[202] Diagnoses are symptomatic; as it relates to pre-existing symptoms, diagnoses are asymptomatic. Also, most diagnoses in the arena related to mental health.

The American Psychological Association's Diagnostic and Statistical Manual (DSM) of Mental Disorders is expressing a breakthrough in dealing with religion, spirituality, and psychiatry issues. Clinicians and researchers on the Committee on Religion, Spirituality, and Psychiatry have had some success in their attempt to address the spiritual and philosophical issues in distinguishing a psychiatry disorder from a spiritual condition.[203]

However, it is beyond the capabilities of these professionals to treat all patients of all religious and spiritual persuasions, especially when religion and spirituality are viewed from a humanistic perspective.

The DSM-IV and DSM-V have included new work focusing on the areas of

- mystical experiences.
- new religious movements.
- visionary experiences.
- kundalini awakening.
- near-death experiences.
- possession experiences.
- shamanic crises.
- loss of faith.
- alien encounters.
- terminal and life-threatening illnesses.
- changes in membership, practices, and beliefs.[204]

These breakthroughs seem to focus on manmade religious and spirituality, and I find that they are most relevant to the practices of Hinduism, Buddhism, and Taoism, among other religions.

---

202. Charity Neejide Onyishi, Leonard Chidi Ilechukwu, Vera Victor-Aigbodion, and Chiedu Eseadi, "Impact of Spiritual Beliefs and Faith-Based Interventions on Diabetes Management." *World Journal Diabetes 12(5)*, May 15, 2021, 630.

203. John R. Peteet, Francis G. Lu, and William E. Narrow, *Religious and Spiritual Issues in Psychiatric Diagnosis: A Research Agenda for DSM-V* (Arlington, VA: American Psychiatric Association, 2011).

204. *Diagnostic and Statistical Manual of Mental Disorders, Fifth Edition* (Washington, DC: American Psychological Association, 2013).

How would a Hindu psychiatrist, who does not believe in the existence of God, use these approaches to diagnose the religious and spiritual conditions of a Christian or Muslim patient? Many people believe that religion and spirituality exist in one big tent that contains all the ideologies and beliefs of the world.

But these areas of research may not be relevant, nor may they represent a source of mental and psychiatry healing, for Bible-believing Christians.

Genuine Christians believe in satanic activities that affect our physical and mental health (John 10:10). However, they don't believe in mystical experiences, psychic openings, demonic possession experiences, religious cult movements, etc. The gateway to understanding and practicing faith in Yahweh must take root in Jesus Christ. A believer's faith, relationship with God, and trust in the authority and power of Christ are the criteria for spiritual, mental, and physical diagnoses and healing (James 5:13).

## III. TREATMENT

Most religious and spiritual treatments are practiced without the use of medication and fall into the following categories: psychotherapy; obedience to religious norms; consultation with nature, energy, and spirit world; and counselling.

Fasting and chanting are encouraged when one seeks the face of a god or type of energy, but fasting and chanting alone are not good enough criteria for securing answers to prayer. For Christians, no amount of good works will earn God's favor. Rather, it's all about what the blood of Christ has earned for humanity; that's what enables breakthroughs in prayer.

## IV. HEALING CAPABILITY

In their articles, Koenig and Korreich and Aubin write that religion and spirituality influence healing in mental and social support and substance abuse, among other areas.[205] Furthermore, they express the opinion that religion and spirituality have the capacity to provide hope, optimism, meaning, and purpose, while allowing people to cope with depression, suicide, anxiety, psychosis, marital instability, alcohol and drug abuse, and infidelity.

WHAT DRIVES THE PRACTICE OF RELIGIOUS/SPIRITUAL HEALING?
There are many factors that drive the practice of religious/spiritual healing.

---

205. Koenig, "Religion and Medicine II: Religion, Mental Health, and Related Behaviors"; and Kornreich and Aubin, "Religion and Brain Functioning (Part 2): Does Religion Positively Impact Mental Health?"

**Rejection of the Creator.** Those who reject God, the source of righteousness, end up producing the fruit of unrighteousness. The rejection of the Creator, and tolerance of unrighteousness, has allowed Satan to permeate the lives of unbelievers with demons and false spirits, tricking them into believing that the power to heal sickness resides within themselves due to their interactions with the spirit world. As a result, wickedness, hatred, and ill health are rapidly increasing in the world.

**Satan is the prince of all ungodliness.** Satan has one main agenda: the destruction of all appearances of godliness. He uses creatures, including humans, to achieve this goal (John 10:10).

But those led by the Spirit of Christ produce the fruits of the Spirit, including health and well-being. The Holy Spirit indwells believers and becomes a dominating force in their imaginations, words, and deeds (John 14:16–17, 1 Corinthians 6:19–20, Ephesians 4:30).

**Lack of knowledge of truth and authentic faith.** Knowledge of the truth sets a person free from any form of domination, enslavement, or deception. The most outstanding work of Satan throughout the generations has been the production of falsehoods—and specifically, atheism. The explosion of false teachings about the existence of God, the reality of authentic truth, and the humanistic view of our universe are catalysts for satanic activities.

The writer of Hebrews warns believers to watch out for unbelief in godly instruction and beware the perplexity of malicious activities in the world.

> *Beware, brethren, lest there be in any of you an evil heart of unbelief in departing from the living God; but exhort one another daily, while it is called "Today," lest any of you be hardened through the deceitfulness of sin.* (Hebrews 3:12–13, NKJV)

WHY DOESN'T MANUFACTURED RELIGION/SPIRITUALITY GUARANTEE HEALING?
Authentic healing is not based on manufactured spirituality. The original healing prayer depends on the spirituality of the one speaking it.

We do not eliminate sickness and suffering by right philosophical, ideological, and psychological thinking in man's wisdom alone. The Bible declares that human religiosity and spirituality are filthy rags before the righteousness of God.

> *All of us have become like one who is unclean, and all our righteous acts are like filthy rags; we all shrivel up like a leaf, and like the wind our sins sweep us away.* (Isaiah 64:6, NIV)

## THE ROLE OF GOD'S GRACE IN HEALING AND WELLNESS

Those in the field of modern medicine and mental health deal with many physical and mental afflictions. They need to understand that in Christianity, human religiosity and spirituality are not behind God's acts of healing. Because we have been created in the image and likeness of God, we enjoy his common grace.

Grace is the essence of the divine being of God and his actions regarding creation. Moses acknowledged that God is *"compassionate and gracious… slow to anger, abounding in love and faithfulness"* (Exodus 34:6, NIV). Peter said that the Lord is *"the God of all grace"* (1 Peter 5:10, NIV). We also read,

> *In past generations he allowed all the nations to walk in their own ways. Yet he did not leave himself without witness, for he did good by giving you rains from heaven and fruitful seasons, satisfying your hearts with food and gladness* (Acts 14:16–17, ESV)

God's gift of common grace extends to all living creatures, including humans. As humans, we all have the same quality and quantity of oxygen. We enjoy the same sunshine and weather conditions. The breath in our lungs is God's breath (Genesis 2:7). The Bible tells us that God *"makes his sun rise on the evil and on the good, and sends rain on the just and on the unjust"* (Matthew 5:45, ESV).

We enjoy these things not because we are good religious and spiritual people. God's common grace is equally distributed to the atheists and agnostics, who deny the existence of the Creator. Murderers, thieves, idolaters, adulterers, and haters of good enjoy all the blessings of God's common grace regarding their well-being. God heals them of their diseases. Why? Not because they pray or perform certain actions. He heals them through his favor, extended to everyone.

When Christians talk about the authority and power of Christ, it is an acknowledgement that the suffering Servant, Jesus Christ, paid the price for our sickness. Through the presbytery prayer ministry, he has asked believers to report to him the afflictions of members of the church for healing and forgiveness of sin through prayer (Philippians 4:6–7, James 5:13–18).

CHAPTER NINE
# The Presbytery Crisis Prayer Ministry

> We can cure physical diseases with medicine, but the only cure for loneliness, despair, and hopelessness is love. There are many in the world who are dying for a piece of bread, but there are many more dying for a little love.[206] —Mother Teresa

THE PCPM DEPENDS on the participation of the Trinity, the promise in God's word, and the redeemed presbytery. The Triune God is involved in the healing of any sickness. The presbytery prays to God the Father, describing the crisis member's condition through the name of God the Son. The Holy Spirit then directs that prayer within the scope of the will of the Godhead to the presbytery.

UNDERSTANDING PRESBYTERY CRISIS PRAYER MINISTRY FOR HEALING
Research into human efforts to pursue healing and maintain holistic health from a biblical perspective shows that disease took root with the curse of sin. Every disease and sickness is a consequences of sin, a curse that affects the perfect state of the universe.

As a result, the Creator severed his relationship with mankind. Since that time, humanity has come to depend on plants and its own intelligence to source remedies for the tyranny of disease, sickness, and death.

The first four healing approaches explained in this book have offered prescribed treatments for healing sickness. Almost all of these have been based on material substances. Patients obey their healer's directions, and failure to follow them can result in harm—even death.

These other approaches have little knowledge of the root cause of the human predicament. They operate on trial and error, using God's creation, including plants and intelligence, to produce drugs and other treatments. Religiosity and spirituality depend on natural wisdom, ideology, and philosophy, often in consultation with spirits, to invoke healing.

The Creator instituted everything that exists in our world and its prescribed treatment for ill health is the righteous prayer of faith through the accomplished work of Jesus Christ on the cross. The presbytery crisis prayer ministry is the available provision that can heal our physical, mental, and spiritual conditions.

---

206. Mother Teresa, "We can cure physical…" *AZ Quotes*. Date of access: June 2, 2023 (https://www.azquotes.com/quote/553793).

Throughout the pages of Scripture, God's standard prescription for resolving every problem comes down to the acknowledgment, confession, and forgiveness of sin, having faith in God's promises standing in the righteousness of Christ (James 5:15–18, 1 John 1:8–10).

With the PCPM, God has put in place a procedure for maximizing divine results.

**God is the institute, and the church is the implementor.** God instituted the PCPM in his church and uses his human-ordained representatives to defeat the effect of sin in a believer's life.

**God sets the method of healing: righteous prayer in the local church.** According to his divine prerogative, God has set forth the instrument for healing. He has revealed in his word that prayer of the righteous presbytery is his sacred resource for restoring health in lives of crisis members.

**God provides the formula: faith, confession of sin, and forgiveness.** God has revealed the formula for overcoming any physical or spiritual deficiency. We are to have faith in Christ Jesus, confess and forsake our sin, and receiving the forgiveness of sin.

**God ordained the healing source: the righteousness, authority, and power of Christ.** God has revealed in his word that the source of healing is the righteousness, authority, and power inherent in the name of Jesus Christ.

**God's intended goal of healing: the destruction of the works of Satan.** God summarizes in his word that Christ came to destroy Satan's works. The foundation of the results of Satan's work is sin, and the product of sin is human suffering, for sin destroys the physical and spiritual health of a child of God. We must rest assured that Christ's victory on the cross will provide us with success at every step of our journey of faith in Christ.

**God's divine outcome for restoring health: a healthy church and the glory of God.** Providing physical and spiritual healing results in the destruction of the works of Satan. This is accomplished for the single purpose of glorifying God.

**God ordained this healing process without the involvement of the material world.** Entirely on the leading of the Holy Spirit, God instructs us through his word about prayer for crisis members. The chief supervisor of this process is the third person in the Godhead. All his works are perfectly accurate and useful in redeeming human crises.

## I. HEALING SOURCE

The healing source of the PCPM is found in the Holy Spirit, the Bible, the presbytery prayer of faith, and reasoning according to God's promises and counsel. The Holy Spirit directs the presbytery's effective prayer to the will of God through the Lord Jesus Christ. The Holy Spirit knows the promises of God in the Bible and presbytery counselling, based on God's promises, helps to turn things around in the life of a crisis member.

## II. METHOD OF DIAGNOSIS

Like the other healing approaches, diagnosis is an important aspect of presbytery crisis prayer. It must include assessing, questioning, and testing the crisis member for their health condition. Here is the general road map:

- The presbytery must establish the church member's spiritual relationship with Christ. They are to be Christ's possession because of the benefit of Christ's redemptive work in them (John 3:3–5).
- The presbytery must be in good standing with the Lord and themselves. The elders should self-diagnose their own spiritual health with God and others and deal with any problems that are discovered (Psalm 32:3–5).
- All parties must have faith in the authority and power of Christ for healing to occur. The Godhead is involved in the presbytery's righteous prayer if that prayer is presented in the name of Jesus Christ.
- The presbytery must deal with sin in order to defeat the accuser, Satan and his demons, who have no basis on which to hinder God's response to prayer if sin is dealt with before the healing prayer is made.
- The presbytery must address the presence of the evil one in the victim's life. They also check the individual's past spiritual relationship with God and fellow man so that they may go before God confidently.
- They must identify the root of the crisis. The presbytery works with the crisis member to identify the cause of the sickness and deal with it (Romans 6:12, James 5:16).
- The presbytery must cry out to God for healing. This demonstrates our complete dependence on his grace, mercy, power, and authority to heal.
- The presbytery must anoint the crisis member with oil and pray by the laying on of hands. This is the solution for healing, fulfilling the biblical instruction and to demonstrate obedience to God.

## III. TREATMENT

To heal a crisis church member, there are many criteria that will bring forth healing, including following the word of God, praying, fasting, having faith, and undergoing counselling. The presbytery must:

- Ensure both their own consecration and that of the crisis member. In addition, the board of elders must deal with any personal obstruction/sin between God, the crisis member, and themselves.
- Use relevant Scripture. God's word is the gateway to his heart, promises, and miracles in a believer's life. God's word reveals that he magnifies his character, promises, name, and sufficiency above everything (Psalm 138:2).
- Fast when it appears necessary and possible. Praying with fasting is a Bible requirement for a miracle to occur. In addition, fasting indicates one's commitment to and confidence in the promises of God (Matthew 17:21).
- Have faith in and belief in God's impossibility. Healing is absolutely an act of God.
- Do its part to have faith, pray, confess sin, forgive, and obey all procedures for healing. However, the presbytery must then leave the act of healing to God, because healing is his divine prerogative.
- Address God in the second person, as opposed to the third person. For example, "You have said" instead of "He has said," "You have promised" instead "He has promised," and "You are my Healer" instead of "He is my Healer." The use of the second person personalizes one's close relationship to God.

## IV. HEALING CAPACITY

GOD'S HEALING PLAN CANNOT BE THWARTED
We must recognize and appreciate God's gifts of plants, animals, and human intelligence. Everything comes from God, who empowers us.

It is important to know that the PCPM does not depend on any human source of power, but rather depends on Christ. Healing of the sick takes place on account of God through the righteousness of his Son.

In his testimony of the joy and peace of knowing the power and authority of his name, Jesus said,

> *Truly, truly, I say to you, whatever you ask of the Father in my name, he will give it to you. Until now you have asked nothing in my name. Ask, and you will receive, that your joy may be full.* (John 16:23–24, ESV)

The church has authority and power over all human disease (Matthew 10:1). Believers are to pray for a total restoration of health (Psalm 41:3), having been empowered to do more excellent work (John 14:12).

There are fatal sicknesses. Even in these cases, God can extend grace to the sick in order to their lives (2 Kings 20:3, Isaiah 38:5). Also, prayer offers us the potential to be healed and made whole of any disease. Prayer and faith in Christ are God's channels of response. Therefore, it is essential to understand that only prayer and faith in Jesus Christ has the capacity to heal human affliction.

Healing through the PCPM does not result in any side effects. However, side effects are part and parcel of the other four approaches to healing discussed in this book.

Where God chooses not to heal a sickness, the apostle Peter affirms God's eternal plan for the believer's wellness: *"And the God of all grace, who called you to his eternal glory in Christ, after you have suffered a little while, will himself restore you and make you strong, firm and steadfast"* (1 Peter 5:10, NIV).

Healing is God's prerogative; nonetheless, there is no limits to what is possible through the healing power of the PCPM. This is true because there is nothing too great, too big, too strong, too complex, or too complicated for God. Nothing and no one can thwart his purpose as long as it aligns with his divine plan (Genesis 18:14, Jeremiah 32:17, Isaiah 41:10, Job 42:2, Matthew 19:26, Mark 11:24).

God has authority and power over and beyond every human condition. But if the presbytery prayer does not produce a positive result, there are several possible reasons.

**Disobedience exists.** The presbytery must bring prayer before the Lord in an unrebellious attitude. God ignores an attitude of disobedience. Peter writes: *"For the eyes of the Lord are on the righteous and his ears are attentive to their prayer, but the face of the Lord is against those who do evil"* (1 Peter 3:12, NIV).

**One has failed to right a wrong with both God and man.** The presbytery must live in the core truth that God will not respond to a prayer if unconfessed sin and unforgiveness exists. The presbytery must ascertain that no known sin exists before engaging in the crisis prayer. Existing iniquities are barriers to God's presence (Psalm 66:18, Isaiah 56:2)

**One has not demonstrated faith in Jesus.** The root of any successful Christian ministry is faith in Christ Jesus. Faith in him moves God to a suppositive response to presbytery crisis prayer. Conversely, the Bible says that a lack of confidence results in the failure to attract miraculous answers (Matthew 21:22, Mark 11:24, Hebrews 11:6, James 1:6).

**God does all things to glorify his name.** Whatever God does, he does it for his name's sake and his exaltation (Acts 12:21–23).

**God does not heal certain human conditions.** For example, instead of healing a sickness he may use that sickness to take his child to rest in his eternal home.

**God may not effect healing to showcase the effect of sin and man's need for redemption.** As a sovereign Lord, God has all things under his control. Nevertheless, he doesn't choose to heal every instance of human suffering. This serves as a marker for mankind's fall from God's righteousness and points to our need for redemption.

**God will not honor the prayer of presbytery if an unholy relationship exists in that person's family.** One of the severe reasons for unanswered presbytery crisis prayer is that the crisis member is guilty of abusing his or her spouse. On the other hand, honoring one's spouse produces an answer to prayer (1 Peter 3:7). Every member of the presbytery must at all times work out any difference with their spouse that could result in blocking the aroma of the Holy Spirit in pleasing God.

**God distances the presbytery's self-confidence and ill will.** The Lord turns off his healing power when the presbytery crisis prayer is proud, hypocritical or motivated by ungodliness. Crisis prayer that rest on such a foundation is like a filthy rag in the presence of God (Proverbs 29:23, Matthew 6:5, James 4:3).

**God loves strong persistence in crisis prayer of faith.** A lack of persistence in crisis prayer could result in unanswered prayer. Scripture reveals that God releases unusual miracles when the presbytery is persistent in knocking at the door of his divine throne. Persistence crisis prayer seems to be synonymous with persistent faith (1 Thessalonians 5:17–18).

**God demonstrates his greater loving purpose in choosing not to heal sickness.** God's prerogative not to heal a particular sickness may serve to showcase his more excellent plan and purpose in an individual's life and ministry.

The choice not to heal a particular sickness should not be taken to describe any incapacity or limitation on God's part. We know he is Jehovah Rapha, and his love for his church is unconditional.

Scripture shows us many examples of this. Jesus decided to delay the recovery of Lazarus to demonstrate his authority and power over the dead and resurrection. He then used artificial medicine to heal Timothy rather than a word of miraculous declaration. He also allowed Job's afflictions to teach Satan that only God himself controls curses and blessings. Paul, too, had to linger with his affliction because God wanted to show the sufficiency of his grace.

PRESBYTERY FAITH PRAYER ACTS ON WORKING FAITH
Understanding the central importance of faith in Christ, as well as Christ's faithfulness, anchors believers' saving and working faith. The anointing work of Christ is the only

requirement for being redeemed of sin. He took our sins and gave us his righteousness.

Christ Jesus satisfied God's justice and righteousness. Because righteousness and justice are two sides of the same coin, he cannot fulfill his imputed righteousness without satisfying justice. So when the PCPM operates, it is done in righteousness and justice. We in the ministry have no role of our own in delivering saving faith; we only have a role in working our faith.

Paul's defence of this biblical truth can be found in Romans 3:21–26:

> But now God has shown us a way to be made right with him without keeping the requirements of the law, as was promised in the writings of Moses and the prophets long ago. We are made right with God by placing our faith in Jesus Christ. And this is true for everyone who believes, no matter who we are.
>
> For everyone has sinned; we all fall short of God's glorious standard. Yet God, in his grace, freely makes us right in his sight. He did this through Christ Jesus when he freed us from the penalty for our sins. For God presented Jesus as the sacrifice for sin. People are made right with God when they believe that Jesus sacrificed his life, shedding his blood. This sacrifice shows that God was being fair when he held back and did not punish those who sinned in times past, for he was looking ahead and including them in what he would do in this present time. God did this to demonstrate his righteousness, for he himself is fair and just, and he makes sinners right in his sight when they believe in Jesus. (NLT)

Therefore, the PCPM is a prayer in the faith of Jesus Christ. Prayer is not a spiritual gift but a characteristic of growing Christian faith, without which there can be no breakthrough.

All the forces of darkness are utterly submissive to the Lord's sovereignty through prayer. The same is true when something that is impossible is put into action and made practical by God in accomplishing his word.

Andrade and Radhakrishnan, despite not sharing Christian faith, write that prayer describes thoughts, words, or deeds that address or petition a divine entity or force. Christ is above all evil forces: he is the Lord of all that exists.[207]

---

207. Andrade and Radhakrishnan, "Prayer and Healing: A Medical and Scientific Perspective on Randomized Controlled Trials."

So the presbytery prayer of faith in Christ establishes that God is always in control of the daily affairs of men and women—and God's involvement in our welfare does not stop when we are saved.

The Bible teaches many things we do not know about God and his dealing with humanity.

> *However, as it is written: "What no eye has seen, what no ear has heard, and what no human mind has conceived"—the things God has prepared for those who love him—these are the things God has revealed to us by his Spirit.* (1 Corinthians 2:9–10, NIV)

Satan does not understand the unseen, unheard, and unconceived things of God. Neither do human senses understand it. The Holy Spirit alone does. Therefore, he is at work in his church to fulfill God's divine plans, even the unseen and the incomprehensible.

Believers should operate with their intellect as well as faith in the things of God in relationship to the PCPM. According to Mark Dombeck and John Karl, "A prayer of faith is unifying force, unfolding mystery, and inner strength, such as joy and peace in the inner man; creating harmonious interconnectedness with the presbytery, crisis member, and a higher power—God"[208]

At all times, crisis prayer must focus more on faith in what God has promised to do. He is faithful to perform it. The fact is that faith in Jesus must be present in order for us to receive anything from God (Hebrews 11:6). We must believe that he exists, that he is good, and that he will be good to us if we pray to him.

In concluding this chapter, it is crucial to observe that medical scientists, psychologists, and mental health professionals have been researching the scientific evidence on the correlation between religious faith and health achievement for many decades. Furthermore, research shows that spiritual faith does influence health outcomes.[209]

Therefore, the church needs both saving faith and working faith to dispute any claims that faith prayers are ineffective in healing. The story of the Bible has endured aggressive criticism. Many attempts have been made by many forces to thwart the mission of God in Jesus Christ, but divine miracles have resisted every attempt.

---

208. Mary Dombeck and John Karl, "Spiritual Issues in Mental Health Care," *Journal of Religion and Health 26(3)*, 1987, 183–97.

209. Thomas G. Plante and Naveen K. Sharma, "Religious Faith and Mental Health Outcomes," *Faith and Health: Psychological Perspectives*, eds. Thomas G. Plante and Allen C. Sherman (New York, NY: Guilford Press, 2001), 240–261.

Satan attempted it in the Garden of Eden, but he failed. The Egyptian Pharaoh tried to deny the progression of God's plan for humanity, but he died at the Red Sea without achieving his anti-righteous goal. Herod attempted the elimination of the Child Jesus, but he failed because God manipulated his destructive plan. Finally, Satan is destroying the works of Jesus Christ on earth through polytheistic beliefs, pluralistic religion, and mystic worship.

Christianity today is a living miracle of the relationship between a sinless God and a sinful man.

**Traditional healers mock the church for hypocrisy.** Monotheistic religions around the world are antagonistic to the mission and Person of Jesus Christ and describe him as just one of many mere prophets and a famous character in human history.

**Religious and spiritual practitioners view Christianity as being part of western culture and secularism.** They view the Christian faith as being lower than the culture, and a highly antagonistic culture in our modern world. Therefore, they reject the testimony of the apostle Peter:

> *Now to you who believe, this stone is precious. But to those who do not believe, "The stone the builders rejected has become the cornerstone," and, "A stone that causes people to stumble and a rock that makes them fall." They stumble because they disobey the message—which is also what they were destined for.*
>
> *But you are a chosen people, a royal priesthood, a holy nation, God's special possession, that you may declare the praises of him who called you out of darkness into his wonderful light. Once you were not a people, but now you are the people of God; once you had not received mercy, but now you have received mercy.* (1 Peter 2:7–10, NIV)

Western civilization and culture were built on the tenants of biblical faith and have benefited from the blessings of Abraham. Tacey echoes this claim in his article, writing that "Australians are godless, and sometimes we glory in this condition and even boast about it. This behavior comes from our larrikin, skeptical and rebellious streak. The streak has produced xenophobia, sexism, racism…"[210]

Also, there are rising tendencies of Christphobia in our world.

---

210. Tacey, "Spiritual Connectedness and Healing," 1.

**THE PRESBYTERY CRISIS MINISTRY**

## THE PCPM IS NOT BASED ON THE HUMAN PERSPECTIVE OF RELIGIOSITY/SPIRITUALITY

There are several reasons that the PCPM is not based on the human perspective of religiosity/spirituality.

- No one becomes a Christian by human moral standards but rather by faith in Christ alone.
- The source of the Christian faith does not arise from any created being or spirit.
- The PCPM is prayed directly to the living and active God, not any created object or animated spirit.
- The PCPM is an act of obedience followed through clear instructions by Jesus Christ.
- The PCPM is not based on giving alms, making sacrifices, appeasing animal spirits or departed spirits, or observing any set of laws.
- The PCPM has a direct relationship with the living and active God through the person of the Lord Jesus Christ, who promised to respond in times of affliction.

Christian Spirituality Differs from Other Expressions of Religion/Spirituality

- Christianity is not founded on human wisdom, philosophy, and ideology.
- Christians worship the Creator, not the creature.
- Christianity reveals God's hatred for manufactured religion/spirituality.
- Christianity is about the Creator seeking man, not man seeking and searching for the Creator amidst the creation.
- Christians operate by faith in the truth of God's promises through Jesus Christ alone.
- Christians live because their Founder has defeated sin, sickness, and death—and he is alive.

# The Presbytery Faith Healing Ministry

CHAPTER TEN
# Spiritual Insights Regarding James's Prayer

*For we are not fighting against flesh-and-blood enemies, but against evil rulers and authorities of the unseen world, against mighty powers in this dark world, and against evil spirits in the heavenly places.*
(Ephesians 6:12, NLT)

JAMES WAS PRECISE in his writings about the presbytery crisis prayer. He laid out a procedure on how presbytery prayer should function in meeting a crisis member's needs in a local church. In understanding this procedure, we will now discuss some key concepts.

In the Bible, an elder is a special designation. An elder is an elective office with specific functions and a set term or duration. It is also limited to a distinct local congregation. In this sense, elders are a set of spiritual under-shepherds representing the righteousness of Christ and his Lordship over a community of believers for a stipulated period of time (1 Timothy 4:14).

The term "presbyter" is sometimes used interchangeably with words like bishop, elder, or overseer (Acts 20:17–28, Titus 1:5–7). In the table below, you will discover various Greek terms translated as bishop, overseer, shepherd, and steward under the umbrella of eldership.

| FIGURE 2: THE FIVE GREEK TERMS THAT DESCRIBE THE ELDERSHIP OFFICE | | | |
|---|---|---|---|
| GREEK TERM | ENGLISH TRANSLATION | DEFINITION | AREA OF EMPHASIS |
| Presbureros | Elder or presbyter | Older or senior man | Experience |
| Episcopos | Overseer or bishop | Guardian or superintendent | Overseer |
| Poiemen | Shephard or pastor | Tender | Protection |
| Oikonomo | Steward | Treasurer | Trustworthy |
| Presbuterion | Eldership | Older men or elders | Plurality and equality |

Why did the Holy Spirit allow the writers of the Bible to use different Greek words to describe the eldership and its functions? That is a robust question. Let's shed some light on the titles used in the church.

An article on Bible.ca makes several interesting assertions. The word *elder* indicates an older man with wisdom that can only come from age and experience. An *overseer* suggests a position of top authority, one who is in charge and makes all final decisions for the local congregation. *Shepherd* indicates someone who is to show love, care, dedication, and self-sacrifice for the sheep—church members. In comparison, God can trust a *steward* with fabulous treasure, the souls of church members, and any material things associated with the local assembly.[211]

In the case of a local assembly, elders are always spoken of in the plural sense. They are appointed or elected to office through fasting and praying (Acts 11:29–30, 14:23, 15, 16:4, 20:17–28, 21:18, James 5:14, 1 Peter 5:1–3, 1 Titus 4:14, 5:17).

While the presbytery, in the context of James, is not formed based on political, tribal, seniority, age, or position, the Holy Spirit raises spiritual leaders in the knowledge of God's word. Eldership is not a spiritual gift. However, an individual elder's spiritual gift could influence their effectiveness.

Since the focus of presbytery prayer is directed primarily to the local congregation, Vine affirms that elders ascend into this position through the fulfillment of divine qualifications, divine selection, and human confirmation (Titus 1:6–9, 1 Timothy 3:1–7, 1 Peter 5:1).[212]

For example, pastors and teachers at my Nigerian church, ECWA (Evangelical Church Winning All), can be divinely selected, appointed, and called into ministerial offices, but not necessarily appointed through human confirmation. As a denomination, the ECWA affirms the divine selection, appointment, and calling of pastors and teachers, but it exercises the assignment of ministers to local assemblies, institutions, and parachurch ministries. In this organizational sense, the divinely selected, appointed, and called pastors and teachers form the board alongside those who have been appointed by fellow humans.

## I. THE CALLING, FORMULATING, AND FORMATTING OF THE PRESBYTERY

In the context of the book of James, the PCPM operates by both human and divine evocation of faith by the Holy Spirit. When used as a verb, "call" is an action that prompts elders' awareness of the need for crisis prayer in the lives of believers.

---

211. "Organization of the Local Church," *Bible.ca*. Date of access: May 2, 2023 (https://www.bible.ca/ntx-elders-pastors-bishops.htm).

212. W.E. Vine, *An Expository Dictionary of New Testament Words* (Old Tapan, NK: Revell, 1966).

In this chapter, we will engage in some relevant discussion on members' calling for presbytery crisis prayer. Formulating and forming the elders board is crucial if such a church will ever experience true efficacy in the PCPM.

PRAYER

Prayer is the primary source for dealing with any predicament. The heart of biblical prayer is all about asking God to do what he has promised to do through Christ. God has scheduled everything we need, partnering with us for life and godliness (2 Peter 1). God is interested in the prayer and supplications of his saints (Ephesians 6:18). He wants us to pray for everything (1 Timothy 2:1–4). God answers righteous and faithful prayers because he desires for us to pray in this way. Answering prayer is one of his functions.

God's heart turns on the fragrance of the saints' prayers. In a piece written by J.R. Miller more than a century ago, he quoted the words of MacMillan:

> Perfume is the breath of flowers, the sweetest expression of their inmost being, an exhalation of their very life. It is a sign of perfect purity, health and vigor; it is a symptom of full and joyous existence—for disease and decay and death yield, not pleasant—but revolting odors—and, as such, fragrance is in nature, what prayer is in the human world. Prayer is the breath of life, the expression of the soul's best, holiest and heavenliest aspirations, the sign and token of its spiritual health.[213]

Therefore, prayer in the light of James's message is the sweatiest spiritual weapon in the elders' authority to distinguish the control of unpleasant parasites in an afflicted member's life. Prayer is an opportunity for us to take our problems of stress, pain, weakness, guilt, sin, affliction, and difficulty to God for an appropriate divine response (1 Peter 5:7), an opportunity for us to stop looking at the size of a problem and shift our focus to look instead to the size of our sovereign God.

Prayer is the heartfelt and persistent calling of God's promises of healing upon the afflicted. It is a declaration of faith in the sovereignty of God that produces healing results.

James's text emphasizes that the prayer of a righteous presbytery can accomplish much when the faith of Jesus Christ is active and God makes it effective. It is a spiritual dynamic with tremendous power to damage the sin in a believer's life.

---

213. J.R. Miller, "The Sweet Fragrance of Prayer," *Grace Gems*. Date of access: May 1, 2020 (https://gracegems.org/Miller/sweet_fragrance_of_prayer.htm). Quoting MacMillan.

Again, the demonstration of the prayer of faith is a call on the righteousness of Christ. The presbytery cannot go into the presence of God on the merit of their own righteousness, because human righteousness is like a filthy rag before God (Isaiah 64:6).

The God of the Bible is the Lord of specifications, and he seeks such an approach when a believer comes to him in prayer. The PCPM must be specific to the need of the crisis member. This approach is crucial because God is specific in his character.

Crisis prayer focuses on a particular crisis. Biblical prayer on a specific need can easily be aligned with the promises of God. God is interested in the precise desires of a believer's heart.

Author Chris Sparkman stresses that Paul truly believed that there is power in prayer. He prayed specific prayers for specific needs, praying for provision, deliverance, freedom, boldness, salvation, opportunity, and co-workers throughout Acts and his epistles.[214] The art of specificity in prayer is the center of discourse in James 5:13.

The PCPM must involve praying in both the spirit and the mind, depending on the moment's need. In other words, the presbytery could address a crisis by praying in tongues as well as with their minds.

However, the concept of praying in tongues is not referred to as speaking in tongues or speaking in an unknown language which requires an interpreter to benefit the brothers and sisters in Christ. If a person speaks in an unknown language, someone should interpret what was said to strengthen the life and faith of the faith community.

Nevertheless, praying in tongues does not require that this protocol be observed. There are many different doctrinal positions based on interpretation of what the apostle Paul meant here.

We also know that all Scripture is beneficial to the body of Christ. Hence the way this issue is presented by the apostle Paul, the master of speaking in tongues:

> *For if I pray in tongues, my spirit is praying, but I don't understand what I am saying. Well then, what shall I do? I will pray in the spirit, and I will also pray in words I understand. I will sing in the spirit, and I will also sing in words I understand.* (1 Corinthians 14:14–15, NLT)

However, praying in a known or unknown language gives rise to much debate among members of the church of Jesus Christ. Theologians and scholars differ on how and when speaking in tongues should be used, and even whether believers should speak in tongues at all.

---

214. Chris Sparkman, *Praying the Prayer of the Apostle Paul: Discovering God's Power in Your Life* (Nacogdoches, TX: Strategic Book, 2009), 215.

When it comes to the PCPM, the presbytery should not be afraid to pray in both known and unknown tongues and sing in known and unknown tongues if the Holy Spirit prompts such an opportunity. Those who honestly believe that praying in an unknown language constitutes direct spiritual communication with God should obey the leading of the indwelling Holy Spirit.

We know that praying in unknown tongues is neither a ticket to heaven nor a disqualifying note from entering the everlasting reign with Christ. If praying in such a tongue is a means of communicating directly with the Holy Spirit (Romans 8:26), then the church needs to allow believers with this gift to exercise it as deemed necessary. The presbytery should unequivocally engage God, who has the power to heal all forms of sickness.

The presbytery should also pray for knowledge. Praying with mental and spiritual knowledge reveals a profound understanding of God's promises. We have emphasized that God answers all prayers for mental and spiritual wisdom. In other words, God answers prayer according to his will and based on his promises to the church.

Suppose the presbytery has a high probability of receiving an answered prayer. In that case, they must be spiritually pure and mentally knowledgeable in God's word, because the gateway to the mind of God is guiltlessness and explicit knowledge of his word.

## ANOINT

Elwell defines the word *anointing* as rubbing the body after a bath, honoring someone, or setting someone aside for a specific function.[215] Although the act of anointing oil involves both political and medicinal usage, the practice of anointing was given religious significance.

The term is used in the book of James in light of the sacred application and anointing of the sick (Mark 6:13, James 5:14). In this case, the anointing does not involve the act of rubbing; rather it's about anointing the sick for prayer. The spiritual application derived from using oil in healing physical sickness.[216]

## OIL

The anointing oil motif is a significant representation of the involvement of the Holy Spirit in the healing process. In this book, we will not go into details on the biblical teaching

---

215. Walter A. Elwell, *Baker's Evangelical Dictionary of Biblical Theology* (Grand Rapids, MI: Baker Book House, 1997).

216. Charles Pfeiffer and Everett Harrison, *The Wycliffe Bible Commentary* (Grand Rapids, MI: Eerdmans, 2012).

regarding the role of oil. Instead we will attempt to clearly understand the purpose of oil in both the first and the twenty-first centuries.

Generally, oil symbolizes the third person of the Godhead, the Holy Spirit. The use of oil represents several biblical teachings and applications. The common purposes were for medicinal (Luke 10:34), preservative, and cosmetic. Elwell and Vine state that its primary application was to treat wounds, mark corpses, and be applied to either captives and the heads or feet of people being honored.[217]

Oil represents the spiritual-physical connection that symbolizes the presence of the Holy Spirit (Matthew 25:3–8). The Holy Spirit makes the word (rhema) active in a believer's life and ministry. Oil, as a representation of the Holy Spirit, reflects its accompaniment of miraculous power thereof (Mark 6:13).

It is the Holy Spirit who searches and understands the innermost parts of us, including our spiritual, physiological, and psychological afflictions. One of the Holy Spirit's ministries teaches believers how to pray for the will of God (Romans 8:26). He also inspires and directs the PCPM. He directs the members of the presbytery to use the right words and have the right attitude, increasing their faith. This function of the Holy Spirit prompted James to assert, *"The prayer of a righteous person is powerful and effective"* (James 5:16, NIV). The Holy Spirit guarantees the power and effectiveness of the prayers of the saints, not the language we use.

The longings which the Holy Spirit places in our hearts are often too deep for utterance, too deep apparently for believers to clearly comprehend. God himself must search the heart to know the mind of the Spirit. But God does know what is in the mind of the Spirit. He does know what these Spirit-given longings mean, even if we do not. And these longings are in accordance with God's will. Because he grants them, they must come to pass.

One of the ministries of the Holy Spirit connects a sick person's faith with the faith of the praying presbytery (James 5:15), as well as the faith in the intercessory prayer of Christ. We read in Hebrews 7:25 that Christ can save forever those who draw near to God since he lives to make intercession for them. Any intercession the Holy Spirit presents to the Godhead can produce a positive result. Christ cannot present any prayer need that the Godhead cannot answer. Healing is affected when we pray in the Holy Spirit in line with God's will. Therefore, oil symbolizes God's grace of merciful healing.[218]

---

217. Walter A. Elwell, *Evangelical Dictionary of Biblical Theology* (Grand Rapids, MI: Baker Books, 1996); and W.E. Vine, *An Expository Dictionary of New Testament Words* (Old Tapan, NJ: Revell, 1966).

218. Tadros Y. Malaty, *The Epistle of St. James: A Patristic Commentary* (Orange, CA: Coptic Orthodox Christian Center, 2001).

THE LAYING ON OF HANDS

The laying on of hands is part of James's instructions to the PCPM, and it is hotly debated Christian practice in the church today. There are significant differences in the practice of the laying on of hands among Orthodox believers, Evangelicals, Pentecostals, and those of other Bible-believing denominations.

Does the Bible teach against the laying on of hands? Does the church practice the laying on of hands today? The goal here is not to argue against or argue for, but rather to obey the leading of the Holy Spirit. Whether or not we practice the laying on of hands is not the issue. On the contrary. The acceptance or rejection of this practice has rifted some Christian assemblies, with different congregations attaching different significance to the act.

Most Bible scholars know that this practice is not a gift of salvation, great theological discourse, or must-do practice in the church. Nevertheless, some believers misunderstand it, leading to bitter debate.

The Bible is not silent on the subject, just as with other practices such as the anointing through oil, fasting, postures in prayer, and the healing gifts. It is worth mentioning that numerous practices in the church do not add anything to our salvation, but they portray signs of God's authority, grace, and blessing.

To understand the role of the laying on of hands, we must acknowledge what God's word teaches. We will now discuss the three major views.

**View #1: Those who choose not to practice it.** Some Christians believe that the laying on of hands is an unbiblical practice in the church. However, we have mentioned elsewhere that the practice is not theological heresy or hypocrisy. Scripture observed the practice throughout the generations.

Hebrews 6:1–3 presents the text most frequently debated. The writer describes the act as an *"elementary doctrine of Christ"* (ESV). Precept Austin, a website devoted to inductive study of the Bible, focuses this teaching on the superior priestly ministry and doctrine in and about Christ (Hebrews 6:1–6).[219]

The Presbytery should continue the priestly doctrine in and about Jesus Christ, which should both emphasize repentance and the forgiveness of sin by the blood of animals and faith by the blood of Christ for regeneration and growth.

The writer of Hebrews is not saying that his five elementary teachings—the washing of hands, the laying on of hands, the resurrection of the dead, eternal judgment, and the restoration of an apostate—are ineffective, insignificant, or untheological. Instead the Bible prioritizes growth to maturity (Philippians 3:12).

---

219. "Hebrews 6:1–3 Commentary," *Precept Austin*. Date of access: July 18, 2020 (https://www.preceptaustin.org/hebrews_61-3).

One might find it ridiculous to see a member of a church's leadership whose lifestyle and spiritual standing are questionable move quickly to lay their hands on an ordained minister. We should not be too critical about this because blessing, the transfer of ministerial authority, and healing power all belong to Jesus, and he exercises them for his glory. For mankind, it is all about the faith, authority, and power of the risen Christ.

**View #2: Those who choose to practice it in the context of ceremonies.** During ceremonial appointments, the laying on of hands authenticates genuine salvation and healing (Mark 16:16–18) for setting people apart for their spiritual assignments (Acts 19:5–6, 1 Timothy 4:14, 2 Timothy 1:6).

**View #3: Those who choose to practice it.** The Christian faith's patriarchs used the laying on of hands to transfer blessings (Genesis 48:1). This practice points to Christ's ability to redeem and form the foundation of the Christian faith. It is not to be denied but to build the faith towards maturity (Hebrews 6:1–3). Christ encouraged the laying on of hands by laying his hands on the sick and healing them (Mark 6:5, James 5:13). It is an act of taking control of the present power of disease or sin.

The *Hebrew Roots Bible* reveals that the teaching of the New Testament related to the laying on of hands signifies several things:

- Impartation of blessing (Joshua 4:24).
- Anointing for ministry (2 Kings 3:15).
- Judgment (Ezekiel 25:130).
- Deliverance (Deuteronomy 33:7, Isaiah 41:20).
- Authority and power of God and the local church (Acts 6:1–7).
- Healing (Matthew 8:3).[220]

The act of laying on hands is a physical touch with spiritual relevance. The physical touching of the sick was a common practice in the New Testament church. It was done several times by the Lord Jesus Christ. Each time, a healing manifestation and restoration of wellness occurred. He touched Jairus's daughter to heal her (Mark 5:35–43, Matthew 9:23–26). He touched the eyes of two blind men to heal them (Matthew 9:27–31). He touched the leper to heal him (Matthew 8:1–4).

Also, Jacob passed on God's blessing to Ephraim and Manasseh by the laying on of hands (Genesis 48: 13–20, Matthew 8:3).

James does not suggest that touching enables dramatic healing of the sick, but he does teaches that it is one aspect of the healing process.

---

220. *Hebrew Roots Bible (Qodesh Cepher)* (Scotts Valley, CA: CreateSpace, 2012).

## MEDICAL TOUCH THERAPY

Touch therapy is encouraged in the fields of medicine and psychology. In *Psychology Today*, a clinical psychiatry specialist, Mendoza, states that touch provides many benefits for both the dying and the one doing the touching. She explains further that touch increases the level of the hormone oxytocin, which in turn lowers the stress hormone levels in infants. Touch decreases isolation, anxiety, blood pressure, heart rate, and pain. It also promotes sleep and calmness. It is a powerful form of communication as well, because it messages intimate love and exhibits care.[221]

Therefore, the laying on of hands on the sick—touching—should be accompanied by a righteous elder's prayer. This demonstrates that God's authority works through his ministers, the presbytery, to intervene in the crisis of a church member. This serves as one of the basic doctrinal practices of the church. A servant of God who was prayed for through the laying on of hands received gracious salvation and was filled with the Holy Spirit and healed from his blindness. In Acts 9:17–18, we read,

> So Ananias departed and entered the house. And laying his hands on him he said, "Brother Saul, the Lord Jesus who appeared to you on the road by which you came has sent me so that you may regain your sight and be filled with the Holy Spirit." And immediately something like scales fell from his eyes, and he regained his sight. Then he rose and was baptized. (ESV)

When Ananias laid his hands on Saul's head, it was not the dissemination of salvation but the authentication of God's injunction for healing. Scripture reveals that his blindness was lifted when Ananias's hands rested on him.

In another case, the laying of hands on Saul, who became Paul, was accompanied by the confirmation of authority and power for the ministry apportioned to him (Acts 6:1–7, 15:41, 1 Timothy 4:14–15, 2 Timothy 1:6–14). It also serves as a part of prayer and healing for a believer's crisis. Paul had his wellness restored and he was filled with energy by the Holy Spirit to discharge his ministry.

## HEALING

Healing encompasses many kinds of wellness and cuts across different perspectives. The healing ministry existed experientially in the Old Testament, and in the New Testament is formed the third central ministry of our Lord and Savior Jesus Christ.

---

221. Marilyn A. Mendoza, "Touching the Dying," *Psychology Today*. March 2, 2017 (https://www.psychologytoday.com/us/blog/understanding-grief/201703/touching-the-dying).

Healing is part of Trinity's ministry to creation and it was an authentic ministry of the early church.

When the presbytery prays, they say to God, "Please fix this, Daddy." Brokenness can occur anywhere in the human system, but God is our Daddy, always able to fix our brokenness. The healing process involves restoring the body to functional normally. Whether it's removing fever, blindness, leprosy, an unwanted flow of blood, or demonic domination, healing is like taking out a damaging parasite.

In this chapter, we will discuss healing in light of the teaching of the Bible. James saw healing from both a physical and spiritual perspective.

Many human disciplines see healing differently. A group of researchers writing in *Global Advances in Health and Medicine* critique the definitions, usages, and applications of the concept of healing, discovering thousands of definitions. They believe that understanding the concept of healing is inexact. As a result, medical practitioners and patients are overwhelmed within a healthcare system focused on disease over health creation. To promote quality healthcare and the delivery of that care, they acknowledge that we need to take a more holistic, patient-centric approach that emphasizes healing as being just as important as curing.[222]

After rigorous research, I appreciate one of their definitions that seems to reflect the components of the PCPM: "Healing is a holistic, transformative process; it is personal; it is innate or naturally occurring; it is multidimensional; and it involves repair and recovery of mind, body, and spirit… the individual transcends distress."[223] They stress that healing involves the repair and recovery of every aspect of a person. This perspective of healing agrees with this statement from Ted Karpf:

> A dynamic state of complete physical, mental, spiritual and social well-being and not merely the absence of disease or infirmity as defined by WHO. Also, Healing should include "forgiveness, beliefs, spiritual connectedness, personal experience, a feeling of harmony with the past, presence, and future.[224]

From my writer's viewpoint, healing can be described as God's forceful replacement of health after exterminating the crisis in the victim's body, mind, soul, or spirit.

---

222. Kimberly Firth, Katherine Smith, Bonnie R. Sakallaris, Dawn M. Bellanti, Cindy Crawford, and Kay C. Avant, "Healing: A Concept Analysis." *Global Advances in Health and Medicine 4(6)*, November 2015, 33–50.

223. Ibid., 5.

224. Ted Karpf, "Faith and Health: Past and Present of Relations between Faith Communities and the World Health Organization." *Christian Journal for Global Health 1(1)*, June 2014, 22.

If the Son of man sets you free, you are indeed freed from disease and sin. Although believers may not be free from every physical affliction, they are freed from hopeless bewilderment about their eternal destiny. Almost all the biblical healings point to this twofold freedom in the victim's life.

Unfortunately, this type of healing does not exist in the practice of modern scientific medicine or mental healthcare. That is why effective healing must focus on addressing a whole person—physical, mental, and spiritual.

I see healing as God's way of saying, "I am here, I am in control of human affairs, and I am the Healer." The Old Testaments saints were not afraid of declaring God as the Healer of his people and their circumstances. When God healed the bitterness of contaminated well of water, it was a purification healing (Exodus 15:22–27). God made a prophetic offer of healing among his people.

We can wonder why Christ made healing an essential part of his earthly ministry, but the early church demonstrated that the Gospel of Christ is genuine. In fact, every ministry of the church is about healing, whether it's physical, mental, or spiritual. Therefore, the present church must not be afraid to let God continue his miraculous work of healing in our generation.

The church is not promoting this all-important ministry. Some are even discouraging it. Yet the healing ministry cuts across every aspect of God's covenanted relationship with his people. Healing has always been part of equation. It has been Christocentric and now should be church-centric.

One of the things Christ prayed to God the Father was to keep the church safe *"from the evil one"* (John 17:15), who is the source of all affliction. We know from history that religion, faith, and healing are closely tied. The prophetic utterance of Christ's punishment includes our spiritual, mental, and physical healings (Isaiah 53:3–6).

Biblical healing is like a tripod with three legs: the faith of God, the word of God, and the will of God. The central object of this tripod in the PCPM is the crisis—the disease, the sickness, or the pain that's responsible for the patient's dysfunction. The prayer that moves God to action must put his faith, word, and will into perspective.

No prayer works without God's faith. We have established elsewhere that every aspect of the Christian faith is a gift from the Father above. The ability to believe in God, including his word and his will, is given to us by God. He gives this to us as a way to connect with him in times of need.

All answered prayers must align with God's word, what he has said and promised. All answered prayers are also presented in the will of God—and believers can know the will of God through the ministry of the Holy Spirit.

The presbytery must know that faith in God is the word of God, and the word of God is fulfilled within the will of God. He believes by faith according to his word, and his word is the means for executing his will.

## RISE UP

Those are downtrodden by affliction and pain, or enslaved by Satan, are able to rise up from their broken-heartedness. Raising up those who have gone astray and returning them to a state of normal functioning is the single purpose of Christ's mission to the world.

Rising up is a defeat against stress, worry, pain, sadness, and the destructive elements of the body, mind, and spirit. At the same time, it means regaining joy, peace, and a good life. The church presbytery must not be afraid to command that people be raised from the bondage of their sin or sickness through the faith and righteousness of Jesus and be delivered from brokenness.

All that Moses needed to do was say a prayer, which brought the people to the point of wholeness from their afflictions. The healing ministry of Christ fulfills the prophecy of Isaiah 53:4, for he heals the sick by his authority as the Messiah and the Son of God.[225]

Nothing under the sun that would fail to stop and listen were such an order to be declared in the power and authority of Jesus Christ of Nazareth. Therefore, all the presbytery needs to do is pray that the Lord will remove sin and disease from them in the faith of Christ.

## CONFESSION OF SIN

Confessing sin means intentionally and deeply declaring the offences one has carried out against his fellow man or the righteousness and holiness of God. Forgiveness is God's extra offering of grace, promised in 1 John 1:9: *"If we confess our sins, he is faithful and just and will forgive us our sins and purify us from all unrighteousness"* (NIV).

Adam Clarke states,

> If we confess our sins—If, from a deep sense of our guilt, impurity, and helplessness, we humble ourselves before God, acknowledging our iniquity, his holiness, and our own utter helplessness, and implore mercy for his sake who has died for us; he is faithful, because to such he has promised mercy, Psalm 32:5; Proverbs 28:13; and just, for Christ has died for us, and thus made an atonement to the Divine

---

225. John T. Carroll, "Sickness and Healing in the New Testament Gospels." *Journal of Bible and Theology 42(2)*, April 1, 1995, 132.

justice; so that God can now be just, and yet the justifier of him who believeth in Jesus.[226]

This gives the reader a clear understanding of the importance of confessing sin before they approach God in prayer.

## II. PRAYING IN THE NAME OF THE LORD

Praying in the name of Jesus Christ exercises spiritual authority and quickens a divine response. God moves to answer any petition presented to him in the name of Christ through his own will. The presbytery must clearly understand this biblical truth when praying for the sick. It is significant to pray in the name of the Lord for healing.

The word "name" appears more than a thousand times in the Bible. The frequency of this word's use attests to its theological importance. Names were not mere labels; they were equivalent to whoever or whatever bore them, standing for concepts such as reputation, authority, power, and character (Exodus 3:14–15, Mark 6:14, Matthew 6:9, 7:22, and Revelation 3:1).

We read in Exodus 3:14–15,

> *God said to Moses, "I AM WHO I AM. This is what you are to say to the Israelites: 'I am has sent me to you.'"*
> 
> *God also said to Moses, "Say to the Israelites, 'The Lord, the God of your fathers—the God of Abraham, the God of Isaac and the God of Jacob—has sent me to you.' This is my name forever, the name you shall call me from generation to generation." (Exodus 3:14–15, NIV)*

The name of the Lord is the connecting point of Yahweh's authority and control over every family. In theologizing the divine idea that every family derives its name from heaven, Paul wrote, *"In him and through faith in him we may approach God with freedom and confidence… For this reason I kneel before the Father, from whom every family in heaven and on earth derives its name"* (Ephesians 3:12, 14–15, NIV).

So when you pray in the name of the Lord, you are praying in his character, mind, purpose, and promise. The purpose that brought Jesus Christ into the world was to destroy the works of Satan, including sickness and every form of sinful affliction (1 John 3:8). Therefore, any prayer of healing must come through the name of Jesus Christ our Lord (John 14:13–14, 16:23–24).

---

226. Adam Clarke, "Clarke's Notes on the Bible, 1 John 1:9," *Bible Portal*. Date of access: May 3, 2023 (https://bibleportal.com/commentary/section/adam-clarke/564179).

When the presbytery uses God's name in the prayer of intervention, they declare the nature, sovereignty, and acts of God in the life of the church. Using the names of the Lord in presbytery prayer is a divine decoration of our spiritual rock of victory. Just as young David told Goliath, *"You come to me with a sword, with a spear, and with a javelin. But I come to you in the name of the Lord of hosts, the God of the armies of Israel, whom you have defied"* (1 Samuel 17:45, NKJV).

When the presbytery moves in to pray for the afflicted, it is essential to understand what the name of the Lord can do. I have chosen five of God's names that declare who he is and his acts to showcase the benefits we get by invoking them.

**El Elyon (God Almighty).** This name reveals God as being supreme. No other gods stand before him. None are equal to him or can be compared to him, either in heaven or on earth, beneath the earth, or in the water.

Exodus 20:4 shows us Moses acknowledging that God's mightiness has no similitude. Genesis 14:18–19 contains the teaching that Melchizedek, king of Salem, brought out bread and wine. He described Abram as the priest of the Most High God and then blessed Abram: *"Blessed be Abram by God Most High, Creator of heaven and earth"* (Genesis 14:19, NIV).

Daniel 3:26 tells us, "Nebuchadnezzar then approached the opening of the blazing furnace and shouted, 'Shadrach, Meshach and Abednego, servants of the Most High God, come out! Come here!'" (NIV)

David and Luke declared the Lord to be the "God Most High, fulfilling his purpose in his children. The presbytery must bear in mind that El Elyon never changes, nor can he be subverted by the fleeting power of the earth. The Almighty God who reigns in eternal majesty is our heavenly Father.[227]

**Jehovah Rapha (the Lord who heals).** The presbytery needs to be aware that Jehovah Rapha has a divine plan for the sick who call for such ministry. Therefore, our prayer needs to be spoken in the name of Jehovah Rapha, the Lord who heals, restores, and makes us healthful (Exodus 15:25–26).

One of the characteristics of God is healing. This is who he is. Healing is one of the ministries of the Godhead given to the church for eliminating suffering and elevating wellness. Healing is a promise of God to his people if they live obediently to his word.

**Jehovah Shammah (God is there).** This refers to several names of God in Jerusalem (Ezekiel 48:36) and indicates God's presence in the new city.[228] God assures

---

227. D.R. Barnhart, *Contending for the Faith* (Orleans, ON: Abiding Word Publications, 1994).

228. "Jehovah Shammah: The Lord Is There," *Precept Austin*. Date of access: May 3, 2023 (https://www.preceptaustin.org/jehovah_shammah-the_lord_is_there).

the presbytery and the sick that the great God is always there for them. Christ expressed this name in this promise to the church: *"Never will I leave you; never will I forsake you"* (Hebrews 13:5, NIV). The indwelling of the Holy Spirit in believers shows the presence of God in our midst.

**Jehovah Shalom (God is our peace).** The peace that reigns during difficult situations comes only from Jehovah Shalom. When the presbytery prayers through this name, a painful moment is transformed into a peaceful one.

The peace of God heals troubled hearts (John 14:27). Jesus promised to leave us with his peace, and he gave us his peace. He did not promise to leave us with disease and sickness. Even in the midst of tribulation and suffering, he declared to the church that he is our Overcomer (John 16:33).

**Jehovah Tsidkenu (God is our righteousness).** First, pray in the righteousness of Christ. D.R. Barnhart writes that we have no righteousness except that which comes through Jesus Christ. Therefore, we stand to pray in the righteousness of the Lord through the atoning work of Christ, and we stand on the dominant divine platform when our prayer brings results because the accomplishment of Christ has brought everything under his feet.[229]

Second, James appeals very strongly for us to act in the will of the Lord—and the presbytery prayer is no exception. We must understand that God's will is his promised word. However, the Lord responds to all requests through his perfect will. The fact that we have no assurance of being able to infallibly discern God's will in every situation does not relieve us of the responsibility to actively seek his will so we can pray, to the best of our knowledge, according to his will.

RIGHTEOUS MAN IN GOD'S EYES

A righteous man is not one who is totally free of guilt or human fallibility. Rather, it's a reference to God's righteousness, which is dynamic and filled with tremendous power to break the unpleasant yoke of sin and sickness.

God meets human needs through the righteousness that comes through Christ, for the righteousness of Christ makes all things possible. It is transformative, holistic, transcendent, and multidimensional.

The presbytery is qualified to petition, supplicate, and present prayer to God for healing when they stand on the transformative righteousness of Jesus Christ. It is holistic because the righteous prayer can heal sickness and any sin, making the crisis member whole from spiritual and physical disease. Such a healing is transcendent and miraculous, enduring as an act of God that comes down from the heavenly Father. It is

---

229. Barnhart, *Contending for the Faith*.

also multidimensional because the human body consists of various parts; if one is sick, the others are affected.

Finally, the PCPM does not operate according to the faith and righteousness of the presbytery but in the faith and righteousness of Jesus, which makes the righteous prayer powerful and miraculous.

**The infilling of the Holy Spirit.** The Bible teaches that no one can say "Jesus is Lord," unless they are authorized by the Holy Spirit (1 Corinthians 12:3). Since the Holy Spirit acts as a person, praying and performing miracles using a human instrument (Romans 8:26, Acts 8:39), the presbytery needs his active control in the ministry of prayer. Elders will not be able to have a breakthrough prayer without the infilling of the Holy Spirit.

Being filled means submitting to the Holy Spirit, handing over control to him as he deems fit. The Holy Spirit knows the mind of God the Father and God the Son, so when he fills a soul he impacts every aspect to appropriately reach the minds of God in a moment of trouble. Each time we are filled with the Holy Spirit, we also experience a miracle (Acts 2:4, Ephesians 5:18).

**Excellent moral character.** Humans must leave no room to question the presbytery's excellent moral character. Instead the presbytery must endeavor to fulfill the biblical qualifications recorded in 1 Timothy 3.

**The spirit of Judas Iscariot.** A deviant spirit in the presbytery shows the spirit of Judas Iscariot. The presbytery's prayer of intervention will have no effect if a person is controlled by a demon. Therefore, the Holy Spirit must search and find a unity of spirit and purpose in prayer. One must have no double-minded submission to the Holy Spirit's control.

**Holding fast to godly righteousness.** Holding fast to godly righteousness as a lifestyle is crucial to interventional prayer. Godly righteousness in the life of the presbytery fosters intimacy with God and builds spiritual strength and stability (Psalm 15:1–6). It pleases God when his children live holy lives. Holy living produces the fruit of effective service (Ephesians 5:1–17).

**Role of believing in faith.** Faith seems to have three faces that all take their roots from the same Greek word, translated as "faith." One is *faith* (Matthew 9:29, 17:20, 21:21), another is *belief* (Mark 9:23, 11:23), and the third is *power* (Ephesians 3:20).

Any prayer that changes a situation must be spoken on the platform of faith (Hebrews 11:6). Our praying faith must be anchored to the faith of Jesus Christ. One of the most important factors that moves God to action is when a righteous man cries out in faith and the one who receives the prayer is also filled with the faith of Christ.

Faith in Jesus is that which overcame death and the grave. God has given the presbytery the authority and power to conquer crises by the blood of the Lamb and the testimony of his Lordship (Revelation. 12:10–11).

The writer of Hebrews states that *"without faith, it is impossible to please God"* (Hebrews 11:6, NIV). The one who says the prayer and the one who receives it must believe in God and know that he will do what he says he will do.

Today's presbytery, the church, is the modern-day Elijah. Tadros Malaty writes that heaven submitted to Elijah when he issued an order for no rain and got a spontaneous response (1 Kings 18).[230]

Suppose God responded to a single man's prayer to do something supernatural. What would stop the Godhead from responding spontaneously when the presbytery, the leaders of the Bride of Christ, fulfills the charge of James? Although the presbytery, like Elijah, is weak and natural, Jehovah Rapha has demonstrated his sovereignty when crisis prayer is spoken in the faith, righteousness, and name of the undefeated Christ.

God demonstrated his power and authority for healing in the ministry of the apostle Peter. The healing energy was so contagious that even Peter's shadow expelled disease, and his handkerchief healed sickness.

The same authority and power have been delegated to the church presbytery for the healing ministry in the local church.

> *And as ye go, preach, saying, The kingdom of heaven is at hand. Heal the sick, cleanse the lepers, raise the dead, cast out devils: freely ye have received, freely give.* (Matthew 10:7–8, KJV)

Healing is one of the salvation gifts to those who believe. The diagram below shows that the presbytery, praying for a crisis member in the faith of Jesus Christ, produces results.

If there's anything we wish to do or say to please God and move his heart to respond, our prayer of faith must channel through the faith of Jesus. Romans 5:2 says, *"through whom also we have had our access by faith into this grace wherein we stand; and we rejoice in hope of the glory of God"* (ASV).

In her article on the impact of faith and spirituality, Fawne Hansen says that she believes faith generates optimism, enriches interpersonal relationships, creates support systems, and enhances our quality of life.[231]

**The faith of Jesus Christ.** The redemptive work of Christ and unconditional love of God are the means through which God relates to his church. Nothing human outside

---

230. Malaty, *The Epistle of St. James: A Patristic Commentary*.

231. Fawne Hansen, "7 Common Adrenal Fatigue Symptoms (and How to Treat Them!)" *The Adrenal Fatigue Solution*. July 10, 2021 (https://adrenalfatiguesolution.com/adrenal-fatigue-symptoms).

Christ's accomplishment on the cross qualifies believers to be adopted as sons and daughters into the kingdom of Christ.

The prophet Isaiah, the greatest acknowledger of the holiness of God, taught that any righteousness outside the imputed righteousness of Christ is akin to filthy rags (Isaiah 64:6). Moses reiterates this idea: *"He is your life. And he will let you live many years in the land. This is the land he promised to give your ancestors Abraham, Isaac and Jacob"* (Deuteronomy 30:20, ICB). Job also acknowledges, *"In his hand is the life of every creature and the breath of all mankind"* (Job 12:10, NIV). And Paul restates: *"For in him we live and move about and exist, as even some of your own poets have said, 'For we too are his offspring'"* (Acts 17:28, NET).

Therefore, the Holy Spirit anointed Jesus with authority and power to enable his human nature to do the good work of healing. The disciples of Christ always ministered in the same fashion as Christ, who said, *"Get up! Pick up your mat and walk"* (John 5:8, NIV). Later, Peter spoke in a like-minded way: *"In the name of Jesus Christ of Nazareth, walk"* (Acts 3:6, NIV).

The Bible teaches that the Holy Spirit anoints the presbytery as Christ's representatives in the church to minister healing to the sick (Matthew 4:23–24, 8:16, 12:15, Acts 10:38). God gave the presbytery authority and power to enter the presence of God with any form of crisis through the faith and righteousness of Christ.

Nothing is more highly exalted before God than the holy name of the crucified and resurrected Christ. So Satan loses control of disease and sickness when sick people are declared healed in Christ's name.

**The role of the presbytery in righteous prayer.** The PCPM is rooted in the faith of Jesus Christ. Jesus declared, *"Daughter, your faith has healed you. Go in peace and be freed from your suffering"* (Mark 5:34, NIV). Elsewhere in the gospels, a woman teaches us about the kind of faith that focuses entirely on the authority and power of Christ (Luke 7:50, 17:11–19, Mark 5:34, 10:46–52).

It is the righteousness of Christ that transforms our circumstances. Therefore, the presbytery's self-righteousness must be emptied and filled with the righteousness of Christ, through which they can do anything.

**The role of faith in receiving righteous presbytery prayer.** All things are received by faith, which is our only bridge to the realm of the impossible. Miracles are produced when the recipient of prayer demonstrates faith in Christ's authority and power. All miraculous acts must come from believing that Christ exists and is the One who rewards our trust in him.

When the presbytery anoints a crisis member with oil, lays their hands upon the sick, and declares the authority and power of Christ imputed in them, the receiver of that prayer must connect and focus entirely on Christ, whose mission is to destroy the devil's works and make the victim whole.

**The word and will of God is the basis for answering prayer.** The word of God helps us to know his promises and builds our faith through it. In Scripture, we know what God has done, what he is doing, in our world and the church, and what He will continue to do. This helps us to know how to present a prayer.

It also teaches us why God does not answer specific prayers. There are many possible reasons, including a sinful lifestyle, unbelief, faithlessness, and doubt.

**God's response to our prayers of faith.** Jesus gives the presbytery and the crisis member the faith of Jesus through which people receive healing of every kind of sickness. God responds to all prayers through the faith and righteousness of Christ, for it is the faith of Christ that makes all things possible.

Moreover, without depending on the faith of Jesus Christ, it is impossible to please God. Therefore, the presbytery who comes to God in prayer and believes that God is a rewarder of those who seek him (Hebrews 11:6).

God reacts in our defense against sin and sickness through the authority and power in the righteousness of Christ, destroying the authority and power of sin, disease, and sickness—because Christ paid the penalty of sin and sickness through his death and resurrection. God is pleased to perform any number of impossibilities for saints who are covered by the righteousness of Christ.

God will always act on any circumstance that brings glory and honor to his name. The purpose of all recorded supernatural acts in the Bible is to point to God's glory. Therefore, when the PCPM is directed and focused on the exaltation and glory of God, he will act.

**God's love provides freedom and healing from sin and sickness.** If God had not sent Christ, his only begotten and sinless Son, to die a shameful death and redeem the souls of sinful mankind, he would not have destroyed the work of Satan.

He lavishes his love on his children. John reveals this state of character toward sinners: *"See what great love the Father has lavished on us, that we should be called children of God!"* (1 John 3:1, NIV)

**Your faith heals you.** If the Son of God sets you free, you are free indeed. Every child of God has received spiritual and physical healing at one point in their life. After individual salvation, what the Godhead does to a believer is nurture them through his word. Your healing experience may not be spontaneous, but we all know that we have received the healing ministry from above. God is at work.

**God is at work.** He promises to minister to the needs of the saints, a promise which will continue to the end (Hebrews 1:14).

CHAPTER ELEVEN
# The Task of the Presbytery Crisis Prayer Ministry

*Confess your trespasses to one another, and pray for one another, that you may be healed. The effective, fervent prayer of a righteous man avails much.* (James 5:16, NKJV)

## I. THE CARRYOVER OF RABBINIC PRAYER

WE HAVE ESTABLISHED that the epistle of James is addressed to Jewish believers. Therefore, he wrote as a Jew and contextualized his message on Jewish tradition based on rabbinical spiritual practice. His charge for the PCPM cannot be divorced from his understanding of the rabbinical practice of prayer.

Rabbis offer different types of prayer to Yahweh. Although it's difficult to trace the conception of rabbinic prayer step by step, an article in *The Jewish Quarterly Review* addresses this idea. It offers some tips on the development of rabbinic prayer, which is linked to the belief that one has a reason for pride, not shame, and that human nature has shown itself capable, under the impulse of the divine spirit, of transforming the ugly into the beautiful, magic into religion.[232]

The origin of Hebraic prayer, which developed into the doctrine of Pharisaic practice, is fettered to rigid mechanism. Pharisaic practice believes in the efficacy of prolonged prayers of the righteous and gifted individuals who influence the powers from above. This led the spiritual leaders of the synagogue to believe that righteous men of prayer could force their desire on a reluctant people.[233]

This view of prayer holds that God's purpose is affected, and his intention repositioned, by prayer. This position is significant to the understanding of the message of James: *"The effectual fervent prayer of a righteous man availeth much"* (James 5:16, KJV). Like the Jewish spiritual leaders, James sees prayer as an antidote for prevailing over the ugly situations in the lives of Christians. He sees prayer as a means for managing and prevailing in times of difficulty.

Rabbis believed that God, the Holy One, yearns for the prayer of the righteous.[234] (p. 6). God is a God of practicality. He did not just say, "Let there be light" in a theoretical fashion without there being a practical source of light.

---

232. I. Abraham, "Some Rabbinic Ideas on Prayer." *The Jewish Quarterly Review 20(2)*, January 1908, 281.

233. Ibid., 272.

234. Ibid., 277.

Besides our gift of salvation, nothing is capable of moving a Christian into the supernatural except prayer. Prayer is the only way for the church to bring down the divine will of God to be done on earth: This phrase in the Lord's Prayer: *"Thy kingdom come, Thy will be done in earth, as it is in heaven"* (Matthew 6:10, KJV).

The unrighteousness of believers stands between God and the accomplishment of his word. Our rebellion stands against the working power of the Holy Spirit.

J.D. Greears stresses that some theologians and scholars believe that the epistle of James is essentially a practical book designed to correct observed Christian behaviors regarding healing prayer.[235]

Sam Allberry reveals why the church should study and precisely practice five important truths in the epistle of James. He underscores that James provides believers with practical, direct, vivid, stretching, and encouraging truths for everyday living. According to Allberry, James "is all about what it means truly to follow [Christ]. It will show us what genuine faith looks like in real life—and it will challenge us about how real faith works hard and lives distinctively."[236]

The spiritual presbytery in the synagogue was comprised of rabbis, God's representatives to the people. Their task was to oversee the well-being of believers and instill in them God's word to guide their daily lives.

The presbytery needed to function within the framework of the righteousness and faith of Jesus Christ to be effective. Every operation of the PCPM, whether in attaining wisdom from above, withstanding trials, chasing away demonic operations, or uprooting the causes of sickness, had to be understood through the lens that working faith is made perfect through the medium of prayer.

For D.H. Wells, James's letter to the church "incarnates the whole of the life of God."[237] After the believer's salvation, the Spirit of God spends its time in ministry nourishing that believer's spiritual growth and physical well-being.

The rabbis in the synagogue believed that God yearned to respond to the praise and prayer of his righteous Israel. *The Jewish Quarterly Review* asked, "Why did God bring Israel into extremity of danger at the Red Sea before effecting a deliverance?" The answer is that God did it because he longed to hear Israel's prayer.[238]

---

235. J.D. Greear, *Essential Christianity: The Heart of the Gospel in Ten Words* (Surrey, UK: The Good Book Company, 2023).

236. Sam Allberry, "Five Reasons to Love the Letter of James," *The Good Book*. January 19, 2016 (https://www.thegoodbook.com/blog/usefulresources/2016/01/19/five-reasons-to-love-the-letter-of-james).

237. D.H. Wells, "Behavioral Dimensions of Creative Responses." *The Journal of Creative Behavior 20(1)*, March 1986, 61–65.

238. Ibid., 280.

This illustrates that God hesitantly flames into action at the outcry of his children. His ears itch to hear his child cry out for help.

When the Egyptians enslaved the Israelites in Egypt, they cried out to the Lord because of their bondage. The Bible says,

> *The Israelites groaned in their slavery and cried out, and their cry for help because of their slavery went up to God. God heard their groaning and he remembered his covenant with Abraham, with Isaac and with Jacob. So God looked on the Israelites and was concerned about them.* (Exodus 2:23–25, NIV)

So he took them from Egypt with a strong hand and an outstretched arm.

God does not break covenants or promises. He renews a relationship gladly when a man breaks God's covenant and returns to him for reconciliation (James 4:8).

> *The Lord was very angry with your fathers. Therefore say to them, Thus says the Lord of hosts: Return to me, says the Lord of hosts, and I will return to you, says the Lord of hosts.* (Zechariah 1:2–3, RSV)

If you want God back in your life, despite your ugly circumstance, the Lord never wavers in fulfilling his covenant. When we pray by God's covenant or promise, he defends and rescues his children.

The rabbinical ministry asserts the importance of the prayer of the righteous. Since God called Moses as his representative among his chosen people, he has always honored the prayer of his representatives—from Moses to Joshua, his chosen kings, priests, prophets, disciples, and apostles to the church presbytery. The presbytery is God's representative in the present-day church.

## II. THE PRESBYTERY CHARGE

In this book, the use of the word presbytery, which can be defined as a group of elders, is deliberate in order to narrow the scope of the discussion. Christian denominations use a Greek word for the presbytery, πρεσβυτέριον (presbuterion). The noun form πρεσβύτερος, is translated as "elder."

It may be helpful to mention some synonyms, such as bishop, overseer, or leader. The original Greek word for bishop, ἐπίσκοπος (episcopos), could generically be translated as an overseer.[239]

---

239. J.W. Berry, "Acculturation as Varieties of Adaptation," *Acculturation: Theory, Models and Findings*, ed. A. Padilla (Boulder, CO: Westview, 1980), 9–25.

## THE PRESBYTERY CRISIS MINISTRY

The word bishop in this book does not connote the meaning meant by some leaders in church leadership today. Neither does it necessarily describe how loosely the word is understood among some exalted Christian ministries.

In the modern and postmodern Pentecostal and faith movements, the words "bishop" and "overseer" are highly esteemed and used with great integrity. However, they are not used in the context that many Evangelicals would. The word is valued more than other ecclesiastical titles such as pastor, evangelist, or elder.

The words bishop and overseer are often used to recognize individual leaders who occupy high ministerial office. Such leaders are generally considered unapproachable, pious, and challenging by ordinary believers. Note that some ambitious leaders have created spiritual leadership terms to satisfy their spiritual ego. Today, the church has terms such as pope, patriarch, cardinal, archbishop, reverend, eminence, reverend, and father. The list could go on. All these spiritual terms are somewhat unscriptural. In some cases, a list of protocols are put in place before believers can gain access to such leaders. James did not use the term "presbytery" in such an elusive context.

Administratively, these words could include the offices of an ordained minister or church elder. For the sake of our discussion, the words elder, bishop, and overseer could be used interchangeably. In some evangelical denominations, the more common term is elder. Whatever the title, they provide pastoral care and exercise oversight on the holistic health of a congregation alongside an ordained minister.

This position is inherently understood from both Peter's and Paul's writings. For example, Peter writes,

> *To the elders among you, I appeal as a fellow elder and a witness of Christ's sufferings who also will share in the glory to be revealed: be shepherds of God's flock that is under your care, watching over them—not because you must, but because you are willing, as God wants you to be; not pursuing dishonest gain, but eager to serve.* (1 Peter 5:1–2 NIV)

In the same context, the apostle Paul writes:

> *From Miletus, Paul sent to Ephesus for the elders of the church. When they arrived, he said to them: "You know how I lived the whole time I was with you, from the first day I came into the province of Asia..."*
>
> *Keep watch over yourselves and all the flock of which the Holy Spirit has made you overseers. Be shepherds of the church of God, which he bought with his own blood.* (Acts 20:17–18, 28, NIV)

It seems clear that the key aspect of these leaders' ministries is intercessory prayer that is presented alongside teaching and preaching the word.

In my opinion, prayer must supersede the study of the word. Because prayer provides the platform for understanding each aspect of church ministry, it is the master key that opens every spiritual activity and leads to our noble faith.

I believe completely that Jesus Christ both started and ended his ministry with prayer. Examples include the occasion when he prayed during his baptism as open confirmation of the beginning of his ministry (Luke 3:21). He also prayed when he gave up his Spirit into the Father's hand on the cross (Luke 23:46).

James also describes the indispensable place of prayer in any spiritual endeavor. And yet this aspect of the elders' ministry isn't much emphasized and practiced among Christian congregations today.

The beauty of James's teaching on prayer shows that it demonstrates both faith and works on the part of a crisis member and the presbytery. The teachings in this book serve as a wake-up call for church leaders to adhere to this all-important ministry and bring about the physical health and spiritual well-being of the church's crisis members.

In discharging this all-important ministry of church elders, I subscribe to John Piper's view on a threefold understanding of James's prayer: the elders' self-praying, the elders' prayer for the sick, and the elders' prayer for others.[240]

In the case of true divine inspiration, spiritual overseers are the product of the work of the Holy Spirit (Acts 20:17, 1 Peter 5:1–2). Therefore, the appointment of the miracle-working presbytery must be the art of the Holy Spirit.

Unfortunately, some churches choose leaders to serve as overseers based on human qualities; they are good-looking, have a certain tribal affiliation, demonstrate solidarity to leadership, enjoy a prosperous economic status, and are influential in the community. Sometimes unregenerate people are chosen to serve in the church. No wonder the emphasis on the divine role of the PCPM is less encouraged and practiced in the church today.

## III. THE PRESBYTERY'S AND CRISIS MEMBER'S SELF-CRISIS PRAYER

James 5:13 says, *"Is anyone among you suffering? Then he must pray"* (NASB). Objectively, this is a direct reference to physical and mental afflictions. However, a believer can also have a spiritual affliction (Romans 14:1). James 5 does not specify which type of weakness he is talking about, which suggests that the presbytery or sick church member must first pray for himself or herself first. Believers entrusted with leadership

---

240. John Piper, "The Elders, the People, and the Prayer of Faith," *Desiring God*. March 11, 1990 (https://www.desiringgod.org/messages/the-elders-the-people-and-the-prayer-of-faith).

should exercise the authority to take members' afflictions to the Lord through the ministry of the Holy Spirit.

THE CRISIS MEMBER'S SELF-PRAYER

Believers are instructed to take charge of their affliction and call the elders when a crisis persists. Unfortunately, demonic forces may block or delay a prayer from getting through to the Lord, or block the Lord's answer from returning. It's important to note here that it can be a battle to receive responses to prayer. Daniel's struggle presents a case in point.

> *A hand touched me and set me trembling on my hands and knees. He said, "Daniel, you who are highly esteemed, consider carefully the words I am about to speak to you, and stand up, for I have now been sent to you." And when he said this to me, I stood up trembling.*
>
> *Then he continued, "Do not be afraid, Daniel. Since the first day that you set your mind to gain understanding and to humble yourself before your God, your words were heard, and I have come in response to them. But the prince of the Persian kingdom resisted me twenty-one days. Then Michael, one of the chief princes, came to help me, because I was detained there with the king of Persia.* (Daniel 10:10–13, NIV)

It is clear from the above text that Daniel's prayer was answered in heaven, but Satan thwarted its delivery. We know that Satan has assigned his demons to watch believers and accuse us before God when we miss a step in our lives; they make sure that none of our prayers are answered, or at least that the answer is delayed.

Daniel's prayer was delayed for good three weeks. However, he maintained his confidence in a covenant-keeping God.

In seeking God's healing in problematic situations, a crisis member needs to observe the following biblical principles.

**Focus on who you are in Christ.** Crisis members ought to know that God has chosen them and called them into a relationship with Christ Jesus (Romans. 8:29, 1 Thessalonians 1:4, 1 Peter 2:9, Romans 9:11). Believers, not just random people. As true believer you have Christ's unique characteristics in you. You are a masterpiece in the hand of an all-knowing and all-powerful God. The Holy Spirit dwells within you. You live in Christ, and Christ is in God (Ephesians 1:11–14, Romans 8:11).

**Focus on what God's word says about you.** In times of affliction, don't be afraid, because God is a healer. The Lord says that you should declare strength when you feel weak (Psalm 18:32), knowing that You're a masterpiece in the hands of the undefeated God.

**Be persistent and consistent in God's presence.** God never abandons his children in the their time of affliction. Instead he has promised to deliver them (Psalm 34:19).

The passage from Daniel 10 reveals the importance of persistence and consistency of prayer. Crisis members and the PCPM must not stop until a clear response from God is made manifest and be understood as such.

It is noteworthy to remember that a believer's assigned angel will fight for their breakthrough for answered prayer from the Lord, just like in the case of Daniel.

**Be sensitive to the enemy's contradictions.** Remember that the primary task of the evil one is to contradict the truth that God has spoken concerning our body, mind, and spirit. Whenever a believer expresses the faithfulness of God and his promises, the devil contradicts God's word.

Satan sows lies, misinformation, doubt, and discouragement about God's faithfulness. Satan creates a spirit of faithlessness in the believer's relationship with God Almighty. If he did it to Christ in his temptations, he will do it to any believer in their moment of affliction.

**Do not blame yourself for your affliction.** A crisis member may declare the devil's own lie that he is a sinner, but God says that we have been forgiven, adopted, and saved (Ephesians 1:5, 1 John 2:12). God sees us as significant and purposeful people whom Christ died for (Jeremiah 29:11, 1 Peter 2:9). We are beloved members in God's family (Ephesians 2:19).

Satan loves when believers blame their problems on themselves. He lies to us and causes us to feel guilty and believe God to be unfaithful.

Henry Wright states that Satan plants in us fear, guilt, shame, and accusations toward God. He tries to convince us that our disease comes from God, or that we aren't good enough to receive his love, care, and healing.[241]

The enemy wants believers to think that they must perform to receive God's love, but the word says otherwise. God's word says that nothing can separate God's children from his love. Believers are encouraged to come into the presence of God just as they are and know that God is always willing to cleanse and transform their filthiness into the righteousness of Christ.

---

241. Henry W. Wright, *Exposing the Spiritual Roots of Disease: Powerful Answers to Your Questions About Healing and Disease Prevention* (Kensington, PA: Whitaker House, 2019).

## THE PRESBYTERY CRISIS MINISTRY

### THE PRESBYTERY'S SELF-PRAYER

We have established that the Presbytery represents the Old Testament rabbis and the New Testament apostles.

In the Old Testament, the rabbis took care of their sins before intervening in other people's sins. Therefore, calling the presbytery to pray over a sick member is a big deal that has physical and spiritual significance.

When a believer cries out, the angels assigned to each member of the presbytery are swift to act, upholding the PCPM to access the presence of God and ensure that the forces of darkness don't block or delay answered prayer.

Daniel and his angel needed more angelic backup to drive away the demons seeking to block his prayer.

The PCPM activates the presence of the Healer, Jesus Christ, putting the promises of God to the test. This is a demonstration of the prayer of faith by spiritual leadership. The presbytery's self-prayer allows them to examine themselves, deal with any sin of commission or omission, and avoid Satan's false accusations. At this point, they are prepared to put on their full spiritual armor to disarm the flying and flaming arrows of any opposition (Psalm 91:3–6).

Paul instructs the faithful to engage the gears of answer prayer with these words: *"In all circumstances take up the shield of faith, with which you can extinguish all the flaming darts of the evil one"* (Ephesians 6:16, ESV).

### THE PRAYER FOR CRISIS MEMBERS

Having spoken a self-searching prayer, believers become elders when they meet the stipulated qualifications laid out in the Bible. These elders are equipped to pray in the authority and power of Jesus Christ for crisis members.

Remember, James 5:14–15 says, *"Is anyone among you sick? Let him call for the elders of the church, and let them pray over him, anointing him with oil in the name of the Lord. 15 And the prayer of faith will save the one who is sick..."* (NIV)

Such a crisis demands that the presbytery exercise authority and power over it to remedy the situation. When the elders are called, the situation could involve a spiritual and physical condition that keeps a person from getting up, and this is where we must think back to Jesus's earthly ministry, which was twofold.

First, most of his healings took place in situations when the afflicted were brought to him. The gospel writers record phrases such as "They brought..." or "They came..." or "They sought..." or "They followed..." When they came to him, believing in his power and authority, as well as in his compassion, he healed them all.

We have talked about the importance of using anointing oil elsewhere. Oil symbolizes the presence of the Holy Spirit. So let the presbytery use it. It is a biblical practice.

When the presbytery moves to pray for the crisis member, it is a movement of war-like prayer. It represents the Godhead in a battle to free the victim from parasitic domination. It also represents the unity of the local church that has appointed, selected, or elected a body of the presbytery.

## THE CRISIS PRAYER FOR OTHER MEMBERS

James 5:16 gives us an idea of what is included in this prayer mandate: *"Therefore, confess your sins to one another and pray for one another, that you may be healed"* (NIV). James includes healing for the elders and parishioners.

Through the Holy Spirit, Christ has given the church specific authority and power over particular needs. A Christian's body is a house in which the Holy Spirit dwells. Believers have the authority and power of Christ to denounce any stressors to leave their body. But that authority and power must be exercised in the name of Jesus Christ of Nazareth.

The apostle Paul encourages believers to know that they have been given the Holy Spirit and God's authority and power. Believers have the mind of Christ to help them understand the mind of the Trinity in matters concerning the ministry (2 Corinthians 2:6–12).

The presbytery has been given the right to know the deep things of the Lord because they have the Spirit of God dwelling in them. The Spirit knows every imagination, thought, and act of God about his creation. Therefore, the Holy Spirit-led presbytery has the power and authority to know and judge the affairs of local church members. The presbytery is encouraged to increase their perseverance and not give up on God in difficult moments but instead give gratitude to God, who has jurisdiction over all human illness (1 Thessalonians 5:16–18).

The prayer of the presbytery accomplishes healing and keeps the soul well. It provides enough patience to endure and persevere in pain. It overrules the enemy's thoughts about God's faithfulness in keeping his promises. A careful study of Scripture also reveals that prayer offers the forgiveness of sin, and spiritual healing can result in physical healing (Mark 2:9, James 5:15).

## IV. BASIC TOOLS OF THE PCPM

Malaty describes the church as a compassionate mother toward her children. Therefore, the church must meet the needs of its members in both joy and pain.[242]

In every local assembly, God calls a presbytery to oversee the well-being of his children. But Satan attacks and causes all kinds of crises in the family of God, including

---

242. Malaty, *The Epistle of St. James: A Patristic Commentary*, 71.

## THE PRESBYTERY CRISIS MINISTRY

illness, abuse, broken relationships, betrayal, sorrows, pain, injury, disappointment, barrenness, heartache, joblessness, unfaithfulness, hatred, anger, anxiety, depression, etc. The list could go on and on.

This list must not frighten the presbytery from fulfilling its divine calling to carry out the ministry of crisis prayer. As a thief, Satan's primary objective is to steal all that has been given to the church to benefit its relationship with Christ. Satan blocks the church's blessings, hinders good health, kills active faith, weakens brotherly love, and aids the quenching of the fire of the Holy Ghost.

In the following section, we will discuss some of the basic tools available to the PCPM.

## GOD BAPTIZES BELIEVERS WITH THE HOLY SPIRIT AND FIRE

**Baptized with the Holy Spirit.** It is incredible to know that at the time of a believer's regeneration, God takes charge, controlling and empowering the believer's life according to his will through the active ministry of the Holy Spirit.

This is interpreted in different ways. Some believers accept that the baptism of the Holy Spirit occurs spontaneously with the believer's regeneration. Some believe it occurs at a later time.

Whatever your position on this matter, one thing stands out: the indwelling presence and power of the Holy Spirit exists in a regenerated life.

I believe that in the moment of a believer's regeneration, God anoints a believer, sets his seal of ownership on him, and puts his Spirit in that person's heart as a deposit, guaranteeing what is to come (2 Corinthians 1:21–22). This deposit signifies that Christ is the Lord and Controller over such souls. In such a moment, the image and likeness of God is renewed in a regenerated life.

This baptism of the Holy Spirit connects a believer to the throne of God, giving them access to the presence of God and all the benefits thereof. The Holy Spirit reveals the mind of God to a believer and helps a believer to pray effectively.

Baptism of the Holy Spirit also helps believers to operate beyond the natural and into the supernatural. Connection with God through the indwelling Holy Spirit paves the way for godly wisdom, might, and understanding of the deep and hidden things of God. When the Spirit indwelled Daniel, he wrote,

> *Blessed be the name of God forever and ever, to whom belong wisdom and might. He changes times and seasons; he removes kings and sets up kings; he gives wisdom to the wise and knowledge to those who have understanding; he reveals deep and hidden things; he*

*knows what is in the darkness, and the light dwells with him.* (Daniel 2:20–22, ESV)

Isaiah said this about the presence of the Holy Spirit and his role in helping us to know the mind of God:

*And the Spirit of the Lord shall rest upon him, the Spirit of wisdom and understanding, the Spirit of counsel and might, the Spirit of knowledge and the fear of the Lord.* (Isaiah 11:1–2, ESV)

The apostle Paul acknowledges that believers are given the Spirit of God. He teaches that the things of God can be received only through the working of the Holy Spirit:

*For the Spirit searches everything, even the depths of God. For who knows a person's thoughts except the spirit of that person, which is in him? So also no one comprehends the thoughts of God except the Spirit of God. Now we have received not the spirit of the world, but the Spirit who is from God, that we might understand the things freely given us by God.* (1 Corinthians 2:10–12, ESV)

**Baptized with fire.** The believer is not only baptized with the Holy Spirit; every believer is baptized with fire. Matthew 3:11 reads, *"But after me comes one who is more powerful than I, whose sandals I am not worthy to carry. He will baptize you with the Holy Spirit and fire"* (NIV).

What does fire do? It purifies. It can also refer to judgment, wrath, or vengeance.

*The Commentary Critical and Explanatory on the Whole Bible* explains fire: "it is but the fiery character of the Spirit's operations upon the soul—searching, consuming, refining, sublimating…"[243] This guarantees the effectiveness of the ministry. Fire refines and purifies believers into new strength and energy. The Spirit of God fans the presbytery crisis prayer into a healing flame.

Christians are empowered by the Holy Spirit and his fiery character empowers them. This understanding of Matthew 3:11 brings God into the present.

---

243. Robert Jamieson, Andrew Fausset, and David Brown, "Commentary Critical and Explanatory on the Whole Bible, Matthew 3:11," *Study Light*. Date of access: May 3, 2023 (https://www.studylight.org/commentaries/eng/jfb/matthew-3.html).

## GOD NEVER INTENDS FOR CONFUSION AMONG BELIEVERS

The presbytery should understand that all Bible-based ministers of God must believe in the inerrancy of God's word. People hold different theological, doctrinal, hermeneutical, and homiletical interpretations of the Bible. Whatever experts do to understand the accuracy of the biblical text, the basis of understanding God's word has always been the leading of the Holy Spirit. If the Holy Spirit, who is God, is the Chief Explainer of the Bible, then confusion is no longer part of the equation.

However, these different interpretations and applications of the Bible affect people's lifestyles. For example, suppose a scholar believes that prayers no longer result in spontaneous miracles. In that case, such a theologian would have no choice but to struggle to see the authority and power of Christ to bear fruit in the PCPM.

The character and work of God in our world have not changed, but they are increasing. The effect of prayer determines the outcome of a Christian's belief and interpretation of the text.

## CRISIS PRAYER PROPAGATES HEALING

We know that our salvation is based entirely on supernatural healing from the deadliest human sickness—namely, our sins. The art of getting healed from the bondage of sin is far more complex than getting healed from physical afflictions.

This truth is attested to by Christ's rebuke of the scribes who accused him of blaspheming because he forgave the sins of a paralytic man.

> *Knowing their thoughts, Jesus said, "Why do you entertain evil thoughts in your hearts? Which is easier: to say, 'Your sins are forgiven,' or to say, 'Get up and walk'? But I want you to know that the Son of Man has authority on earth to forgive sins." So he said to the paralyzed man, "Get up, take your mat and go home."* (Matthew 9:3–5, NIV)

Spiritual healing further confirms physical and emotional healing.

Prayer is a spiritual exercise. The apostle Peter puts it this way: *"'He himself bore our sins' in his body on the cross, so that we might die to sins and live for righteousness; 'by his wounds you have been healed'"* (1 Peter 2:24, NIV).

Our redemption is made complete by Christ's spiritual and physical wounds. In spiritual pain, he told the Father to take from him the weight of the cup of human sin (Luke 22:42). However, at the same time he showed Thomas the wounds on his hands to showcase the physical pain he had endured (John 20:29).

According to John Gill in his commentary,

> What Christ bore were "sins," even all sorts of sin, original and actual, and every act of sin of his people; and all that is in sin, all that belongs to it, arises from it, and is the demerit of it, as both filth, guilt, and punishment; and a multitude of sins did he bear, even all the iniquities of all the elect; and a prodigious load and weight it was; and than which nothing could be more nauseous and disagreeable to him, who loves righteousness, and hates iniquity…[244]

Christ's pain included his spirit, soul, and body. What he accomplished on the cross conquered all sicknesses affecting the spirit, soul, and body.

THE PCPM STRENGTHENS RECONCILIATORY RELATIONSHIPS IN THE CHURCH

The presbytery serves as representatives of God in the God's royal priesthood (1 Peter 2:9), or *ecclesia*, meaning all the believers in Christ. Prayer anchors every ministry in the church. The PCPM empowers the leadership to heal sickness, increase believers' vitality, and glorify the Lord (James 5:14, Acts 6:4).

God desires for his children to make their requests known to Him in moments of trouble. This kind of a prayer:

- Is an act of obedience to what God has commanded of the church (Psalm 50:15, Jeremiah 15:21). God is always waiting for the church to call on him in prayer.
- Is an opportunity for God to fulfill his promises. Crying out to God in prayer means activating a channel he has created in order to pass along to the church all the promises he has made.
- Is a means for God's glory to be seen. Man is the only created being who understands God's glory, and man is able to express such glory to God. God wants us to pray because he wants to fulfill his promises so we can honor, worship, and glorify him.

The presbytery must not lose sight of these words pertaining to our relationship with God:

---

244. John Gill, "John Gill's Exposition of the Bible, 1 Peter 2:24," *Bible Study Tools*. Date of access: May 3, 2023 (https://www.biblestudytools.com/commentaries/gills-exposition-of-the-bible/1-peter-2-24.html).

> What a friend we have in Jesus, all our sins and griefs to bear! What a privilege to carry everything to God in prayer! O what peace we often forfeit, O what needless pain we bear, all because we do not carry everything to God in prayer![245]

The presbytery has been given the power and authority of Christ to pray for healing because sin, sickness, and ill health does not come from God. Jesus does not cause sickness; he heals sickness. Christ demonstrated this truth when the source of his authority and power was questioned after the casting out of a demonically oppressed person:

> *When his family heard about this, they went to take charge of him, for they said, "He is out of his mind."*
> *And the teachers of the law who came down from Jerusalem said, "He is possessed by Beelzebul! By the prince of demons he is driving out demons."*
> *So Jesus called them over to him and began to speak to them in parables: "How can Satan drive out Satan? If a kingdom is divided against itself, that kingdom cannot stand. If a house is divided against itself, that house cannot stand.* (Mark 3:21–25, NIV)

The presbytery has the authority and power to pray the affliction out of a person's life because sickness does not come from God. On the contrary, healing is all about returning disease and sickness back to the sender: the evil one.

## GOD DOES NOT CAUSE CRISES FOR HIS CHILDREN

Since every human was created in the image and likeness of God, his love for every human is unconditional. But not all humans embrace and appreciate the unconditionality of God's love, and not all humans have an eternal relationship with him. The moment believers are reconciled to God the Father through faith in God's gracious Son, they are declared to be adopted children of God with all benefits of having an eternal relationship with Him.

No, God does not cause any crisis to befall his children. He is upright and has no wickedness. Rather, he can destroy crises in his children's lives. And the authority and power to do so in the church age has been given to the presbytery.

---

245. Joseph Medlicott Scriven, "What a Friend We Have in Jesus," 1855.

## GOD HAS A GOOD PLAN OF PROSPERITY FOR HIS CHILDREN

God does not count it as joy to see his children in crisis, but he takes pleasure when they live in good health, body, soul, and spirit. His plans are of prosperity, hope, and a good future, not harm. His promises are for the well-being of His children. Whenever calamity befalls a child of God, it displays God's justice for that person's erroneous behavior.

## GOD GIVES HIS BEST TO HIS CHILDREN

God has promised to grant the desires of his righteous children. He will always give his child that which is good and beneficial.

The presbytery has been granted the righteousness and faith of Jesus Christ so that the they are able to pray based on the righteousness and faith of Christ, thus giving the gift of healing and restoration in the lives of crisis members. No gift from God does adds any sorrow to a person's life; the presence of God in us takes away sorrow and gives us peace unlike anything else found in the world.

## GOD WISHES WELLNESS FOR HIS CHILDREN

When the Bible talks about God's power given to the presbytery to stand in the gap, we are talking about restoring the holistic functioning of crisis members. Matthew 6:33 reads, *"But seek first his kingdom and his righteousness, and all these things will be given to you as well"* (NIV).

John Gill describes righteousness as "what God approves of, accepts, and imputes, and which only can justify in his sight, and give an abundant entrance into his Kingdom and glory."[246]

The term "these things" refers to the physical needs and earthly resources we need in order to journey through our righteous lives in Christ—which includes mental healing from worry, anxiety, and depression. It comes to us due to depending on the righteousness of Jesus Christ.

## GOD RESPONDS TO CRISES IN HIS CHILDREN'S LIVES

A believer's crisis makes a mockery of God's sovereignty, since God does not want his children to suffer bitterness, anguish, disarray, and torment. When he has committed to fulfilling the desire of his child's heart, he takes action to prove his sovereignty over human predicaments.

---

246. John Gill, "John Gill's Exposition of the Bible, Matthew 6:33," *Bible Study Tools*. Date of access: May 4, 2023 (https://www.biblestudytools.com/commentaries/gills-exposition-of-the-bible/matthew-6-33.html).

## THE PRESBYTERY CRISIS MINISTRY

Consider the cases of Hannah, Job, Daniel, and Elijah. They faced desperation and found themselves in distress. Such situations make the PCPM even more compelling. If such a prayer is answered, God is moved to respond in specific ways to resolve the crisis.

Hannah's mind before God, bitter and deeply troubled, turned God's state of mind and produced a positive response. God hates to see his child and his name dragged through the mud due to a crisis.

No wonder a young shepherd, David, was furious at Goliath for ridiculing the sovereign God of Israel. God told King David, *"Pray to me in time of trouble. I will rescue you, and you will honor me"* (Psalm 50:15, CEV).

Concerning his children, Jesus says, *"So if you sinful people know how to give good gifts to your children, how much more will your heavenly Father give good gifts to those who ask him"* (Matthew 7:11, NLT).

## GOD ANSWERS RIGHTEOUS CRISIS PRAYERS IN MULTIPLE WAYS

Scholars have identified three ways through which God answers the prayer of his child.

- "Yes."
- "No, but I will give you the grace to bear through."
- "No."

Some have added the fourth one:

- "I cannot hear you."

The reason for this fourth answer is found in Psalm 66 and Isaiah 5. Sin prevents God from hearing our prayer.

In the PCPM, however, God responds to righteous prayer in just two-way answers—and he guarantees an answer.

- "Yes." He then terminates the crisis and perfects the healing.

A typical example of this can be seen in the life of Jacob (Genesis 32:23–34).

I believe that God responds positively to any crisis prayer if the prayer demonstrates four qualities: repentance, faith, persistence, and alignment with the will of God.

Crises do not represent the positive side of God's love and glorious plan for his children, and he always has a good and prosperous plan. We should also remember that Satan doesn't want God's children to live prosperously. Therefore, God answers all prayers when those prayers are in tune with him.

However, our selfishness and lack of connection with God can prevent our prayers from being received, which is what leads to the second possible answer:

- "No." He then guarantees the sufficiency of his divine grace.

In the case of Paul, God said, "No. You will have a thorn in your flesh, but I have supplied abundant grace and peace of heart to get you through." This can be seen in 2 Corinthians 12:9–19.

Some people think another possible answer to the PCPM is "Wait." But making his children wait for an answer to prayer is not in God's character. He does not have a "wait time" in his divine plan. If you are waiting for a response, it means that the prayer does not align with the will and promise of God.

Therefore, all answered prayers exist within God's sovereign plan, divine schedule, will, and promise. All unanswered prayers stand in opposition to his plan, schedule, will, and promise.

The Bible says that God answers any prayer by his will (Matthew 10:29). The will of God concerns his sovereign governance over everything that comes to pass. The church needs to understand that the promises of God demonstrate his will for believers. If we ask something according to his will, it is the same as asking for something according to his promises. He operates in heaven and on the earth according to his will and divine schedules (Daniel 4:35).

As we read in the Lord's Prayer, paraphrased, "Let thy will in heaven and thy will on the earth be the same and fulfill what you have promised in heaven to come to pass on the earth."

## WHEN MORE THAN ONE PERSON PUTS FORTH A REQUEST, GOD RESPONDS

God established an answer to Hannah's prayer when Eli, the priest, confirmed her request. Repeatedly we see God establish his willingness to act when there is a bond of unity.

God loves collective prayer and worship. The presbytery prayer suits this divine desire, representing a collective spiritual force. When we cry out in prayer in accord with one another, God hears us and responds. He loves to see his people seek his remedy to a crisis.

## GOD HONORS PRAYER PRESENTED WITH AN EXCELLENT MOTIVE

No godly presbytery would seek God's intervention with a motive other than to uplift the kingdom of God among men. Like Hannah's case, God is pleased when an answered prayer results in praise, worship, and service of him.

Miracles are part of God's character, and God himself is a Miracle. The word of God is a miracle. God demonstrated his miraculous power in the creation of the universe. It is also a miracle that we are saved by faith in Christ. God's love for sinners is a miracle, too.

David wanted the world to know that God is a miracle-working God. He declares,

> *This day the Lord will deliver you into my hands, and I'll strike you down and cut off your head. This very day I will give the carcasses of the Philistine army to the birds and the wild animals, and the whole world will know that there is a God in Israel.* (1 Samuel 17:46, NIV)

God himself wants the world to know that he is in control of our lives and destiny, even in the church age.

## GOD ANSWERS PRAYER FOR HIS OWN GLORY

Whatever God does in heaven and on the earth, it is done for the sake of his glory. In God, there is no malice. Even when he allows negative happenings in our world, he does so for his sake. A perfect scripture echoing this divine intention is found in Isaiah 48:9–11:

> *For my name's sake I defer my anger; for the sake of my praise I restrain it for you, that I may not cut you off. Behold, I have refined you, but not as silver; I have tried you in the furnace of affliction. For my own sake, for my own sake, I do it, for how should my name be profaned? My glory I will not give to another.* (ESV)

This includes his creation, our salvation, our well-being, our successes, and our existence.

> *Whatever you ask in my name, this I will do, that the Father may be glorified in the Son.* (John 14:13, ESV)

Our saving and working faith are possible because they bring glory to God (John 5:44). When the presbytery prays, God responds supernaturally, turning an ugly crisis into a river of praise to the Lord.

## GOD HONORS PRAYERS THAT SHOW CONSISTENCY AND PERSISTENCE

Jacob could not let go of an angel of God until he was blessed, and Hannah told the Lord that her son would bring honor to him through priestly service. The Lord honored her request.

On the other hand, she would not stop pestering the king for justice until her answer came through. She made him crazy with her restless prayer until she got the result she was looking for (Luke 18:5).

Sometimes persistence and consistency in prayer is not enough. The presbytery may need to go the extra mile to break through the blocking power of the adversary, the devil.

## GOD ESTABLISHES HIS PERFECT PEACE

We know that the human body, spirit, and soul were corrupted at the fall, transforming from blamelessness to blameworthiness. Also, we know that our blameworthiness affects the perfected body, soul, and spirit.

It is also true that sickness and pain do not produce peace in our body, soul, and spirit. Therefore, sickness is an outcome of blameworthiness.

The PCPM has the power to preserve the body, soul, and spirit from the dominance of ill health. We know this divine truth from James's testimony: *"And the prayer offered in faith will make the sick person well; the Lord will raise them up. If they have sinned, they will be forgiven"* (James 5:15, NIV).

Because God's constant and consistent desire for his children is a state of blamelessness in spirit, soul, and body, he never desires that we be kept in a state of bewilderment.

## THE PRESBYTERY GRANTS CARE, GOD GRANTS CURES

God is behind every physical and spiritual healing. He is in control of the healing process, scientifically and prayerfully. He causes scientific medicine and faith prayer to cure disease and sickness. Modern medicine is the product of human effort, but healing through faith prayer is the product of divine restoration.

Therefore, all authentic healings are acts of the authentic God. God's healing acts are never counterfeit.

The members of the presbytery are ordained instruments used by God to manifest himself as Jehovah Rapha. David told Goliath to refrain from mocking the living God. Elijah defeated the prophets of Baal when he acknowledged that God was acting. Daniel and his friends brought Nebuchadnezzar to his knees. Peter said, *"But what I do have, I give you: in the name of Jesus Christ of Nazareth, walk!"* (Acts 3:6, MSG)

The availing power of presbytery crisis prayer is an act of God's power that changes things.

## GOD RESPONDS POSITIVELY BASED ON OUR LOVE AND ACKNOWLEDGEMENT

God promises to protect, deliver, honor, and satisfy the desires of the presbytery who calls on Him with righteous supplication. He will not withhold what we ask for through the honor of his name and his love for the church, because God is always on the move to watch and perform his word. The Lord's all-time promise to his children is stated in Psalm 91:14–16:

> "Because he loves me," says the Lord, "I will rescue him; I will protect him, for he acknowledges my name. He will call on me, and I will answer him; I will be with him in trouble, I will deliver him and honor him. With long life I will satisfy him and show him my salvation." (NIV)

## GOD GIVES HIS SPIRIT TO CHOSEN VESSELS AND HIS PRESBYTERY

Daniel is set up as God's servant above all the officials of Babylon, and his distinguishing feature is the excellent Spirit that God deposited in him. The is the same Holy Spirit that indwells the presbytery. This has numerous effects on a person.

**It gives you the mind of Christ (Philippians 2:5).** This allows the presbytery to discern the things of God, bestowing his practical wisdom and insightful leadership in spiritual warfare and winning spiritual battles. The presbytery is also enabled to speak the things of God through the Holy Spirit (1 Corinthians 2:13–16). Having the mind of Christ is to minister to the needs of a parishioner through the explicit instruction of Christ with complete humility (2 Corinthian 2:16).

**It allows you to hear directly from the Lord about every situation (Daniel 6:3, John 16:13).** The presence of the Spirit speaks to the presbytery about what he hears, and he declares what is to come. Isaiah wrote about this function of the Spirit: *"The Spirit of the Lord will rest on him—the Spirit of wisdom and of understanding, the Spirit of counsel and of might, the Spirit of the knowledge and fear of the Lord"* (Isaiah 11:2, NIV).

**It enables you to use God's power for unusual miracles.** Every spiritual ministry is appropriately empowered by the Holy Spirit, as he works for and encourages the work of the ministry (Luke 4:14, 1 Corinthians 12:11).

**It enables you to see situations beyond your natural wisdom.** One of the most critical aspects of the PCPOM is having the spiritual insight to see things beyond natural wisdom. Daniel and the other Hebrew youths with him could see and understand dreams and visions that originated from the mind of God (Daniel 1:17).

**It enables you to command the absolute obedience of demons.** If the presbytery is given the Spirit, the power of darkness listens. Paul writes:

> *For the weapons of our warfare are not carnal but mighty in God for pulling down strongholds, casting down arguments and every high thing that exalts itself against the knowledge of God, bringing every*

## The Task of the Presbytery Crisis Prayer Ministry

*thought into captivity to the obedience of Christ, and being ready to punish all disobedience when your obedience is fulfilled.* (2 Corinthians 10:4–6, NKJV)

When the presbytery fulfills its obedience to Christ and is endowed with the Spirit, it is able to minister to needy members effectively without demonic harassment (Acts 19:15). Instead it operates according to these active words from Paul, challenging any obstruction to successful crisis prayer. With the leadership of the Spirit, the presbytery can:

- Pull down the stronghold of the member's situation.
- Cast down arguments from demonic opposition.
- Put down every high thing that exalts itself against the knowledge of God. For example, God has promised to protect his children from deadly sickness, such as Ebola, Lasa Fever, HIV/AIDS, COVID-19, among other pestilences. God told Jeremiah, *"I will restore you to health and heal your wounds"* (Jeremiah 30:17, NIV). The church has given the power and authority to cast out evil spirits and heal every kind of disease and illness (Matthew 10:1).
- Bring every thought into captivity to the obedience of Christ.

God has promised complete forgiveness and healing with the use of righteous presbytery prayer (2 Chronicles 7:1). He can enact healing through goodness and mercy when the presbytery is humble and righteous. We read this conditional affirmation from God:

*If I shut up heaven that there be no rain, or if I command the locusts to devour the land, or if I send pestilence among my people; if my people, which are called by my name, shall humble themselves, and pray, and seek my face, and turn from their wicked ways; then will I hear from heaven, and will forgive their sin, and will heal their land.* (2 Corinthians 7:13–14, KJV)

The qualities of humility, seeking, and turning are the divine ingredients of righteousness for those who ride the will of God. Today the presbytery must be encouraged to know that the Lord is closer to his people than he was in King Solomon's days. Solomon saw God's awesomeness in the temple; the presbytery sees God in the tablets of their own hearts.

## GOD'S PROVISION FOR HEALING WAS ACCOMPLISHED ON THE CROSS

Throughout Scripture, we find that God's state of willing mind is not to cut off the desire of the righteous when they do their part. God extends a universal provision for physiological and spiritual healing. Universal provision was prophesied and fulfilled on the cross by Christ Jesus and passed on to the presbytery.

Some may say this is heresy! Well, let us investigate this further.

**The prophetic utterance.** The central mission for God in becoming man was to provide physical, mental, and spiritual healing. Sin affects the spiritual being whereas infirmities and disease concern a person's physiological components. This divine mission was foretold a long time ago by men of God before the fulfillment came true through the life and ministry of the Lord Jesus Christ.

Prophets of the Old Testament wrote that Christ's ministry would include destroying the devil's works. Genesis 3:15 reads,

> *I [God] will put enmity between you [Satan] and the woman [mother of the human race], and between your offspring [fallen demonic forces] and her offspring [human descendants]; he [the Son of God] shall bruise your head [Satan], and you shall bruise [cause sin, disease and death] his heel.* (ESV)

In the New Testament, we read in 1 John 3:8, *"The one who does what is sinful is of the devil, because the devil has been sinning from the beginning. The reason the Son of God appeared was to destroy the devil's work"* (NIV).

Matthew 8:16–17 declares the ways in which Isaiah 53 foretold the redemptive work of Christ, including spiritual, mental, and physical healings.

However, some scholars believe that the Isaiah 53 prophecy has nothing to do with healing; they claim that it refers only to spiritual healing. Nevertheless, Matthew 8 talks about both types of healing: *"When the even was come, they brought unto him many that were possessed with devils: and he cast out the spirits with his word, and healed all that were sick..."* (Matthew 8:16, KJV) The text of the follow verse then fulfills Isaiah's prophecy: *"...that it might be fulfilled which was spoken by Esaias the prophet, saying, Himself took our infirmities, and bare our sicknesses"* (Matthew 8:17, KJV).

Indeed, healing is not just spiritual healing but also mental and physiological.

**The fulfillment of prophecy.** Besides the Matthew 8:16–17 text, many passages from the Bible attest to the physical and spiritual ministries of the Lord Jesus Christ. We will include two such scriptures here:

> News about him spread all over Syria, and people brought to him all who were ill with various diseases, those suffering severe pain, the demon-possessed, those having seizures, and the paralyzed; and he healed them. (Matthew 4:24, NIV)

> When evening came, many who were demon-possessed were brought to him, and he drove out the spirits with a word and healed all the sick. This was to fulfill what was spoken through the prophet Isaiah: "He took up our infirmities and bore our diseases." (Matthew 8:16–17, NIV)

**The transfer of authority and power of Christ to fulfill prophecy.** The church must come to terms with the violence and pestilence that unfolds in our broken and rebellious world. The sicknesses are beyond the capability of traditional and scientific medicine to cope with.

The prevalence of disease is too great for us to fully comprehend; scientific medicine is no match for many of the mysterious diseases that befall humanity. Traditional and scientific medicine can cure some visible, but they cannot prevent the terror and devastation of every type of cancer and pandemic.

But this does not mean that traditional and scientific medicine do not fulfill their role in promoting health. Scientific intelligence, I believe, is part of God's plan to meet the needs of humanity. Therefore, we must embrace, encourage, and celebrate human achievement through traditional and scientific research. This development and expansion of knowledge fulfills what has been foretold by the inerrant word (Daniel 12:4).

God in Christ has given the church the authority and power to seek his face in everything, including to restrain pestilence and cure all manner of diseases through the faithful prayer of the righteous presbytery.

Know that God has not changed his mind about his promises regarding our healing. Unfortunately, the church has failed to follow these divine principles and instructions.

GOD REFUSES NO POSITION WHEN MAN'S FAITH ALIGNS WITH HIS HEART
We have discussed elsewhere in this book that the will and promises of God are the same. Therefore, God answers any prayer that aligns with his promises. There are many testimonies in the Scripture about the unchanging character of God:

> God is not human, that he should lie, not a human being, that he should change his mind. Does he speak and then not act? Does he promise and not fulfil? (Numbers 23:19, NIV)

> ...if we are faithless, he remains faithful, for he cannot disown himself.
> (2 Timothy 2:13, NIV)

> Or do you think Scripture says without reason that he jealously longs for the spirit he has caused to dwell in us? (James 4:5, NIV)

The Holy Spirit cannot wait for us to declare God's promises in prayer so that he can bring them to fulfillment.

## GOD'S HEALING IS SUFFICIENT FOR ALL

God owns everything, including all healing power and authority. Two powerful texts attest to this fact:

> Cast your burden on the Lord, and he will sustain you; he will never permit the righteous to be moved. (Psalm 55:22, ESV)

> Cast all your anxiety on him because he cares for you. (1 Peter 5:7, NIV)

These theologies teach about casting one's burden on the Lord. This is an act of prostrating oneself in the presence of the Lord, our Healer. It reflects a prayer of putting down our anguish, pain, and sickness and asking for mercy and redemption.

We are encouraged that the Lord will *"never permit the righteous to be moved."* Our faith and righteousness are all accomplished in the faith and righteousness of Christ. The two must be interwoven for supernatural healing to occur.

*The Expositor's Bible Commentary* explains this interwoven relationship: "Faith mentioned before righteousness. The two must go together, for trust which not accompanied by righteousness is no true trust, and righteousness which not grounded in trust is no stable or real righteousness."[247]

Faith in the authority and power of Jesus Christ is a central criterion for all physical, mental, and spiritual healing. Whether an individual wants physical or spiritual healing, it must be done through the authority and power of faith accomplished on the cross. No healing will be effected without going through the faith of Christ. God will act on the prayer of any sickness by lining up our faith with the faith of Jesus Christ. The presbytery

---

247. Alexander Maclaren, "The Expositor's Bible Commentary, Psalm 55." *Blue Letter Bible*. Date of access: May 4, 2023 (https://www.blueletterbible.org/comm/maclaren_alexander/the-expositors-bible/psalms-volume-two/psalm-fifty-five.cfm).

must operate with the understanding and belief that the faith of Christ exists (Hebrew 11:1).

In acknowledging Jesus Christ as a special healer, Father James McTavish encourages the church to embrace the Christology of healing—physically, psychologically, and spiritually:

> As for specialties, we could say his healing work encompassed ophthalmology (opening the eyes of the blind), ENT (curing the deaf), dermatology (healing leprosy), rehabilitation (curing paralysis), hand surgery (healing a withered hand), plastics and reconstruction (repairing a severed ear), neurology (treating a boy with convulsions), critical care (saving the slave of a centurion who was about to die)…[248]

The Lord God Almighty revealed Isaiah's healing plan. He received it and spoke it. Jesus fulfilled it and transferred it to the presbytery. Therefore, the church presbytery has received it and should practice the PCPM to any needy member who calls for it.

## GOD RESPONDS TO ALL PRAYERS BASED ON GRACE, NOT THE LAW

God relates to the church based not on what it has done but on what God has done in believers. Our spiritual and physical blessings are not acquired based on any righteous content in our lives but on God's grace, mercy, and love. No righteousness in us is enough to fulfill the standard of God's righteousness and move him to answer prayer.

So when the presbytery calls for a crisis prayer, they must understand that they must mix faith and the righteousness of Christ to obtain the desired result. The act of justice is conformity to the will of God, and faith is the supreme act of righteousness and unity with Christ the Righteous (1 Corinthians 1:30–32).

## GOD'S DESTINY FOR A MAN IS TAILORED TO GLORIFY HIMSELF

Every human has a God-given destiny. Destiny is God's plan for an individual's life, and it is tailored to honor and glorify himself.

Before Job got sick, God had already set the destiny of his sickness outside the realm of human knowledge and understanding. A man operates within the perimeter of affliction, and their reports measure their circumstances, seeing limitations and impossibilities. The presbytery should instead see possibilities.

---

248. James McTavish, "Jesus the Divine Physician." *The Linacre Quarterly 851(1)*, February 2018, 18.

## THE PRESBYTERY CRISIS MINISTRY

GOD GIVES THE PRESBYTERY THE POWER OF PROPHECY

Ask God for a continued increase of faith (Matthew 7:7–11, Mark 11:22–24, Romans 10:17, James 1:6). Faith that has the potential to increase is not saving faith but working faith. Saving faith is positional, and it's sometimes called justification faith.

Faith is an act of God. It's not something a believer does. So increasing faith is to stop belittling God and his promises and no longer deny or doubt his faithfulness in accomplishing his children's desires. We must understand that these desires are accomplished only by faith and that God gives to those who ask.

Next, read and study what makes the heroes of faith become heroes (Hebrews 13:1). Also read the testimonial faith of church reformers, such as Martin Luther, Charles Finney, John Wesley, Billy Graham, and a host of others.

Also read and study the scriptures that pertain to biblical miracles.

> *He is the one you praise; he is your God, who performed for you those great and awesome wonders you saw with your own eyes.* (Deuteronomy 10:21, NIV)

> *He said, "If you listen carefully to the Lord your God and do what is right in his eyes, if you pay attention to his commands and keep all his decrees, I will not bring on you any of the diseases I brought on the Egyptians, for I am the Lord, who heals you."* (Exodus 15:26, NIV)

> *When Jesus saw that a crowd was running to the scene, he rebuked the impure spirit. "You deaf and mute spirit," he said, "I command you, come out of him and never enter him again."*
>
> *The spirit shrieked, convulsed him violently and came out. The boy looked so much like a corpse that many said, "He's dead."* (Mark 9:25–26, NIV)

Pray, call the disease and sickness by its name, and acknowledge that Christ's name is above every name.

> *By faith in the name of Jesus, this man whom you see and know was made strong. It is Jesus' name and the faith that comes through him that has completely healed him, as you can all see.* (Acts 3:16, NIV)

Then read and study scriptures on the subject of self-daily renewal (Romans 12: 1–2). God keeps stays in contact and maintains a consistent relationship with the presbytery because of self-daily renewal—in other words, the presbytery's ability to say to the Lord, "You have searched me, Lord, and you know me.... Search me, God, and know my heart; test me and know my anxious thoughts" (Psalm 139:1, 23, NIV).

Read and study the depth of the Father-child relationship when crying to God in times of affliction (Matthew 7:11). Be familiar with the promises of God about times of afflictions (Psalm 33:12). Know that God sees his children in every generation as his possession. The church is a chosen people to serve as God's inheritance.

The scripture that stands out most about God's promise in afflicting time is Psalm 34:17–20:

> *The righteous cry out, and the Lord hears them; he delivers them from all their troubles. The Lord is close to the brokenhearted and saves those who are crushed in spirit. The righteous person may have many troubles, but the Lord delivers him from them all; he protects all his bones, not one of them will be broken.* (NIV)

What moves God to action is the proper standing of his child who comes to him with a heartbreaking need. Having a righteous character makes a considerable difference when it comes to the presbytery crisis prayer. The forgiveness of sin, healing, and restoration will occur when honest prayer prevails.

Address any sin of commission and omission to avoid Satan's criticisms. One of the primary results of Satan's anger towards God is his efforts to make life miserable for the children of God. He looks for believers' shortcomings and accuses them before God. He does this to destroy God's elect and to continue to showcase his hatred of anything godly. He brings charges to the church nonstop (Romans 8:33). He is a schemer as well (2 Corinthians 2:11). But we should not fear, because the Lord rebukes him continually on behalf of the church (Zechariah 3:1–2).

Constantly remind yourself that the power and authority of Jesus Christ has been transferred to you (Ephesians 3:22–23). The Bible teaches that not all issues of human health can be addressed with traditional medicine, scientific medicine, mental health provision, and religiosity/spirituality healing methods. We are to carry everything to God in prayer, turning to the divine plan for dealing with human suffering.

In our experiential knowledge, we know that scientific medicine deals with the physiobiological component of man, whereas mental healthcare deals with the psychological component.

Interestingly, only the PCPM can deal with all issues of ill health. Presbytery crisis prayer has the quantitative and qualitative capabilities needed to effect healing in the physiological, psychological, and spiritual arenas. There is nothing too high, too low, too wide, too long, or too complicated for the Lord to understand and treat with great success (Isaiah 59:1, 21; Psalm 139).

Be driven sensitively by the Holy Spirit to deliver the presbytery crisis prayer. The Holy Spirit knows the mind of God and the struggles of man. Remember that the Holy Spirit is the Spirit of prayer; he is always ready to lead believers in the right direction, to the right situation, and stand with God in their time of need (Luke 4:1).

## V. THE PRESBYTERY SERVES AS A DUPLICATE OF CHRIST'S INSTITUTIONAL MINISTRY

As imitators of Christ's spiritual dynasty, the church's central task on earth is to continue the mission of its Master. The presbytery is to continue where others have stopped. Believers in Christ in every generation have an equal ministry of justification by faith through grace (Ephesians 2:7–10). All believers have the same imputed righteousness, justification, and forgiveness of Christ to function in the power and authority of his righteousness (Romans 3:26, 4:25, 5:1–19).

Ever since Acts 2, all true believers have had the indwelling presence of the Holy Spirit and enjoy all the benefits of his power, authority, and ministry gifts. The single purpose of his existence is to enable the church to continue the spiritual heritage of Jesus Christ in all its functions.

The eternal goal of the church is to honor Christ, so the mantle of passing on the ministry is biblical and theological. For example, consider the lineages from Moses to Joshua, Elijah to Elisha, Jesus to his disciples, Paul to Timothy, etc. Everyone is saved to pick up the mantle, head our into the world, and carry out the Master's work (Luke 9:60).

## VI. PROCEDURAL TIPS FOR PRESBYTERY CRISIS PRAYER

### REBUKE THE STRESSOR OF THE SICKNESS

We have established that God does not cause disease and sickness, nor does he tolerate their domination. He may allow them to occur, but he can rebuke and exterminate them when the righteous pray in the power and authority of the name of Jesus Christ of Nazareth.

One upside to life's predicaments is that God knows the cause of every one—and he also knows the cure. He is omniscient and the origin of all knowledge. He controls all understanding and the embodiment of all knowledge.

Neither Job, his wife, nor his friends knew the source of Job's calamities, but God knew. Satan negotiated the perimeter of Job's sickness and God set the boundaries of his afflictions.

In the same way, all disorders have proscribed limitations in our lives. God does not allow disease and infection to cross the boundaries of what his children can handle.

Presbytery crisis prayer needs to start with the rebuke of the stressor of the sickness—in other words, Satan. In a sense, Satan is the ruler of the world's physical and spiritual darkness. His highest goal is stealing, killing, and destroying anything godly (John 10:10). Satan can complete this mission in the world today, and the ultimate result of this mission is human death.

But Christ came to the world to accomplish just the direct opposite: to destroy the mission of Satan (1 John 3:3). Christ's mission is to give life in abundance, physical and spiritual.

Luke revealed the mission of the Lord Jesus Christ to the world, stressing the proclamation of the good news to the poor, freedom for the prisoners, recovery of sight for the blind, and setting the oppressed free. This good news is a double-edged sword that focuses on meeting humanity's spiritual and physical needs (Luke 4:18–19).

For this reason, Satan challenges God's supremacy. Throughout the pages of Scripture, Satan causes calamities to challenge God's sovereign rule. Even the patriarch of our faith was not left unscorched; the prince of the darkness challenged him.

God has raised all the prophets in order to prove his worthiness in the face of the devil's destructive acts. Miracles performed in the Old Testament defend God's sovereignty against his adversary and ours. And in the end God always rises, declaring his limitless power to deal with any crisis triggered by the works of the evil one. God demonstrated sovereignty in the case of Moses and the magicians of Egypt, as well as with Elijah and the prophet of Baal. We also see this with Elisha and Naaman, Moses and the brazen serpent in the wilderness, the Hebrew boys and the King of Babylon, and even with Jonah in the belly of the fish.

When Jesus went to the fig tree to pick up its fruits for dinner and found none, he was dissatisfied, rebuked it by name, and instantaneously cursed it!

After Christ's ascension, every act of miracles has been accomplished using the name of Christ Jesus—specifically, Jesus Christ of Nazareth (Acts 3:6). I must conclude here that the miracles in Scripture were carried out with the missionary purpose of declaring that Yeshua is God.

ADDRESS THE SICKNESS BY ITS NAME

There is something important about names. They have roots, characteristics, and values. Almost all treatments—whether they be traditional, natural, or scientific—are best received when the practitioner knows the name of the sickness and the correct medicine to match it.

## THE PRESBYTERY CRISIS MINISTRY

The diagnostic approach is the heart of scientific medicine. Modern practitioners engage in dialogue through questioning, diagnosing, analyzing, observing, and testing. Knowing the name of the sickness reveals its cause, severity, and treatment. They ask the how, where, when, and what. They also try to discover out how the sick person feels, where the sickness might have started, when the pain first arose, its location, and also what the patient has consumed by way of food and drink.

Every human approach to healing, and maintaining health, mirrors God's approach to finding and knowing our affliction. When Adam became sick with the sin of disobedience, he told God, *"I heard you in the garden, and I was afraid because I was naked; so I hid"* (Genesis 3:10, NIV). God quickly turned to the process of diagnosing their illness.

Scripture records the beauty of God's diagnosing procedure:

> *And they heard the sound of the Lord God walking in the garden in the cool of the day, and the man and his wife hid themselves from the presence of the Lord God among the trees of the garden. But the Lord God called to the man and said to him, "Where are you?" And he said, "I heard the sound of you in the garden, and I was afraid, because I was naked, and I hid myself." He said, "Who told you that you were naked? Have you eaten of the tree of which I commanded you not to eat?"* (Genesis 3:8–11, ESV)

God wanted to research what had caused their nakedness. It's not as if God didn't know what had happened; he chose to use the human process of diagnosis to identify their disease. Having learned the nature of the sickness, God prescribed the healing remedy in Genesis 3:15.

So knowing the name of the sickness is essential to being able to provide the appropriate treatment. We know that conventional wisdom supports this.

One of the advantages of the presbytery can be seen in John 16:23–24:

> *In that day you will no longer ask me anything. Very truly I tell you, my Father will give you whatever you ask in my name. Until now you have not asked for anything in my name. Ask and you will receive, and your joy will be complete.* (NIV)

At all times, God is graciously willing to take away our sorrows and make our joy complete.

## THE AUTHORITY AND POWER OF JESUS CANNOT BE CHALLENGED
Both the presbytery and a crisis member must operate in the authority and power of the faith of Jesus Christ. Satan cannot contest the enormous victory of Christ's presence or divine sovereignty to act at will. Christ is the only one who can bind and loose God's heavenly and earthly activities among men. This is the believer's platform for success.

## GOD'S PROMISES CONCERNING A CRISIS
The whole of Christian faith operates on the promises of God in Scripture. One of the most decisive, courageous, and foundational verses is Acts 17:25, 28: *"Rather, he himself gives everyone life and breath and everything else… For in him we live and move and have our being…"* (NIV) In other words, the life we have, the breath we breathe, and anything else concerning our lives are specified by God, who calls us his offspring.

The presbytery needs to understand that God is able to transform every ugly human situation. Since God is not a liar (Number 23:29, Romans 3:4) and is faithful to keep his covenants to a thousand generations (Deuteronomy 7:9), he has not changed. It is biblical to let God know about the wonders he has done on behalf of his children.

King David writes,

> *In that day you will no longer ask me anything. Very truly I tell you, my Father will give you whatever you ask in my name. Until now you have not asked for anything in my name. Ask and you will receive, and your joy will be complete.* (Psalm 40:5, NLT)

Habakkuk declares, *"Lord, I have heard of your fame; I stand in awe of your deeds, Lord. Repeat them in our day, in our time make them known; in wrath remember mercy"* (Habakkuk 3:2, NIV).

The presbytery should be familiar with the promises of God on particular issues relating to a crisis member's needs.

## DEMAND THE CRISIS BE RELINQUISHED IN THE NAME OF CHRIST
The demand for the power of sickness to be relinquished is possible by the authority and power of Jesus Christ.

The centurion's servant was healed instantaneously because of his faith in the authority and power of Jesus over sickness (Luke 7:3–9). We read in Luke 9:1–2 how Christ gave his disciples the same authority and capacity to demand that the power of illness be relinquished (Matthew 10:8).

Satan recognizes the authority and power of Jesus Christ when the church declares them over afflictions. The presbytery crisis prayer of faith, spoken in the authority and power of Jesus, is the only tool in the toolbox of healing that is capable of dismantling the dominance of sickness. Scientific medicine is making tremendous advancements and discoveries, but prayers must not be replaced by scientific medicine. Likewise, we must not seek to replace our faith in God. Jesus says that if we have faith in God, we can move mountains (Mark 11:22–23).

## VII. WHAT CONSTITUTES PRESBYTERY ANSWERED PRAYER

The Bible declares God's willingness to answer the prayers of those children who are in right standing in him. The following qualities means that a person is in right standing with God.

### A TRANSFORMED HEART

A transformational heart is a born-again heart (John 3:3). It is a righteous heart covered with the imputed righteousness of Jesus Christ.

We have noted elsewhere in this book that God responds to humanity through his common grace. A transformational heart enjoys God's acts of special grace. Special grace can only be used effectively through the righteousness of Christ. No prayer is effective to God unless it comes through the righteousness of Christ.

The Bible says that no one is good enough to stand before God based on his or her righteous actions (Romans 3:23, 4:22–25, 6:23, 2 Corinthians 5:21). Therefore, effectual prayer produces a result. The presbytery must envelop itself in the righteousness of Christ.

### A RIGHTEOUS LIFESTYLE

The psalmist writes, *"If I had cherished sin in my heart, the Lord would not have listened"* (Psalm 66:18, NIV). Upon checking several Bible commentaries and studies on this verse, I made some significant observations. Among them are some truths that the presbytery ought to know if they are to deliver prayers that have a positive outcome.

Commentator Joseph Benson states,

> God's hearing and granting my petitions hath brought along with it a testimony of my sincerity in serving him, far more valuable than my kingdom; for, if I had been guilty of known iniquity, or had entertained in my heart a desire or intention to commit it, the Lord, who hates iniquity, would have denied my request.[249]

---

249. Joseph Benson, "Benson's Commentary of the Old and New Testaments, Psalm 66:18," *Study Light*. Date of access: May 4, 2023 (https://studylight.org/commentaries/eng/rbc/psalms-66.html).

Another commentator, Albert Barnes, writes,

> **If I regard iniquity in my heart**—literally, "If I have seen iniquity in my heart." That is, If I have indulged in a purpose of iniquity; if I have had a wicked end in view; if I have not been willing to forsake all sin; if I have cherished a purpose of pollution or wrong. The meaning is not literally, If I have "seen" any iniquity in my heart—for no one can look into his own heart, and not see that it is defiled by sin; but, If I have cherished it in my soul; if I have gloated over past sins; if I am purposing to commit sin again; if I am not willing to abandon all sin, and to be holy.
>
> **The Lord will not hear me**—That is, He will not regard and answer my prayer. The idea is, that in order that prayer may be heard, there must be a purpose to forsake all forms of sin. This is a great and most important principle in regard to prayer.[250]

A righteous lifestyle is achieved by completely obeying what God's word says about you and your situation. Nothing can stand in the way of the Lord and his child if he is completely obedient to the spirit of practicing the word, and not just the spirit of hearing of it. A righteous lifestyle is attainable when there is no barrier between God and his child.

AN EFFECTUAL, FERVENT PRAYER
Prayer attracts God's attention when it is effectual and fervent. A fervent prayer has the power to produce the required effect. At the same time, efficacy is the active power that produces the intended result.

If a powerful prayer must produce the intended result, an effectual and fervent prayer must be free of self-righteousness. In other words, all effectual and fervent prayers must pass through the righteousness of Christ in order for the kingdom's result to be released. No matter the passionate intensity of a prayer, it has no relevance in the presence of God except through the righteousness of his resurrected Son.

AN UNCONTAMINATED BROTHERLY RELATIONSHIP
James knew that a toxic brotherly relationship stood as a mountain in the way of accessing the presence of God. Therefore, he instructed the presbytery to confess their sin to one another.

---

250. Albert Barnes, "Barnes' Notes on the Whole Bible, Psalm 66:18," *Study Light*. Date of access: May 4, 2023 (https://www.studylight.org/commentaries/eng/bnb/psalms-66.html).

Confession and the forgiveness of wrongs dispels this mountain of human unrighteousness and blocks Satan's ability to accuse us before God. This confession removes any hindrance to our effectual, fervent, results-producing prayer.

## THE RIGHT MOTIVE FOR APPROACHING PRAYER

The Bible teaches that whatever God does is purposed for his glory, honor, and worship. Therefore, the motive behind our prayer matters a great deal in the presence of God.

The Bible also tells us that he knows our motive. Everything a child of God does, even in simple matters like eating, drinking, tidying a home, is to be done for God's glory (1 Corinthians 10:31).

God seeks glory for himself (John 8:50). Creation exists to honor God. All righteous actions emanate from him and through him and for him forever (Romans 11:36).

It is encouraging to know that God allows some suffering and affliction to glorify himself, even the death of Christ (Exodus 9:8–9, Isaiah 48:10, John 9:3, 11:4, 21:19). Jude expresses this truth:

> *Now to him who is able to keep you from falling and to present you without blemish before the presence of his glory with rejoicing, to the only God, our Savior through Jesus Christ our Lord, be glory, majesty, dominion, and authority, before all time and now and for ever. Amen* (Jude 1:24–25, RSV)

CHAPTER TWELVE
# Background of the Presbytery Crisis Prayer Ministry

*Neglect not the gift that is in thee, which was given thee by prophecy, with the laying on of the hands of the presbytery.* (1 Timothy 4:14, KJV)

*Now to him who is able to do immeasurably more than all we ask or imagine, according to his power that is at work within us, to him be glory in the church and in Christ Jesus throughout all generations, for ever and ever! Amen.* (Ephesians 3:20–21, NIV)

## I. THE AUTHENTICITY OF PRESBYTERY PRAYER MINISTRY

GENERALLY, WRITTEN INFORMATION is believed to be authentic only when the source of information is genuine and trustworthy. The Bible establishes the authenticity of presbytery prayer ministry, declaring that a sick member of the body of Christ should call the presbytery for crisis prayer.

Seth Dalby has researched the definitions and sources of authenticity and authentication. He asserts that if a piece of information is to be authentic, its original must be proven. So to be authentic is to be authoritative, reliable, trustworthy, honest, pure, accurate, or genuine, having the quality of what a thing is purported to be.[251]

No assertion could be more trustworthy than the Scriptural record. The Bible is authentic because its narrative source is the Holy Spirit himself using real human authors. Paul records, *"All Scripture is God-breathed and is useful for teaching, rebuking, correcting and training in righteousness, so that the servant of God may be thoroughly equipped for every good work"* (2 Timothy 3:16–17, NIV).

No one is more qualified and has the charisma to write about the practical Christian life than James. No one has more reliable information and experiential knowledge.

God has mandated that believers call the presbytery for interventional crisis prayer (James 5:14), and James passed along this vital message to the church. James didn't only pass on theoretical knowledge; he also shared his experience about the ministry of Jesus Christ. He both wrote what he knew to be accurate and added what he had experienced firsthand. He had been a leader in the church of Christ in Jerusalem and received inspiration from the Holy Spirit, the Revealer of all true things (John 16:13). James was the best eyewitness of Christ's earthly life and ministries.

---

251. Seth Dalby, "Authenticity/Authentication: Definition and Sources." *International Research on Permanent Authentic Records in Electronic Systems*, December 2004, 3, 5.

## THE PRESBYTERY CRISIS MINISTRY

I consider his ministry to have been authentic because he wrote more about his practical and personal relationship with Christ than all other eyewitnesses recorded in Scripture. James *knew* about Jesus Christ as God, the one who became flesh and dwelled among humans (John 1:14, 18, Philippians 2:5–6). He *knew* that God the Father had sent God the Son of God as the propitiator for sinners (John 3:16–18, 1 John 4:10) and that Christ had come into the world to save mankind from the bondage of sin (John 4:42, 12:17, 1 John 4:14). He *knew* Jesus, the most outstanding miracle worker, the most famous Being who ever lived.

> *Isn't this the carpenter's son? Isn't his mother's name Mary, and aren't his brothers James, Joseph, Simon and Judas?* (Matthew 13:55, NIV)

If any biblical account must be taken seriously by the PCPM, it should be James's testimony. His eyewitness accounts followed Jesus from the beginning, during his coming and going, and up to his resurrection and ascension (John 1:1, Luke 1:3).

John's eyewitness is also astonishing:

> *What existed from the beginning, what we have heard, what we have seen with our eyes, what we observed and touched with our own hands—this is the Word of life! This life was revealed to us, and we have seen it and testify about it. We declare to you this eternal life that was with the Father and was revealed to us. What we have seen and heard we declare to you so that you, too, can have fellowship with us. Now this fellowship of ours is with the Father and with his Son, Jesus, the Messiah.* (1 John 1:1–3, ISV)

The apostle Paul probably didn't have the same credentials as James regarding his knowledge of Christ. However, his genuine encounter with Christ while on his way to Damascus, and the revelation he received through the Holy Spirit, qualified him. Even though Paul heard Christ when he was called into the ministry of the kingdom, he did not get to see, observe, and touch Jesus at the same level of intimacy as the disciples.

James, on the other hand, knew the Lord Jesus Christ from the beginning of his ministry, including his childhood life. Having been at the forefront among the presbytery, and having served as a leading figure in the judicial council in the early Christian community in Jerusalem, James watched his preaching, teaching, and healing ministries. He had the perfect authority to recommend certain functions on fervent healing prayer from the presbytery. He was the senior pastor in the congregational setting and knew the relationship between a righteous prayer and the healing of a crisis member.

## II. IDENTITY OF JAMES

Who was James? There are records of four men in the New Testament with this name. Some biblical scholars believe that only three individuals were called James.[252] In comparison, others maintain that only two individuals bear the name James.

The reader should know that the focus here is not to evaluate the credentials behind each claim. Instead the goal is to find every detail relevant to a discussion on the writer of James's epistle.

Here are the identities of five people called James in the Bible.

**James, son of Zebedee.** This man was called James the apostle, the brother of the apostle John, and one of the sons of Boanerges (Thunder). He was also known as James the Greater, one of the twelve disciples of Christ (Mark 3:17).

**James, the son of Alphaeus or Clopas.** Author William Steuart McBirnie[253] has written that this James is one of the twelve disciples, an apostle and known as James the Younger. He was a brother of the apostle Matthew and a son of Mary, although there is no specification as to which Mary. He was a native of Capernaum and probably came from the Jewish tribe of Levi.

**James, whose mother is another Mary.** The identity of this "other Mary" appears elsewhere in the gospels and Acts. She seems to be an auntie to the Lord Jesus Christ, and her son James is likely to have been a cousin to the Lord (John 19:25).

**James, father of the apostle Judas.** There seems to be no recorded activity about this James, only that he was the father of Judas.

**James, the brother of Jesus and bishop/pastor of Jerusalem church.** In James 1:1, we read that the writer is called James. He describes himself as *"a servant of God and of the Lord Jesus Christ"* (NIV). During the earthly ministry of Christ, James was an unbelieving Jew, but after Christ rose from the dead James became one of his followers (Acts 1:14 1 Corinthians 15:7). The "unbelieving" assertion here is debated; it could be that he disbelieved the concept of the Messiah in Judaism, or it could be that he disbelieved Jesus Christ being the Messiah.

Despite his non-spiritual connection to Christ's earthly ministries, this James saw Christ in his glorious nature. He did not see him as just a physical brother but also a Savior with a godly appearance. No wonder he described himself as a brother and servant of Christ.

---

252. Michael Hunt, "The Men Named James in the New Testament," *Agape Bible Study.* Date of access: April 2, 2021 (https://www.agapebiblestudy.com/charts/The%20James%20of%20the%20New%20Testament.htm).

253. William Steuart McBirnie, *The Search for the Twelve Apostles* (New York, NY: Penguin, 1973).

He was probably the eldest among several brothers of our Lord Jesus Christ (Matthew 13:55).

The leaders of the early church described James as a unique and highly respected individual. The Bible reports that some feared coming near him because he was very pious, a pillar of the church in Jerusalem, and a prayer warrior (Galatians 2:9).

Tadros Malaty writes that he was called James the righteous because he loved to worship. From his tendency to frequently kneel in prayer, his knees were apparently like the knees of a camel. It is also said that St. Jerome mentioned in his writings that the Jews greatly feared him and hastened to touch his clothes. At one time, they brought him to the top of the temple to witness against Christ, and he told them, "Christ now is sitting in the highest at the right hand of the Father, and He will judge the people." When they heard him, some screamed, "Hosannas to the Son of David."[254]

As a younger brother of the Lord, in the flesh, I suppose it would not be out a step to say that James probably knew everything related to his miraculous birth. Their mom, Mary, might have told her sons about her mysterious and divine experience.

Perhaps Jesus and James were involved in helping their father, Joseph, in the carpentry workshop. Jesus not only helped in the carpentry workshop but was called "the carpenter."

> *Isn't this the carpenter? Isn't this Mary's son and the brother of James, Joseph, Judas and Simon? Aren't his sisters here with us? (Mark 6:3, NIV)*

> *Isn't this the carpenter's son? Isn't his mother's name Mary, and aren't his brothers James, Joseph, Simon and Judas? (Matthew 13:55, NIV)*

It might not be an exaggeration to believe that James saw and experienced the human development of Christ. One can imagine them eating, playing together, and going to the synagogue as a family. They might have been involved in kitchen table conversations, slept, and accomplished homework together.

James might have noticed the absence of those sinful human childhood tendencies in their daily relationships. The tendencies to cheat, abuse, steal, lie, bully, and disobey were just not present in the life of Christ. James might therefore have seen in him the exceptional qualities of a super spiritual Being, including distinguished moral behaviors and his obedience to the heavenly Father.

---

254. Malaty, *The Epistle of St. James: A Patristic Commentary*, 5.

Luke's record of Christ wisdom affirms his human exceptionalism. He grew with exceptional knowledge, increasing grace, significant strength, and was abundantly favored (Luke 2:40, 52). He knew that godly wisdom could only be obtained from above (James 3:13). He saw his patience when familiar people mocked him, spit at him, slapped him, and ripped his clothes. No wonder James wrote,

> Let perseverance finish its work so that you may be mature and complete, not lacking anything. If any of you lacks wisdom, you should ask God, who gives generously to all without finding fault, and it will be given to you. (James 1:4–5, NIV)

As a younger sibling to Christ, James might have had questions about his unique lifestyle without being bold enough to ask them. He would have known by the age of twelve that Jesus could no longer hide his divine heritage, wisdom, and quest to fulfill his heavenly Father's mission That's the age when Jesus stayed behind in the temple to declare his divine Sonship and inform the religious intellectuals that he was fulfilling the prophecy of Prophet Micah (Micah 5:2, Matthew. 2:1–2).

James not only experienced the childhood of Christ; he might have listened, watched, acknowledged his miraculous works and divine knowledge. James knew that his brother had turned water into wine, cast out demonic spirits, fed the crowds, healed the sick, raised the dead, defeated the grave, and triumphantly ascended into heaven with a promise to return. James was very familiar with the teachings of Christ and used much of this education in his epistle. For example, his teachings on testing, suffering, wisdom, faith, and wealth are in James 1:12–27. He used quotations from the sermon on the mount as well, teaching on trials, righteousness, and encouragement.

It seems evident that James was familiar with Christ's promises about what his name could accomplish for the church in his absence. He knew that Christ was highly exalted over, above, beneath, and beyond every other character on earth and in heaven. He believed that every knee should bow and every tongue confesses his Lordship so that God the Father would be glorified (Philippians.2:9–11). He knew that whatever a righteous believer asks of the Father according to his will in the name of Jesus Christ would be done (John 14:13–14, Matthew 21:2, 1 John 5:14).

Tadros Malaty also affirms that James was a Nazarite of the Lord and didn't drink any wine or intoxicating drink. He never shaved his head. In his epistle, he later urged the presbytery to pray over the sick, anointing the afflicted with oil in the name of the Lord Jesus Christ (James 5:14).[255]

---

255. Ibid., 6.

It was easy for James to make such powerful assertions that the sick should call on the presbytery to offer prayers of intervention.

> *Now this is the confidence that we have in Him, that if we ask anything according to His will, He hears us. And if we know that He hears us, whatever we ask, we know that we have the petitions that we have asked of Him.* (1 John 5:14–15, NKJV)

James believed that John spoke these words in the Holy Spirit. Hence, it was the will of God for him to make his command about the PCPM. It was the will of God for the presbytery to offer such intercessory prayers for crisis members of the church.

## III. THE EPISTLE OF JAMES

The epistle of James is an essential letter that the church needs today. It is more ethical instruction than theological discourse. Since the Lord Jesus Christ's ascension and the promise of his return to rapture the church unto the Father's house (John 14:1–3), the church has increasingly faced hardship and persecution. Both Jesus Christ and the apostle Paul foretold that the life of the church wouldn't get better until he returned.

James didn't want to dwell on issues of salvation because the recipients of his letter were already believers. Instead he revealed that God chose his children to be holy, tender-hearted, merciful, kind, humble, gentle, and patient (Colossians 3:12). Peter declared that believers are *"a chosen people, a royal priesthood, a holy nation, God's special possession… called out of darkness into his wonderful light"* (1 Peter 2:9, NIV). The protestant reformer Martin Luther described the epistle of James as "a right strawy epistle."[256]

James's epistle deals with three main subjects: faith and works, the function of speaking in tongues, and role of presbytery prayer in the Christian journey. Instead of focusing on evangelistic messages, its message settles on issues of faith, life, hope, and the truth about Christian living. He believes that presbytery prayer is a crucial instrument in challenging times. Prayer is a solid divine instrument given to the Lord to connect a believer's faith with the faith of Jesus Christ in difficult moments.

## IV. RECIPIENTS OF THE EPISTLE

Most biblical scholars maintain that the recipients of the epistle of James were probably the believers. However, the twelve tribes of Israel were in dispersion at the time (James 1:1). The text does not suggest that James was writing to the scattered children of Israel.

---

256. Ibid., 9.

Instead James seems to have been addressing the plight of Christian Jews. The use of *"my brothers and sisters"* (James 1:2) and *"believers"* (James 1:9) clearly indicate this—that he was writing to Jews who had placed their faith in the finished work of Christ's salvation.

Whenever an apostle used the term "brethren," this was the group of people it referred to (1 Peter 1:22, 1 John 2:7). Therefore, James was addressing followers of Christ in the household of Israel (James 1:1), as well as followers of Christ in all generations.

James wants his recipients to distinguish between working faith and saving faith, understanding their differences, so that they can live practically live out the Christian lifestyle in our complex world. He wants the church to understand the power of transformational faith—the faith of regeneration, obedience to Christ, the working of miracles, and so forth. He rebukes the church against simple professions of faith that aren't accompanied with heart change or obedience to Christ.

James believed that a believer with righteous working faith would transform a crisis into the glory of God. He didn't want a faith that only had a form of godliness but denied its power (2 Timothy 3:5).

In discussing the faith of so-called easy belief, the reverend Billy Graham said,

> There is a mindset today that if people believe in God and do good works, they are going to Heaven. But there are many questions that must be answered. It should not be surprising if people believe easily in a God who makes no demands, but this is not the God of the Bible.[257]

God has given the church the power of believing faith and the authority of the working faith to do more significant works in undoing the works of Satan.

## V. THE MESSAGE ABOUT PRACTICAL CHRISTIAN LIVING

The PCPM is a fantastic revelation on the message of prayer. The local elders have the authority and power to pray for healing in Jesus's name. It appears that the presbytery is to operate as the under-physician of Christ, who is the great Physician.

Therefore, it is time for faith to be read, talked about, and practically exhibited. In the twentieth-first century, the power and authority of the Trinity has diminished and become less abundant and effective. Nevertheless, Jesus is willing to act supernaturally

---

257. Billy Graham, "What Does the Term 'Easy Believism' Really Mean?" *Billy Graham Evangelistic Association*. January 29, 2019 (https://billygraham.org/answer/what-does-the-term-easy-believism-really-mean).

in his church as he has done in the past. Believers who hold to the unchanging nature of God can and do experience overwhelming healing miracles. Believers with the spirit of doubting Thomas, however, have chosen to disbelieve the works of practical faith.

The Bible talks about faith that moves mountains, causes the blind to see, and enables the lame to walk. God never said that these works of miracles would stop happening. We have not been limited to just reading about the great results of faith in Scripture.

James urges the presbytery to understand this and take a significant step of faith, continuing the ministry of saving souls *and* healing the sick. The dead works mentioned by James don't just refer to the presbytery's failure in the areas of visitation, good gifts, and respecting and loving one another; the presbytery is also meant to free people from the bondage of affliction.

God talks of abundance, not an imitation of goodness. He is rich in mercy and love toward the total well-being of his children.

CHAPTER THIRTEEN
# Bible Characters on Crisis Prayer

Father helps us to move from being unruly children to the place where you don't need to discipline us so much. Helps us to be like your servant Hezekiah, who trusted in you and your promises with all his heart, and wasn't afraid to ask you for what he needed.[258] —Dr. R.F. Wilson

## I. CRISIS

DIFFERENT PEOPLE USE different words to describe a crisis. It could be understood as a helpless, hopeless, dangerous, or out of control situation in need of a swift intervention.

I believe that a crisis is understood from a range of different perspectives. It's an urgent, unresolvable impediment or turning point in a person's life. A crisis is usually seated on the bedrock of sin. Also, a crisis isn't always a bad experience, since it represents both danger and opportunity. It offer an opportunity for calmness and sober thought.[259]

The crisis threatens to overwhelm its victim and paralyzes them into confusion, helplessness, pain, dysfunction, and even death. Therefore, the presbytery must be ready at a moment's notice to offer intervention prayer.

The presbytery's prayerful role is key to the health of church members, who should be oriented toward understanding that the presbytery is there for them. A crisis member has the task of calling on the presbytery in times of crisis and inviting the elders to pray. They must have faith in the authority of the presbytery and the power of prayer in the name of Christ Jesus to prevail.

No wonder one of the most outstanding Christian leaders in recent years, Billy Graham, has said,

> Prayer is the most powerful weapon we have in our spiritual arsenal to stand against the world's greatest enemy, the one who presents himself as an angel of light… No matter how dark and hopeless a situation might seem, never stop praying.[260]

---

258. Ralph F. Wilson, "Hezekiah's Petitions for Deliverance and Healing," *JesusWalk*. Date of access: May 22, 2023 (https://www.jesuswalk.com/greatprayers/6_hezekiah_petition.htm).

259. Donna C. Aguilera, Janice M. Messick, and Marlene S. Farrell, *Crisis Intervention, Theory, and Methodology* (Maryland Heights, MO: Bosby, 1986).

260. "Prayer Quotes—Billy Graham," *Prayer Coach*. Date of access: May 6, 2023 (https://prayer-coach.com/prayer-quote-billy-graham/).

Prayer is the only antidote instituted by God to help believers destroy the thoughts, maneuvers, and displays of the evil one.

In this regard, the job of the presbytery is to oversee the holistic well-being of the saints. The apostle Paul said, *"Let each of you look not only to his own interests, but also to the interests of others"* (Philippians 2:4, ESV). From another perspective, we need to understand that no matter how chronic and traumatized a crisis member may be, actively and selflessly serving others in prayer can bring about God's perfect healing, producing the kind of peace that fills a victim's body, soul, and spirit.

Developed nations—like the United States, Canada, the United Kingdom, and Germany, to mention a few—place the welfare of humans above all things. For example, when a motorist hears an ambulance's siren on the highway, they pull over; the siren signals urgency and therefore danger. All other traffic gives way to allow the ambulance to pass. The ministry of the presbytery cannot be different.

Local church members can only contribute productively to their Christian journeys if their bodies, souls/minds, and spirits are healthy. An unhealthy condition leads to a weak soul, spiritual dwarfism, and even physical death.

Human crises are treated according to three approaches: naturistic, scientific, and spiritual. In this chapter, we will discuss each in turn.

## NATURISTIC PERSPECTIVE

When people think of a crisis, they think of negative and feelings, poor decision-making, and unpredictable circumstances.

In a crisis situation, we should ask a couple of different questions. Where does the crisis in the human heart come from? What makes human thinking harmful rather than purely positive?

It has been established in Chapters Three and Four that a crisis originates from mankind's breaking of divine rules. As a result, he loses the righteousness of God's divine image and likeness.

Dustin K. MacDonald describes three stages of crisis formation:

1. A negative event occurs which leading to a feeling of subjective distress
2. This distress leads to an impairment in functioning
3. Coping skills fail to improve functioning[261]

---

261. Dustin K. MacDonald, "Crisis Theory and Types of Crisis," *Dustin K MacDonald*. June 13, 2016 (www.dustinkmacdonald.com/crisis-theory-types-crisis).

According to my research, a crisis is built on mankind's loss of divine perfection. Troubled thoughts proceed from a hostile heart, and a hostile heart gives birth to negative feelings (Jeremiah 17:1). Using unreliable human wisdom, any attempt to deal with these troubled thoughts, hostile hearts, and negative feelings can make a crisis worse.

The Lord says,

> *Cursed is the one who trusts in man, who draws strength from mere flesh and whose heart turns away from the Lord. That person will be like a bush in the wastelands; they will not see prosperity when it comes. They will dwell in the parched places of the desert, in a salt land where no one lives...*
>
> *The heart is deceitful above all things and beyond cure. Who can understand it? "I the Lord search the heart and examine the mind, to reward each person according to their conduct, according to what their deeds deserve."*
>
> *...Heal me, Lord, and I will be healed; save me and I will be saved, for you are the one I praise.* (Jeremiah 17:5–6, 9–10, 14, NIV)

A man's negative thoughts, decisions, and feelings are the product of his deceitful heart. Therefore, a naturistic approach to prayer prevents the Lord far from responding to the request.

## SCIENTIFIC PERSPECTIVE

A crisis as an unhealthy human condition that challenges our human endeavors—and it comes in many forms.

Professionals view and understand crises within the framework of their profession. As a result, practitioners of modern medicine understand and approach crises differently than a practitioner of traditional medicine.

However, the primary goal of all practitioners is to redeem a situation, restore health, and save one's life.

Scientists such as physicians, psychologists, psychiatrists, and psychotherapists wrestle with the effect of the law of sin, which is weak and has subjected human physiology to affliction and death (Romans 8:1–6). Their perspective focuses on physiology.

**Physicians.** Physicians deal mainly with physiological disease and sickness and don't deal with human crises from a spiritual perspective.

Herm believes that the term crisis is used in many medical senses.[262] He describes a medical crisis as a decisive turning point in an illness. In medicine, the physiological symptoms of sickness are of primary concern. These symptoms are confirmed either physically or in the laboratory before a treatment is administered.

Physicians are helpless when it comes to dealing with an illness of the soul or spirit, for which there can be no laboratory diagnosis or analysis. A laboratory cannot test to learn about a person's sadness, unforgiveness, or hatred. Rather, physiological crises are handled physiologically.

However, a crisis member's faith, together with a presbytery that is anchored in the faith of Jesus Christ, can make all the difference.

**Psychologists/psychiatrists/psychotherapists.** Mental healthcare providers deal primarily with personal, relational, and family issues. These issues range from fear and worries to stress, anxiety, and depression. They focus on psychological disorders and cognitive problems. They also deal with many damaging behaviors.

Some of these crises can only be handled through spiritual therapy and the PCPM. Unfortunately, we know that there is no medication for behaviors like lying, stealing, and cheating.

In a crisis, a mental health professional will work quickly to identify symptoms diligently save and restore their patient. They use the scientific method to transform ill health into good health, dissatisfaction into satisfaction, and pain into a pain-free life. They do this because their profession demands it, not to mention their respect for the dignity and sanctity of human life.

SPIRITUAL PERSPECTIVE

The spiritual perspective references the biblical approach to dealing with mankind's crises. A crisis in the biblical view is described as bondage, or a situation that enslaves its victim.

Scripture records many testimonies of crisis prayer changing a terrible situation into one full of enrichment, vitality, and growth.

The presbytery has been granted God-given talents and access to the Holy Spirit, who helps us to pray by God's will. James understood the critical role played by church leaders. His goal was to testify of God's willingness to grant us both spiritual health and healthy bodies.

The apostle John emphasized our need for complete health—spirit, soul, and body: *"Beloved, I wish above all things that thou mayest prosper and be in health, even as thy*

---

262. Erlend Hem, "The Medical Crisis," *Tidsskrift for den Norske laegeforening 138(1)*, January 8, 2018.

*soul prospereth"* (3 John 2, KJV). But what does *"above all things"* mean? There are various interpretations.

Finis J. Dake sees John's prayer here as God's standard will work for all saints.[253]

Richard C. Lenski reveals that 3 John 1–15 refers to one's physical health. John was praying that Gaius, who was spiritually well-off, would have physical health to match his spiritual health. Therefore, spiritual health is the standard by which one's physical health is measured, not the other way around.[264]

According to Adam Clarke's biblical commentary, this prayer includes three priorities: health of the body, health of the soul, and prosperity in secular affairs:

> These three things so necessary to the comfort of life, every Christian may in a certain measure expect, and for them every Christian is authorized to pray; and we should have more of all three if we devoutly prayed for them.[265]

In this passage, John prays that the man named Gaius would prosper in all respects and continue in good health. The Lord was to keep Gaius prosperous, so that his physical health would match his spiritual health. John makes the well-being of the man's soul the governing concern.

## II. FIVE GREAT CRISIS PRAYERS IN THE BIBLE

There are many crisis prayers of intervention and intercession in the Bible. In the following pages, I will focus on five which serve as effective examples.

### MOSES'S CRISIS PRAYER

The following passage record the crisis prayer of Moses:

> *"I have seen these people,"* the Lord said to Moses, *"and they are a stiff-necked people. Now leave me alone so that my anger may burn against them and that I may destroy them. Then I will make you into a great nation."*

---

263. Finis J. Dake, *Dake Annotated Reference Bible* (Lawrence, GA: Dake Publishing, 1999).

264. Richard C. Lenski, *Commentary on the New Testament* (Peabody, MA: Hendrickson Publishers, 1998).

265. Adam Clarke, "Clarke's Notes on the Bible, 3 John 1:2," *Study Light*. Date of access: May 6, 2023 (https://www.studylight.org/bible/lat/nvl/3-john/1-2.html).

> But Moses sought the favor of the Lord his God. "Lord," he said, "why should your anger burn against your people, whom you brought out of Egypt with great power and a mighty hand? Why should the Egyptians say, 'It was with evil intent that he brought them out, to kill them in the mountains and to wipe them off the face of the earth'? Turn from your fierce anger; relent and do not bring disaster on your people. Remember your servants Abraham, Isaac and Israel, to whom you swore by your own self: 'I will make your descendants as numerous as the stars in the sky and I will give your descendants all this land I promised them, and it will be their inheritance forever.'" Then the Lord relented and did not bring on his people the disaster he had threatened. (Exodus 32:9–14, NIV)

> I lay prostrate before the Lord those forty days and forty nights because the Lord had said he would destroy you. I prayed to the Lord and said, "Sovereign Lord, do not destroy your people, your own inheritance that you redeemed by your great power and brought out of Egypt with a mighty hand. Remember your servants Abraham, Isaac and Jacob. Overlook the stubbornness of this people, their wickedness and their sin. (Deuteronomy 9:25–27, NIV)

Moses faced the anger of God against his people to the point that their punishment was to be complete destruction. God rebuked Moses, desiring to be left alone to lash out his wrath against the rebellious Israelites for being stiff-necked.

In this instance, God attempted to alter his promise to Abraham, Isaac, and Jacob. He had promised to make Abraham's descendants the stars of heaven and sand at the seashore. Moses therefore reminded him of that promise. The result is that God promised Moses a royal position to make him *"a great nation."*

When a righteous person prays, God moves to action. Moses swiftly flattened himself to the ground facedown and prayed.

It's interesting to read of this conversation between God and Moses. Moses was so confident of his place in God's heart that he transformed God's negative feelings about the Israelites into a positive outcome. He transformed anger and wrath into mercy and grace.

The intercessor needs to focus on God's promises, compassion, and grace to gain results from a crisis prayer:

> *Turn from your fierce anger; relent and do not bring disaster on your people. Remember your servants Abraham, Isaac and Israel, to whom you swore by your own self: "I will make your descendants as numerous as the stars in the sky and I will give your descendants all this land I promised them, and it will be their inheritance forever."* (Exodus 32:12–13, NIV)

What can we learn about how Moses approached his crisis prayer? To turn the crisis around, Moses made a number of appeals.

**He reminded God that he owned the Israelites as his people.** God's purpose for Israel was established in an everlasting covenant. He called Israel his people: *"This is what the Lord says: Israel is my firstborn son"* (Exodus 4:22, NIV). Israel was God's possession and a covenant people. So when Moses wept in the presence of God forty days and forty nights, God remembered his mercy, love, and purpose for humanity and forgave them instead of destroying them.

**He reminded God of his promise with Abraham.** The Bible teaches that God confirm his word when signs of it are done in his name (Mark 16:20). Because God's name is holy, he has chosen to sanctify and honor his word above his name. His word is his being—and he keeps the promises he has made in his word.

Moses knew precisely about the relationships between God's word and God himself. He knew God would be faithful in executing what he had said he would do. So Moses put that ownership statement before the very presence of God, pleading for God to understand that he had sworn his promise long ago to Abraham, Isaac, and Israel and remind him that their descendants were God's personal possession.

**He reminded God of his outstanding reputation among the heathens.** The heathens in Egypt knew about God's outstanding reputation, power, and mighty hand. In his prayer, Moses reminded God that if he destroyed the Israelites, then the heathens would have a reason to discredit the goodness, mercy, grace, and favor of the Lord toward his children.

It appears that the Lord changed his mind or repented of his wrath against the Israelites. The change here came about through a display of mercy, which means that the intercession of a righteous man of God causes the mercy of God to swell. The prayer of an honest man can have transformative power.

**He reminded God of his character of righteousness, love, and forgiveness.** We have established in this book that there is nothing evil in the character of God. He does not create a human and then opt to act wickedly to such a human. In the righteousness and love of God, he knows that humans are weak, fallible, and self-destructive. He knows humans endure crises and then need forgiveness.

## THE PRESBYTERY CRISIS MINISTRY

When we're in crisis, God wants us to report the ugly situation to him. Because God shows his children mercy and complete forgiveness (Colossians 3:12–14), he values the power of interventional prayer.

As a leader, Moses stood for the Israelites in prayer and obtained God's mercy, forgiveness, and healing.

The spiritual leaders in the local church are the presbytery, which has been called to minister to crisis members and bring about remedies to their situations. Just like Moses, God's representative before the Israelis, the presbytery is God's representative in a local church.

**He reminded God of the consistency of his love, mercy, and justice.** When dealing with sinful man, God operates according to three pillars of his character: his love, mercy, and justice.

He forgives sin, which he sees through his love-based magnifying glasses. Mercy shows the forbearance of God and reveals his generosity of God. In contrast, justice is the righteousness of God. His actions are always right and pure.

So when the presbytery prays for a crisis, God's response is not based on the absolute holiness of the presbytery or sinfulness of the crisis member; his answer is based on his love, mercy, and justice found in Christ. His righteousness makes him show mercy. His consistency of love, mercy, and justice is higher than any crisis we go through. He will fulfill his good and prosperous plan for our well-being.

JEHOSHAPHAT'S CRISIS PRAYER

Jehoshaphat's crisis prayer was for healing, restoration, and increase. God honored his cry, healing Jehoshaphat from his sickness, restoring his leadership role, and increasing his productive years of ministry.

Jehoshaphat prayed,

> O Lord, God of our fathers, are you not God in heaven? You rule over all the kingdoms of the nations. In your hand are power and might, so that none is able to withstand you. Did you not, our God, drive out the inhabitants of this land before your people Israel, and give it forever to the descendants of Abraham your friend? And they have lived in it and have built for you in it a sanctuary for your name, saying, "If disaster comes upon us, the sword, judgment, or pestilence, or famine, we will stand before this house and before you—for your name is in this house—and cry out to you in our affliction, and you will hear and save." And now behold, the men of Ammon and Moab and Mount Seir, whom you would not let Israel invade when they came from the

*land of Egypt, and whom they avoided and did not destroy—behold, they reward us by coming to drive us out of your possession, which you have given us to inherit. O our God, will you not execute judgment on them? For we are powerless against this great horde that is coming against us. We do not know what to do, but our eyes are on you.* (2 Chronicles 20:6–12, ESV)

There are three things the presbytery needs to learn from Jehoshaphat's crisis prayer of intervention.

**He approached the Lord in a relationship of personal ownership.** He used possessive words like "our" and saw God as his own God. He let God know that he was owned by him.

In seeking the face of God in a time of desperation, the presbytery must let God know that they belong to him and that he is their ruler.

We must recognize the sovereignty of God on the earth. He is omniscient, omnipotent, and sovereign, and there is no impossibility in him. The presbytery must adore his Lordship in worship. He loves our praises in worship, declaring his wonder-working power.

**Jehoshaphat acknowledged his dependence on God's.** In his prayer, Jehoshaphat prayed about his powerlessness, limited knowledge, and dependency on God.

God wants his church to declare its helplessness and turns its complete trust in his grace, mercy, and favor. When he sees our faith in action toward him, he comes to our rescue in times of crisis.

The presbytery must acknowledge its powerlessness, dependency, and limited knowledge of a problem. God will deliver health when he knows that he is the only one to whom a crisis member is looking for positive change in a time of affliction, because nothing is impossible with God (Luke 1:37).

**He asked the Lord to remember his faithfulness.** Jehoshaphat reminded the Lord of the records of his faithfulness to deliver victories in times of crisis.

One of the most significant assurances the presbytery has from God is his faithfulness to honor what he has promised to do. He takes delight when the church cries out for a repeat of his commitment to keeping his promises.

The effective prayer of the presbytery is powerful to heal the sick. It brings about the forgiveness of sin and increases the length of our lives in God's kingdom.

## HEZEKIAH'S CRISIS PRAYER

Let's read about the prayer spoken by Hezekiah.

> *In those days Hezekiah became ill and was at the point of death. The prophet Isaiah son of Amoz went to him and said, "This is what the Lord says: Put your house in order, because you are going to die; you will not recover."*
>
> *Hezekiah turned his face to the wall and prayed to the Lord, "Remember, Lord, how I have walked before you faithfully and with wholehearted devotion and have done what is good in your eyes." And Hezekiah wept bitterly.*
>
> *Before Isaiah had left the middle court, the word of the Lord came to him: "Go back and tell Hezekiah, the ruler of my people, 'This is what the Lord, the God of your father David, says: I have heard your prayer and seen your tears; I will heal you. On the third day from now you will go up to the temple of the Lord. I will add fifteen years to your life. And I will deliver you and this city from the hand of the king of Assyria. I will defend this city for my sake and for the sake of my servant David.'"*
>
> *Then Isaiah said, "Prepare a poultice of figs." They did so and applied it to the boil, and he recovered.*
>
> *Hezekiah had asked Isaiah, "What will be the sign that the Lord will heal me and that I will go up to the temple of the Lord on the third day from now?"*
>
> *Isaiah answered, "This is the Lord's sign to you that the Lord will do what he has promised: Shall the shadow go forward ten steps, or shall it go back ten steps?"*
>
> *"It is a simple matter for the shadow to go forward ten steps," said Hezekiah. "Rather, have it go back ten steps."*
>
> *Then the prophet Isaiah called on the Lord, and the Lord made the shadow go back the ten steps it had gone down on the stairway of Ahaz.* (2 Kings 20:1–11, NIV)

Hezekiah's crisis prayer brought about healing, restoration, and the re-establishment of God's glory on the face of the earth. It was the type of presbytery prayer that leads to the extension of life.

The presbytery must understand that God had not changed. He was still Jehovah Rapha, the miracle-working God in every generation. The presbytery was mandated to execute wrath against sickness in the name of the Lord.

There are several things to learn from Hezekiah's righteous crisis prayer.

**He understood that healing prayers are the Lord's battle prayers.** We have established that there is no evil in the nature and character of Yahweh. There is no dirt, sin, or stain in him. So sin and disease must have different sources.

Although 2 Kings 19:14–19 doesn't speak to healing or deliverance, it tells us the desire of God for the well-being of his children. Verses 14 and 16 reads:

> *And Hezekiah received the letter of the hand of the messengers, and read it: and Hezekiah went up into the house of the Lord, and spread it before the Lord. .*
>
> *Lord, bow down thine ear, and hear: open, Lord, thine eyes, and see: and hear the words of Sennacherib, which hath sent him to reproach the living God.* (2 Kings 19:14, 16, KJV)

Spiritual leaders should know that God controls every situation regarding our well-being.

Immediately Hezekiah understood that the letter was an insult to God's sovereignty, a test of his strength and a stain on his glory. God has always presented himself as the Helper in times of trouble and a Fighter for the saints (2 Chronicles 32:8). The Lord loves to win battles, whether it's a struggle against our health or any other victory we deserve.

Therefore, the general in the PCPM is not the presbytery but the Lord.

Let us review how Hezekiah removed himself from the battle.

- He entered the Lord's presence.
- He provided God with details about the battlefield.
- He asked God for his attentive presence.
- He asked for God's transparent attention.

God's children should actively engage in a good relationship with God. In an instance of crisis prayer, the presbytery's primary task is to head into the presence of God after a call has been made and acknowledge that the battle is not theirs but the Lord's. Although our God is omniscient, he wants concise and persistent details of his children's specific burdens.

**He understood that God was in control of all the affairs of men.** Hezekiah's prayer portrays very clearly that he understood the sovereignty of God, that the Lord is in control of every human struggle. He realized that God must be given glory in every situation (1 Thessalonians 5:8).

But he also told God to consider the devotion and faithfulness of his servant David, and the dynasty he established. As a result, God showed Hezekiah mercy, provided instant healing, and blessed him with fifteen more gracious years of life and ministry.

If the presbytery knows something of the devotion and faithful service of the crisis member, God should be reminded of that commitment. We need to tell God about his mission in an individual's life, emphasizing any special gift, ministry task, or essential function the afflicted person is part of achieving.

When believers talk to the Lord about his promises and the faithful service of members of the church, they declare their total dependence on God to rise to the occasion and provide the remedy.

**He understood that living righteously and doing good do not prevent a crisis.** In his prayer, Hezekiah had to remind God that he was living a right and good life, yet that didn't spare him from getting sick.

The presbytery should understand that not all sickness is the result of sin. He prayed, *"Remember, Lord, how I have walked before you faithfully and with wholehearted devotion and have done what is good in your eyes"* (2 Kings 20:3, NIV).

Hezekiah's life teaches the church that neither greatness nor goodness can exempt members from sickness. Hezekiah was favored from heaven above most men, yet he became fatally ill when he was still young. Perhaps he was especially apprehensive because his father had died at around that same age, or perhaps two or three years younger.

Nevertheless, God has ordered that we call on him in times of need, and he will hear us and answer following the abundance of his riches in glory.

**He understood that righteous prayer changes the unrighteous.** Hezekiah's prayer questions whether God changes his plans when considering the special needs of his people. In this story, it's clear that God was giving Hezekiah a death sentence through the prophet Isaiah: *"This is what the Lord says: Put your house in order, because you are going to die; you will not recover"* (2 Kings 20:1, NIV).

That proclamation was given in the perfect tense, showing God's decisiveness regarding the coming end of Hezekiah's earthly life. The final phrase—"you will not recover"—makes it sound like it was already final. The sickness was not curable. God seems to have signed Hezekiah's death sentence before even delivering the message.

Then, knowing the righteousness and mercy of God, Hezekiah engaged God in prayer to reverse the verdict.

> *"Remember, Lord, how I have walked before you faithfully and with wholehearted devotion and have done what is good in your eyes."*
> And Hezekiah wept bitterly… *"Go back and tell Hezekiah, the ruler of*

> my people, 'This is what the Lord, the God of your father David, says: I have heard your prayer and seen your tears; I will heal you. On the third day from now you will go up to the temple of the Lord.'" (2 Kings 20:3, 5, NIV)

Hezekiah's courage and spiritual understanding of God revealed something: he seemed to understand that he had not finished the ministry God had given him. He could not yet prepare for his death, and he saw into the heart of God that a righteous prayer changes an honest plan.

So what changed Hezekiah's death sentence? In righteous prayer, he told God to remember his faithfulness, promises, mercy, and relationship with God.

*Matthew Henry's Bible Commentary* (Concise) describes:

> Hezekiah's piety made his sick-bed easy. "O Lord, remember now;" he does not speak as if God needed to be put in mind of any thing by us; nor, as if the reward might be demanded as due; it is Christ's righteousness only that is the purchase of mercy and grace… God always hears the prayers of the broken in heart, and will give health, length of days, and temporal deliverances, as much and as long as is truly good for them .. This work of wonder shows the power of God in heaven as well as on earth, the great notice he takes of prayer, and the great favour he bears to his chosen.[266]

The way in which the crisis member and the presbytery walk before God, including their faithfulness in ministry, can influence God's healing response. His devotion should remind us that God considers what we do, how we do it, and the level of our dedication to him. It is not an act of price to remind God of the faithfulness of the crisis member (1 John 2:17).

**He understood that sickness has no power to end one's life.** The Lord told the prophet Isaiah to inform Hezekiah about his healing and restoration: *"I have heard your prayer and seen your tears; I will heal you"* (2 Kings 20:5, NIV). Hezekiah's prayer reveals an essential truth about illness and death. Being seriously ill does not guarantee that you will die. Only God has the power of life and death. We came into existence either by his permissive or perfect will, and we die only at the expense of his permissive or ideal plan.

---

266. Matthew Henry, "Matthew Henry's Bible Commentary, 2 Kings 20," *Christianity.com*. Date of access: May 7, 2023 (https://www.christianity.com/bible/commentary/matthew-henry-concise/2-kings/20).

This revelation should strengthen our obedience to James's call to the PCPM. Healing and restoration is not the presbytery's job; it is the Lord's. The task of the presbytery is to act when they receive a call. The presbytery must swiftly move to prayer with the understanding that no deadly sickness has the power to end a person's life. The faith of Jesus Christ can change a crisis from an unpleasant to a pleasant situation.

Every disease obeys the command of Jesus Christ. John Gill wrote,

> Christ was subject to none; and yet he had such power over his soldiers and servants, that if he bid one go, and another come, or ordered them to stand in such a place, and in such a posture, or do this and the other servile work, his orders were immediately obeyed: how much more easily then could Christ, who had all power in heaven and in earth, command off this distemper his servant was afflicted with? He suggests, that as his soldiers were under him, and at his command; so all bodily diseases were under Christ, and to be controlled by him, at his pleasure; and that, if he would but say to that servant of his, the palsy, remove, it would remove at once.[267]

Disease is compared here to a servant of Christ who must obey his command at once.

**He understood that his faithful servant had to accomplish God's assignment.** The Lord acknowledges that Hezekiah's prayer would be answered for his glory.

> *I will add fifteen years to your life. And I will deliver you and this city from the hand of the king of Assyria. I will defend this city for my sake and for the sake of my servant David.* (2 Kings 20:6, NIV)

God does not allow an afflicted person to die if an assignment needs to be done and his name will be glorified. Hezekiah's next fifteen years were years of accomplishment and glory. They were spent leading God's people to victory and out of the hands of the Assyrians.

---

267. John Gill, "John Gill's Exposition of the Bible, Matthew 8:9," *Bible Study Tools*. Date of access: May 7, 2023 (https://www.biblestudytools.com/commentaries/gills-exposition-of-the-bible/matthew-8-9.html).

## DANIEL'S CRISIS PRAYER

The crisis prayer of Daniel was confessional, piety, and gracious. It didn't just taker a theoretical approach; it was a practical call for the systematic involvement of God in dealing with the crisis.

> *Give ear, our God, and hear; open your eyes and see the desolation of the city that bears your Name. We do not make requests of you because we are righteous, but because of your great mercy. (Daniel 9:18, NIV)*

This verse serves as a centerpiece of Daniel's cry for action: the confession of sin, and for the prayer to be answered out of God's grace, not our own merit.

Here is the whole prayer of Daniel:

> *…we have sinned and done wrong. We have been wicked and have rebelled; we have turned away from your commands and laws. We have not listened to your servants the prophets, who spoke in your name to our kings, our princes and our ancestors, and to all the people of the land.*
>
> *Lord, you are righteous, but this day we are covered with shame—the people of Judah and the inhabitants of Jerusalem and all Israel, both near and far, in all the countries where you have scattered us because of our unfaithfulness to you. We and our kings, our princes and our ancestors are covered with shame, Lord, because we have sinned against you. The Lord our God is merciful and forgiving, even though we have rebelled against him; we have not obeyed the Lord our God or kept the laws he gave us through his servants the prophets. All Israel has transgressed your law and turned away, refusing to obey you.*
>
> *Therefore the curses and sworn judgments written in the Law of Moses, the servant of God, have been poured out on us, because we have sinned against you. You have fulfilled the words spoken against us and against our rulers by bringing on us great disaster. Under the whole heaven nothing has ever been done like what has been done to Jerusalem. Just as it is written in the Law of Moses, all this disaster has come on us, yet we have not sought the favor of the Lord our God by turning from our sins and giving attention to your truth. The Lord did not hesitate to bring the disaster on us, for*

*the Lord our God is righteous in everything he does; yet we have not obeyed him.* (Daniel 9:5–14, NIV)

**He acknowledged that no one is righteous enough to come before God on their own merits.** The phrase *"we have"* is mentioned eight times, which reflect the collective confession of sin from God's children. James asserts very strongly that confessing one's sins and those of other people is a defense against the accuser of the brethren, who tries to thwart the righteous prayer from prevailing before God.

Sometimes a member's crisis could be a result of sin. When this is known, collective and individual confession of disobedience may become necessary for breakthroughs to occur.

**He acknowledged the righteousness of God, which alone makes things happen.** The character of God makes him act rightly and perfectly in all human predicaments. Therefore, when the presbytery prays in the Holy Spirit, it prays in the will of God. And God, in his righteousness, will act positively on any prayer made within the perimeter of his choice.

**He acknowledges the mercy and forgiveness of God.** The mercy of God can overrun the justice of God. Yes, the soul that sins shall die. However, many sinful souls have not died because of the mercies of God Almighty.

Because God's mercy appears to be stronger than God's justice, Daniel could remind God of his merciful and forgiving character.

In the revelation of James, sin might be strong enough to hinder healing. It seems clear that the prayer of the righteous presbytery is powerful enough to move God into recovery and forgiving iniquity.

## PAUL'S CRISIS PRAYER

The apostle Paul's crisis prayers are characteristic of many human experiences. Paul played the role of a present-day minister—theologically called, trained, and assigned as pastors to a local church. In contrast, the appointed elders in these churches are the presbytery.

Paul's prayers dwell on the stability of new believers' faith and the importance of fostering a deeper relationship with the Lord Jesus Christ. His crisis prayer suggests some critical matters that the presbytery need to be aware of.

**Prayer is a remedy for affliction and a comfort for troubled souls.** An experiential affliction refines a victim for the ministry of comfort in a journey of an affliction.

**Prayer is a source of enduring hope and comfort.** Romans 15:13 says, *"May the God of hope fill you with all joy and peace as you trust in him, so that you may overflow with hope by the power of the Holy Spirit"* (NIV).

**Prayer is a means of authentic faith.** It is an act of obedience to pray to God, and it is a faithful exercise of faith in God's ability to respond. God loves when his child calls unto him in prayer. He loves to direct this child into greatness when he shows his dependency on him. God may chastise his children when they err, but he will never forsake them if they continue in the authentic faith of prayer. He is interested when they report their afflictions to him.

Exodus 3:7 provides a direct testimony of God's interest in ending his children's afflictions when they pray: *"And the Lord said: "I have surely seen the oppression of My people who are in Egypt, and have heard their cry because of their taskmasters, for I know their sorrows"* (NKJV).

This verse reveals three truths about God: he *sees*, *hears*, and *knows* our affliction. And he is willing to provide rescue and strengthen our faith.

**Prayer of victory is a direct product of the Trinity.** Romans 15:30 says, *"I urge you, brothers and sisters, by our Lord Jesus Christ and by the love of the Spirit, to join me in my struggle by praying to God for me"* (NIV). Paul called the local church presbytery to operate by prayer.

Carefully look at the prayers of the great men and women of the Bible and note that some commonalities cut across the generations of apostles, kings, priests, prophets, pastors, and of course the presbytery. We have seen this in both the writings of Jeremiah in 1 and 2 Kings, Ezra in 1 and 2 Chronicles, Daniel in his eponymous book, the apostle Paul in various epistles, James in his own epistle, etc. We are to share our thanksgiving, confessing one's and others' sins.

Finally, we should petition God, worship his awesomeness, claim ownership of him, acknowledge his sovereignty over all creation, and depend on his grace, mercy, favor, and faithfulness.

## CHAPTER FOURTEEN
# The Presbytery's Mandate for Holistic Ministry

*Lord, I have heard of your fame; I stand in awe of your deeds, Lord. Repeat them in our day, in our time make them known; in wrath remember mercy.* (Habakkuk 3:2, NIV)

IN THIS CHAPTER, we will look at the presbytery's mandate for holistic ministry. James 5:13–17 lays out the mandate for them to handle spiritual matters for the complete edification of the church. These spiritual matters include the ministries of preaching, teaching, and healing.

Religious leaders over the centuries have held a particular respect for the personal epistles written by James and Peter because of their affirmative teachings regarding the ministries of the Lord Jesus Christ. For example, one summary of Christ's earthly ministry states:

> *Jesus went throughout Galilee, teaching in their synagogues, proclaiming the good news of the kingdom, and healing every disease and sickness among the people. News about him spread all over Syria, and people brought to him all who were ill with various diseases, those suffering severe pain, the demon-possessed, those having seizures, and the paralyzed; and he healed them.* (Matthew 4:23–24, NIV)

The proclamation of the good news of Jesus Christ represents out only means of salvation—and salvation is what makes the growth of the church possible. The word builds faith in growth and maturity, and the healing of illnesses provides ground for us as believers to function in good health.

Unfortunately, various denominations of the Christian faith have proclaimed the good news and teaching of the word while denying the efficacy of miraculous healing.

## I. THREEFOLD MINISTRY OF JESUS CHRIST FOR TOTAL NEEDS OF HUMANITY

Just like as the Godhead has a threefold ministry (God the Father, God the Son, and God the Holy Spirit) and Christ had a threefold ministry on the earth (preaching, teaching, and healing), so too does the church have a threefold ministry. The church is responsible to preach, teach, and effect recovery.

The Bible reveals the Godhead's united function. God the Father created heaven and earth. In obedience, God the Son carried out the plan of the Father, taking on human characteristics in order to suffer, die, and rise from the dead to satisfy the requirement of man's reconciliatory relationship with the Father through preaching, teaching, and healing.

In obedience to God the Son, God the Holy Spirit accepted the indwelling ministry to affirm the preaching, teaching, and healing ministries.

Therefore, the church should obey God the Holy Spirit by living out the preaching, teaching, and healing ministries in meeting the need of believers.

## GODHEAD'S DIVINE PLAN FOR MINISTERING TO TOTAL HUMAN NEEDS

**God the Father and the threefold ministries.** Both the Old and New Testaments portray God as the Father, with the commissioning authority to assign tasks. He demonstrated his commissioning authority to the godly men and women in the Old Testament. He is the Father of Israel (Deuteronomy 32:6) who teaches, directs, instructs, heals, and cares for the wellness of his children.

God the Father used preaching, teaching, and healing in ministering to humanity. He demonstrated these abilities through his prophets, priests, and kings, who carried the threefold ministries to the people.

The word preaching occurs in the Bible 125 times while the word teaching appears 404 times. And in his defense of healing on the Sabbath day, Jesus declared to his accusers that the ministries he was carrying out were the same ministries he saw his Father perform. He did not do anything different from his heavenly Father. God wants his will in heaven to be done on earth.

> *So, because Jesus was doing these things on the Sabbath, the Jewish leaders began to persecute him. In his defense Jesus said to them, "My Father is always at his work to this very day, and I too am working." For this reason they tried all the more to kill him; not only was he breaking the Sabbath, but he was even calling God his own Father, making himself equal with God.*
>
> *Jesus gave them this answer: "Very truly I tell you, the Son can do nothing by himself; he can do only what he sees his Father doing, because whatever the Father does the Son also does. (John 5:16–19, NIV)*

How often do theologians and scholars deny the relevancy of Luke 9:1–2 as a designation to Christ's disciples and to the believers who live even now, during the twenty-first century?

> When Jesus had called the Twelve together, he gave them power and authority to drive out all demons and to cure diseases, and he sent them out to proclaim the kingdom of God and to heal the sick. (Luke 9:1–2, NIV)

Today, many theologians say, Christ's authority and power are effective only in the preaching and teaching of the word, not healing by the word. And yet Luke's text seems to summarize the cause of all human problems: demons and diseases.

Isn't that interesting? All that preaching and teaching accomplish is to edify and nurture souls to stand on their victory against deliberate attacks from Satan. This protects us from spiritual derailment. But how can the church prevent us from falling victim to physical derailment if the healing ministry is not taught?

*Preaching.* Christ existed before he took human form; he didn't just become divine at some point in history. He dwelled in heaven with the Father before taking human flesh (John 3:3, 6:38, 8:23, 1 Corinthians 15:47).

God preached through Moses in the creation story (Genesis 1:26) as well as in the story of man's fall (Genesis 3:1–24). Moses seems to have reminded the people of God's authority and power in his life and ministries.

> Your eyes have seen all that the Lord your God has done to these two kings. So will the Lord do to all the kingdoms into which you are crossing. You shall not fear them, for it is the Lord your God who fights for you (Deuteronomy 3:21–22, ESV)

God preached the healing ministry to Hezekiah and Jeremiah (2 Kings 20:5, Jeremiah 30:17, 33:6). The Old Testament prophets constantly reminded their audience that authority and power were beyond themselves but rather came from above.

I believe that the primary mission of Christ was preaching the truth about God's love for sinful humanity and turning man from eternal destruction to abundant eternal life (John 10:10). Preaching explains the mission of Jesus—the way, the truth, and the life (John 14:6). It provides an opportunity for repentance, the forgiveness of sin, and to receive eternal life. It explains the process of being reconciled with God. It affects and influences the spirit and mind to action toward God's word.

*Teaching.* The act of education was one of the primary responsibilities of Moses and the other leaders of Israel through the long years. They taught the Law and sought the people's obedience to the Lord of Hosts. Moses taught them that God was looking for the sign of the covenant to signify and seal spiritual reality in Israel: "And the Lord your God will circumcise your heart and the heart of your offspring, so *that you will love the Lord your God with all your heart and with all your soul, that you may live"* (Deuteronomy 30:6, ESV).

The psalmist understood God as an instructor, teacher, and counselor for his children (Psalm 32:8). Teaching provided the Israelizes the opportunity to embrace a spiritual, moral lifestyle and experience physical health.

*Healing.* Many scriptural texts reveal God's healing ministry to his children, including these two passages:

> *Bless the Lord, O my soul, and forget not all his benefits, who forgives all your iniquity, who heals all your diseases, who redeems your life from the Pit, who crowns you with steadfast love and mercy, who satisfies you with good as long as you live so that your youth is renewed like the eagle's.* (Psalm 103:2–5, RSV)

> *Fools, because of their transgression, and because of their iniquities, were afflicted. Their soul abhorred all manner of food, and they drew near to the gates of death. Then they cried out to the Lord in their trouble, and He saved them out of their distresses. He sent His word and healed them, and **delivered** them from their destructions.* (Psalm 107:17–22, NKJV)

**God the Son and the threefold ministries.** Throughout his three and half years of preaching, teaching, and healing, Christ portrayed the importance of ministry delegation and commissioning. He demonstrated his commissioning authority and power to his disciples to accomplish the preaching, teaching, and healing ministries—with colossal success (Matthew 10:7–9, Luke 9:1–11).

In his commissioning instructions, the Lord delegated authority and power for the church to accomplish his divine preaching, teaching, and healing ministries:

- He commissioned and sent the people to preach/proclaim the good news of the kingdom of God to accomplish the harvest of human souls (Luke 10:9–17).
- He commissioned and sent them to baptize the people into Christ and teach believers to grow into maturity (Matthew 28:18–20, Mark 16:15–16).
- He commissioned and sent the people to cure others of their sin, disease, and sickness (Matthew 4:24; 10:1–2, 7–8).

**God the Holy Spirit and the threefold ministries.** In both the Old and New Testaments, God the Holy Spirit is portrayed as an equal participant in the commissioning process. He demonstrated his commissioning authority and power, calling godly men and women to work together in faith for the kingdom of God (2 Corinthians 6:1).

The disciples, including the chief servant, the apostle Paul, did not have more significant access to the Holy Spirit than church leaders have today. The only difference, I presume, is the obedience and willingness of individual leaders to be filled and used by the same Holy Spirit to fulfill the same mandate—preaching, teaching, and healing.

We have received the delegated authority of Christ when we are indwelled by the Holy Spirit (Acts 1:8). This power is available in aby believer's life and ministry today (Ephesians 3:20).

*Preaching.* This is one of the primary functions of the Holy Spirit, who anoints, enlightens, illuminates, reveals, encourages, gives boldness, and energizes the preacher's heart and mind in communicating the word (Act 4:31). He makes the practice of preaching alive as it transforms people's lives.

*Teaching.* In order for a teaching to have the power to produce a breakthrough in the lives of believers, this is possible through the enablement of the Holy Spirit. The authority and power of the Holy Spirit causes ministries to thrive (John 14:26, 16:13).

*Healing.* The Holy Spirit is a Counsellor, and Healer, providing direction and clarity of instruction and enabling believers. As a member of the Godhead, he knows the mind of God, wields divine power and authority over the works of the enemy, and understand every aspect of the human experience. Therefore, he has equal healing power with Christ.

Donnelly Edward writes about the preaching of Christ from the Old Testament, including in the stories of Abraham, Israel, and David. He notes that even the first verse of the New Testament seems to establish this, describing Jesus as *"the Son of David, the Son of Abraham"* (Matthew 1:1, NIV).[268]

Jesus preached, taught, and healed as a continuation of the ministry of God the Father. Such ministries should be aggressively upheld in every local church.

THE GODHEAD MINISTERS TO MAN'S THREEFOLD NATURE

Earlier, I have covered several topics that showcase the need for equally emphasizing the threefold ministries of the Godhead in the modern church. We have discussed

---

268. Donnelly Edward, "Six Principles for Preaching Christ from the Old Testament," *Banner of Truth*. October 20, 2014 (https://banneroftruth.org/us/resources/articles/2014/six-principles-preaching-christ-old-testament).

the importance that the church places on preaching and teaching God's Word while neglecting the role of healing.

The one thing that is most neglected and de-emphasized in the church today is the healing ministry.

Peter and James, who are both detailed and well-connected to other books in the Bible, emphasize the complete nature of the gospel. The epistle of James puts the Lord Jesus Christ at the center of all prayers. Christ is the center of the preaching ministry, the teaching ministry, and the healing ministry.

Tadros Malaty emphasizes that the Lord Jesus is the center on which we should focus all our attention.[269]

The importance of the PCPM is echoed across all the Christian denominations, whether Orthodox, Evangelical, Charismatic, or Pentecostal, to name only a few. But the emphasis on the practice of prayer for miraculous healing among Orthodox believers and Evangelicals seems to be outdated and unbiblical. With the PCPM, James has given the church a pillar to stand on.

The church, as a mother, is compassionate toward her children and responsible for satisfying all their needs, not only in good and joyful times but also while they carry the cross. If they are sick, they should call the elders of the church.

The early church fathers have delivered to us in the twenty-first century the prayers by which the presbytery can use to pray for the sick. The Holy Spirit inspired these prayers. God does not honor any prayers offered in the Lord's name that derive their righteousness from church elders. The righteousness that satisfies God the Father comes only through the righteousness of God the Son.

Malaty wrote extensively on the apostolic writings of renowned theologians and church fathers who taught about the miracle of healing.

Such early church leaders include Justin Martyr (100–165), Tertullian (160–230), Origin (185–284), and Cyril of Jerusalem (315–386). In the second century A.D., Justin Martyr spoke of demons flying from the touch and breathing of Christians. Two centuries later, Cyril of Jerusalem wrote of demons that fled from Christians "as from a flame that burns them."[270]

Although a crisis brings us into the experience of the Lord for the sin of humankind, both St. Nilos and St. Pachomius believed that crisis prayer allows us to transfer our crises to encounters with the Lord. This serves as medicine and an opportunity to be in his presence in fellowship.[271]

---

269. Malaty, *The Epistle of St. James: A Patristic Commentary*.

270. Ibid.

271. Ibid., 70.

## The Presbytery's Mandate for Holistic Ministry

In times of trouble, believers must discuss their crises with God through prayer. Prayer represents a noble opportunity for God to fulfill his promises and restore our confidence that he is in charge.

In the same vein, Hilary of Arles said that whenever illness comes upon a man, he should be anointed by the presbytery with consecrated oil. The elders should then pray over him in Christ's name. If he does this, he will receive not only bodily health but also the forgiveness of his sins.[272]

St. Augustine of Hippo (354–430) had a decisive view on understanding the effect of the prayer of a righteous presbytery. He believed that prayer is not just a matter of blurting out meaningless words in tongues; rather, he believed that prayer is powerful, living, and inspired by the Spirit. He further stressed that the basis of prayer and supplication is the fulfillment of virtue. Those who receive a prayer must cleanse themselves so that no iniquities stand between their righteous prayer and the righteous God. When the righteousness of Christ is evidenced in both the life of the person who prays and the person who receives that prayer, the prayer becomes solid and full of power.[273]

St. John Climacsu compared a crisis member to a farmer. Using this metaphor, he illustrated the effectiveness of a righteous man's prayer:

> It is like the seeds sown by the farmer. They are planted once, but they do not survive forever unless they are carefully nurtured. Unless the tillers of the soil protect the seeds, they will be exposed to the birds and every seed-eating creature. We are just like this unless we protect what has been sown in us by constant care, for the devil will snatch it away, and our lethargy will destroy it. The sun dries it up, the rain drowns it, and weeds choke it so that it is not enough for the Sower to pass by once only. Instead, he must tend it often, driving away the birds of the air, pulling up the weeds, and filling up the rocky places with much soil. He must prevent, block off and eject any destruction.[274]

Most of the early church fathers took seriously James's call on the responsibility of the presbytery for the well-being of church members. Good spiritual, physical, and mental health is not only the wish of the church; God also desires the complete health of his church.

---

272. Ibid., 72.

273. Ibid., 73.

274. Ibid., 74.

In fact, Jesus gave his disciple the authority and power to access his threefold ministries—preaching, teaching, and healing. Did he ever take these ministries back, removing the church's access to them?

I don't think so. I believe that the church continued to be able to function in the threefold ministries through the authority and power of Jesus. The Holy Spirit indwells believers to enforce the active presence of the authority and power of Christ.

So why does the church embrace the preaching and teaching ministries while rejecting the healing ministry? I believe this happens because of disobedience, faithlessness, and ignorance of its efficacy.

How much authority and power did Jesus give the church? He gave them all of his authority and power, empowering his disciples to perform the same works he himself performed. He even promised that the church would perform even more miracles in his name (John 14:12–14). He called his impartation of authority and power the "greater works."

Christ expected a more significant demonstration of miraculous works in the future than anything he performed during his earthly life. Did Jesus lie, or have we not fulfilled his divine expectations?

To what extent is the church leadership a co-worker with Christ in the threefold ministries today? We read in John 15:5 that apart from Jesus, we can do nothing. The only way we are co-workers with Christ is to continue his preaching, teaching, and healing. The church has been delegated to carry out these ministries through the indwelling of the Holy Spirit.

However, the delegated authority and power of Jesus Christ appears to be less effective in the church today. Our faith seems to be watered down and overly intellectual. We seem to operate according to human know-how, not according to divine authority. The works of Satan will only be destroyed when the church objectively and obediently exercises the mandate of the threefold ministry of Christ.

CHAPTER FIFTEEN
# Defining the PCPM

*"He himself bore our sins" in his body on the cross, so that we might die to sins and live for righteousness; "by his wounds you have been healed."* (1 Peter 2:24, NIV)

## I. THE MEANING OF THE PCPM

As we work to understand what interventional presbytery crisis prayer is and what it is not, we will look more closely at the phrase "presbytery crisis prayer ministry," which we have been abbreviating to PCPM.

Earlier, we discussed that this book's focus is not on theological and doctrinal arguments pertaining to the spiritual gifts. The book does not explore the question of when such gifts may or may not have ceased or whether it's possible for those in the body of Christ to experience those gifts in the ministry today. These questions have divided the church in terms of the Holy Spirit's healing ministry.

The Holy Spirit operates in mysterious ways to meet the needs of believers. Therefore, we should be encouraged to be less critical and leave the ministries of the Holy Spirit to him to operate as he wishes in his church today.

The revelation of God's plan for the salvation of humanity is complete, but we believe there is more to understand about the depth of the revealed word. The same Holy Spirit that worked in the life of Paul and all other servants of God through the generations has not changed. He is still reconciling human souls to himself and expanding his kingdom with the demonstration of miracles in his church and the world.

St. John Climacsu has observed the problem of the church's lethargy. The liturgy, homiletics, and hermeneutics are destroying believers' faith. Some churches are creating a disbelief in miracles through the name of Jesus Christ. Nothing kills the fulfillment of God's promises than a spirit of denial. Such a spirit blocks the flow of Holy Spirit's anointing and prevent effective ministry in the church.

Disbelief serves as the foundation of the theology of cessation of certain spiritual gifts. Some people believe that certain gifts of the Holy Spirit are no longer available to the church. However theologians and scholars need to give the Holy Spirit a chance to carry out his ministry in the lives of believers as the need arises.

The ministry of the Holy Spirit is multigenerational and multidimensional. John declared one of his powerful ministerial characteristics:

*When the Spirit of truth comes, he will guide you into all the truth, for he will not speak on his own authority, but whatever he hears he will speak, and he will declare to you the things that are to come.* (John 16:13, ESV)

Spontaneous miracles still happen in the church today. For example, a student in my class, crippled at birth, stood up on his feet immediately after receiving righteous prayer at the Reinhard Bonnke Crusade in Kaduna, Nigeria. He left his wheelchair and walked. He was declared healed by a servant of God in the name of Jesus Christ of Nazareth. He is still up and walking on his feet today. He has a beautiful wife and children.

The question of whether the servant of God who spoke the prayer has a gift of spiritual healing should not bother anyone. This is simply a case of the Holy Spirit doing his thing in his church. The testimony is always the same: *"One thing I do know, that though I was blind, now I see"* (John 9:25, ESV).

It doesn't matter whether spontaneous acts of God in healing, or other divine manifestations of his character, are the outcome of spiritual gifts. This should not be a contentious matter. No one understands the full depth, width, length, and height of the ministries of the Holy Spirit in the lives of the saints. No one can chain the corporate ministrations of the Trinity in advancing their kingdom among men. So let us relax on this subject.

Having made these observations, we shall now discuss some of the properties of presbytery crisis prayer, including its nature, character, purpose, authority and power, theology, promises, audience, and superb results.

## II. THE NATURE OF THE PCPM

The church must distinguish the PCPM from all other types of prayer enshrined in Scripture. There are different approaches to prayer, and the Lord's Prayer is the crown jewel.

The PCPM differs from so-called pastoral prayer, such as prayer for special financial needs in congregational meetings. It also differs from educational, commissioning, harvest, thanksgiving, and ceremonial prayers. Likewise, the PCPM is not a prayer for offerings, mercy, food, prosperity, success, intellectual abilities, or weather transformation. It is not a general prayer for the relief of natural disasters such as hurricanes, volcanoes, tsunamis, floods, or other calamities. If any of these events were to affect members, there would be nothing wrong with those members calling the church for prayer. These types of interventional prayer do not require the laying on of hands or application of oil by the board of elders.

The result of the PCPM, however, reflects the sovereignty of God, as well as the sufficiency and efficacy of the name of Jesus Christ. This type of prayer involves the act of every kind of healing. When it's based on James's principles, the PCPM promotes a blessed and healthy lifestyle because the crisis member has been raised out of sickness. This prayer is imperative to the board of overseers, who are privileged to participate in intervention; they must be above reproach, prudent, and command Christ's authority and power over sickness (2 Timothy 3:2, 6–7).

No believer in Christ who serves as an overseer should be under the influence of immature faith. The devil can challenge the faith and maturity of an elder who ministers the prayer of intervention for the sick.

Satan challenged the healing ministry of the sons of Sceva because of their unworthy lifestyle in the house of God. The apostle Paul wrote about this experience:

> Then certain of the vagabond Jews, exorcists, took upon them to call over them which had evil spirits the name of the Lord Jesus, saying, We adjure you by Jesus whom Paul preacheth. And there were seven sons of one Sceva, a Jew, and chief of the priests, which did so. And the evil spirit answered and said, Jesus I know, and Paul I know; but who are ye? And the man in whom the evil spirit was leaped on them, and overcame them, and prevailed against them, so that they fled out of that house naked and wounded. (Acts 19:13–16, KJV)

So a presbyter must be mature in the faith, obedient to the word, and be above reproach even to the enemy of the faith, Satan himself.

## III. THE CHARACTER OF THE PCPM

This type of prayer is marked by:

- The faith of Jesus Christ.
- The name of Christ.
- The righteousness of Christ (all prayers smell like rags before God the Father without this righteousness).
- The presence of the Spirit (anointed oil).
- The authority and power of the resurrected Christ (the laying on of hands).

People respond through the preaching of the word. As a result, the word convicts them and they turn away from sin to embrace the righteousness of God unto salvation. The preaching and teaching of the word encourages believers to live godly lives.

The same divine approach causes the prayer of a righteous presbytery to heal the sick and make us mortal beings whole again.

## IV. THE PURPOSE OF THE PCPM

God instituted the PCPM to restore the healing efficacy of his word in the church (James 5:16, Psalm 19). The presbytery is to pray over sick members. Such prayer is robustly successful in bringing about transformation, removing the defects of sickness, and restoring God's intended wellness to man.

God wants us to be completely obedient to the instruction in James, because the presbytery's compliance allows God to bring the benefits of his word to its full manifestation.

Presbytery prayer helps to reveal our sins, perfect and refresh our sick souls, and brings joy to our aching hearts. It provides an opportunity to forgive our hidden faults and produce in us freedom from guilt. The effects of this presbytery prayer are powerful in healing the sick and effective for restoring our uprightness before God and our fellow man.

## V. THE AUTHORITY AND POWER OF THE PCPM

The PCPM is not an idea of the church's; it is an imperative revelation from the Godhead— the Father, the Son, and the Holy Spirit.

God the Holy Spirit teaches and urges believers to call the presbytery for intercessory prayer. The prayer is presented in the name of God the Son to God the Father. God the Father then acts on the believer's request through the Son by his will (John 14:13–16, Ephesians 2:18, Hebrews 4:16).

The Trinity demands that if anyone is in trouble, they call the presbytery for such an interventional intercession. It seems to be an obligation that the victim must seek this prayer. If someone is sick, there must be a call for crisis prayer, and the elders must respond. The instruction reads slightly different depending on the translation of the Bible you are using:

> *Is anyone among you sick? Let him call for the elders of the church...* (James 5:14, NKJV)

> *Is anyone among you sick? He must call for the elders (spiritual leaders) of the church...* (James 5:14, AMP)

> *Is anyone among you sick? Let them call the elders of the church...* (James 5:14, NIV)

> *Are you sick? Call the church leaders together to pray...* (James 5:14, MSG)

The afflicted church member is authorized and empowered to call the leaders of their church. These elders are then authorized and empowered to pray for the sick.

The sick must reach out, and the spiritual leaders must respond and offer fervent prayers of faith over the sick member.

Children of God cannot challenge God on his promises if they cannot first obey his instructions on how to access his promises and obtain results.

Matthew's record on the primary task of Christ's ministries is clear:

> *And Jesus went about all Galilee, teaching in their synagogues, preaching the gospel of the kingdom, and healing all kinds of sickness and all kinds of disease among the people. Then His fame went throughout all Syria; and they brought to Him all sick people who were afflicted with various diseases and torments, and those who were demon-possessed, epileptics, and paralytics; and He healed them.* (Matthew 4:23–24, NKJV)

Christ authorized the presbytery to exercise his authority and power to deal with ungodliness and demonic activity in the church. Here ungodliness refers to any attack on anything in our lives, whether it be our health or anything else concerning our well-being that doesn't bring glory to God. Jesus said, *"Listen carefully: I have given you authority… over all the power of the enemy…"* (Luke 10:19, AMP)

Ill health is an enemy to well-being, isn't it? Of course, it is. Humans must always turn to God for assistance when it comes to a debilitating disorder. We read in Acts 10:38,

> *And you know that God anointed Jesus of Nazareth with the Holy Spirit and with power. Then Jesus went around doing good and healing all who were oppressed by the devil, for God was with him.* (Acts 10:38, NLT)

Every local presbytery has been empowered with the authority that belongs to Christ alone, the authority that can rule over all powers outside the Yahweh's supremacy.

By all indications, there is a massive difference between authority and power. When you have power, it means you have been given the ability to dominate. It is a show of strength, a capacity for forceful accomplishment. Authority, on the other hand, has to do with delegating the right to act and issuing commands on their behavior.

The church, and not only the presbytery, has been given the authority of Christ to function and command his power and authority on issues of ungodliness in the church through the ministries of the Holy Spirit.

Satan has the power to do certain things, but he does not have absolute control since the church has been given the power to act on behalf of the Lord Jesus Christ. When the presbytery acts on the authority and power of the name of Christ, and the word of Christ, they will have the opportunity to eliminate ungodliness in the kingdom of God. The presbytery must engage every situation with a prayer of faith. God will always act with convincing proof when the church operates on his promises.

## VI. THE THEOLOGY OF THE PCPM

The specific prayer needed here was God's idea. Whether the local assembly believes in instantaneous healing, the theology of the healing ministry is that it has been given to the church to meet the physical and spiritual needs of God's children. It must be carried out by faith in the name of the Lord Christ.

The PCPM's results demonstrate the El-Shaddai (All-Sufficient God) and **Jehovah Rapha** (God our Healer) characters of God. The Mighty One of Israel has the power to heal and nourish our brokenness. He desires that we have complete health and abundant life (John 10:10, 3 John 1–2).

John prayed an intentional prayer of intervention for elder Gaius in these words:

> *From the church leader.*
> *To my dear friend Gaius, whom I love because we share the truth.*
> *Dear friend, I know that you are spiritually well. I pray that you're doing well in every other way and that you're healthy.*
> (3 John 1:1–2, GW)

This passage seems to reveal that there is divine intentionality for the health of every child of God.

The word of God is rich in its promises about taking away our disease, sickness, and pain. Obeying God's word increases the opportunity for our spiritual and physical restoration. God has given the presbytery the mandate to be at the forefront of bringing such promises to pass in our lives.

Every possible condition of ill health finds its root in the fall of man in Genesis 3, but the glory goes to God and his word because every one of these conditions has a solution in the Bible. When Christ cried out that, *"It is finished"* (John 19:30, NIV), it marked the ultimate provision of man's spiritual and physical needs.

John T. Carroll outlines the theological importance of the healing ministry today. In his writings, Carroll emphasizes how imperative it is that healing ministry be given its rightful place in the operation of the local church. He lays out three imperatives of the church.

**The local church exists to sustain life and not destroy it.** God recommends caring for and sustaining crisis members over honoring the Sabbath.[275]

One of the most enjoyable parts of my own ministry at ECWA in Nigeria is the practice of holding a prayer meeting or worship service at the residence of a deceased or hurting member of the church. This makes the ministry towards families more meaningful and authentic, allowing the church to bring encouragement and healing to the brokenhearted. It also provides an opportunity to evangelize the community.

Saving a life must always take precedence over obeying the Sabbath. There is no evading this responsibility, for our actions can either to sustain life or destroy it. There is no middle path of benign inaction.

**The local church exists to minister healing as a restoration of the faith community.** The local church either rises to the challenge of her ministry responsibilities or shies away and hurts the members of the body of Christ. We cannot ask God to fulfill his promise while we fail to do ours. Restoring the physical and spiritual needs of crisis members is an opportunity to demonstrate God's historical presence and eschatological reign.[276]

**The local church exists to minister healing as a demonstration of faith in the power and authority of Christ.** Both salvation and healing are possible by faith. Faith has the power to transform any human condition, and it is not possible to please God and create a positive result without faith. We are saved by faith. By faith, we believe in the eschatological events revealed in the book of Revelation. Also, our spiritual and physical healing is accomplished by faith.

Many called and ordained ministers of the gospel of Christ embrace spontaneous acts of faith, but they can be scared to even talk about faith healing. When believers deny the power of faith healing, they miss out on the chance to experience it for themselves. Even the Lord Jesus Christ had to rebuke the residents of Nazareth on the issue of faithlessness (Matthew 13:58) [277]

## VII. THE PROMISES OF THE PCPM

There is nothing God loves to hear more than our reminders of what he has promised to do in his word. He loves to see the written word became the living word (rhema). He loves to showcase his glory and miraculously bring his word to pass. He also admires his children for giving him the adoration he deserves. He wants to hear us declare, like the

---

275. Carroll, "Sickness and Healing in the New Testament Gospels," 138.

276. Ibid.

277. Ibid., 139.

Nehemiah of old, *"Lord, the God of heaven, the great and awesome God, who keeps his covenant of love with those who love him and keep his commandments"* (Nehemiah 1:5–6, NIV).

He never denies or rejects his own promises. He keeps his word and is faithful to perform it. Moses reminded us about the character of God concerning keeping his word:

> *God is not a man, that He should lie, nor a son of man, that He should repent. Has He said, and will He not do it? Or has He spoken and will He not make it good and fulfill it?* (Numbers 23:19, AMP)

He does not change his mind. He honors his word and keeps his promises more than his name (Psalm 138:2), for his character is represented by his faithfulness to honor His word.

It is essential in the PCPM that God magnifies his word, which is his communication channel; his promises are his agenda and a revelation to his people. It's a lamp under the church's feet in a dark and fallen world. God's word is a weapon that distinguishes the firing arrows of the enemy from all manner of human afflictions, even the shield of faith (Ephesians 6:16).

Nehemiah understood the promises of his God when he prayed:

> *Remember the instruction you gave your servant Moses, saying, "If you are unfaithful, I will scatter you among the nations, but if you return to me and obey my commands, then even if your exiled people are at the farthest horizon, I will gather them from there and bring them to the place I have chosen as a dwelling for my Name."* (Nehemiah 1:8–9, NIV)

God will act supernaturally if his children are faithful to his instructions. If Revelation had contained more details about the plan of God for humanity, it would have referred to James 5:13–20 concerning the process of God's promise for healing disease and forgiving sin.

Therefore, the presbytery crisis prayer focuses on what God has said in his word, not on what people assume God desires to do. It is an act of reminding God of his faithfulness, dominion, and acts of wonder throughout history.

## VIII. THE AUDIENCE OF THE PCPM

Any member in the body of Christ is qualified to witness the presbytery crisis prayer of intervention. When a member is in crisis, he or she should call the presbytery. This act of calling is an act of faith in God's promises, and the expectation of such trust shall be met (Psalm 103:3, Matthew 9:1–8).

## IX. THE SUPERB RESULTS OF THE PCPM

Prayer based on the promises of God yields positive results. When the members of a church properly obey the word, the result is glorious; the church is simply acting on what God has promised to do.

The PCPM is a prayer in the living word (rhema) of God, the word in action. This is the active word, the sharp word, and the piercing word. The rhema word brings life to the soul and healing to the body (Proverbs 4:22).

This type of prayer restores life and removes every barrier that stands between peace and sorrow, sadness and joy, guilt and the forgiveness of guilt. Suppose that the fervent prayer of the presbytery changes a situation, moving it in a positive direction—towards a glorious destiny. In that case, the prayer must be spoken through the rhema word of God.

The rhema word of God is the living word that comes through the mouth of the presbytery through the power of the Holy Spirit. The Holy Spirit's empowerment quickens as he searches and knows the desires in the hearts of men. The omniscient God is the one who reveals the deep and hidden things in man's heart.

When a presbyter declares the rhema word based on what the faithful God has said, a door towards a sick person's healing destiny.

The devil understands and obeys the truth spoken from God's rhema word. Satan operates only within the limits God has assigned for him. He could do whatever he wanted with Job, but he was kept within limits (Job 1:1).

On this view of God's word, James wrote, *"The prayer of a person living right with God is something powerful to be reckoned with"* (James 5:16, MSG). When the rhema word is spoken over a sick person by a presbyter who's living right with God, God's power is called into action. God's rhema word does not return without accomplishing the purpose for which it was sent: *"he sent out his word and healed them and delivered them from destruction"* (Psalm 107:20, NRSV).

There is an unimaginable authority and power in the rhema word:

> *For the word of God is living and powerful, and sharper than any two-edged sword, piercing even to the division of soul and spirit, and of joints and marrow, and is a discerner of the thoughts and intents of the heart.* (Hebrews 4:12, NKJV)

The rhema word is the sword of the Holy Spirit. When it is mingled with the presbytery's unweaving shield of faith, the flaming missiles of the evil one are diminished, including his work of causing sickness, pain, and destruction.

The secret power of the rhema word of God that comes out from the mouth of the presbytery in the name of the Lord Jesus Christ is capable of denouncing, destroying, and removing the power of sickness while declaring the glory of God. The glorious wish of God is for us to prosper in everything and be in good health in our spirits, souls, and bodies (3 John 1:2).

God is results-oriented. He causes supernatural events to occur so that he can take the glory. All the acts of miracles performed by men and women of God in the Old Testament were made possible by the use of this rhema phrase: "Thus said the Lord." Almost every servant of God in the Old Testament accomplished God-given tasks through this phrase. When they invoked the Lord in this way, they were speaking the rhema word of God.

# Part Four

## Understanding the Cause and Effect of Sickness

CHAPTER SIXTEEN
# The Cause and Effect of Crises

*The righteous person may have many troubles, but the Lord delivers him from them all.* (Psalm 34:19)

*Vanity of science. Knowledge of physical science will not console me for ignorance of morality in a time of affliction, but knowledge of morality will always console me for ignorance of physical science.*[278]
—Blaise Pascal

## I. DESCRIPTION OF SIN, DISEASE, ILLNESS, AND DEATH

IN THIS CHAPTER, we will attempt to answer several important questions related to illness. What is the origin and purpose of illness? What are its different types? Why do people get ill? The answers will focus more on the biblical perspective than the medical, psychological, or anthropological standpoint. It is worthwhile to understand the root cause of human affliction, including Satan, sin, and the broken world.

According to the Bible, there was a time in human history when the structure of our bodies functioned perfectly. Then the seed of sin interfered with the human system. The biblical pathology of disease, sickness, and death is sin. Sin is the product of man rejecting God and choosing to go his own way.

The *Merriam-Webster Dictionary* defines illness as "an unhealth condition of body or mind."[279] It can occur in any component of the human being—physical, mental, or spiritual.

The *Encyclopedia Britannica* defines disease this way: "any harmful deviation from the normal structural or functional state of an organism, generally associated with certain signs and symptoms and differing in nature from physical injury."[280]

---

278. Bilal Hafeez, "36 One Liners from Blaise Pascal that Will Open Your Mind," *MacroHive*. February 18, 2022 (https://macrohive.com/hive-refreshers/36-one-liners-from-blaise-pasca-that-will-open-your-mind). Quoting Blaise Pascal.

279. "Illness," *Merriam-Webster*. Date of access: May 9, 2023 (https://www.merriam-webster.com/dictionary/illness).

280. "Disease," *Britannica*. Date of access: May 9, 2023 (https://www.britannica.com/science/disease).

By the eighteenth century, illness was defined as "wickedness, depravity, immorality."[281] In another sense, illness is described as "unpleasantness, disagreeableness, and hurtfulness."[282] In the seventeenth century, illness was defined as "ill health, the state of being ill."[283]

Kenneth M. Boyd notes,

> Sickness is a social role, a status, a negotiated position in the world, a bargain struck between the person henceforward called "sick," and a society which is prepared to recognize and sustain him.[284]

According to Boyd, the definitions of disease and sickness offered by the medical community can be complex, vague, and elusive because they embody value judgments. In describing illness, Boyd uses many of the same words used by the Bible to describe the effect of sin.

Medical professionals understand that disease causes sickness and death. However, they do not explain what causes disease. When a patient complains of ill health, doctors will apply a diagnostic label to better understand the problem. Biblically and theologically, it's important to know that sin is the cause of all affliction.

As part of the same discussion, Henry Wright has noted that people wonder why they get sick. He acknowledges that, for some people, getting sick may seem like random chance. Others may think they have been destined to contract illness because of their genetics. As a medical doctor himself, he confirms what we have underscored in this book: disease and sickness are a result of a curse. Satan's primary mission is to undo God's blessings for the human body, mind, and soul/spirit (John 10:10). Disease and sickness do not represent abundance and wholeness of life but the destruction of the human system.[285]

The word teaches, *"A merry heart doeth good like a medicine: but a broken spirit drieth the bones"* (Proverbs 17:22, KJV). This scripture became the focus of Dr. Wright's

---

281. Kenneth M. Boyd, "Disease, Illness, Sickness, Health, Healing, and Wholeness: Exploring Some Elusive Concepts." *Medical Humanities 26(1)*, June 2000, 10.

282. Ibid.

283. "Spiritual Roots of Disease," *Be in Health*. Date of access: December 20, 2022 (https://www.beinhealth.com/spiritual-roots-of-disease). Quoting Dr. Henry Wright.

284. Boyd, "Disease, Illness, Sickness, Health, Healing and Wholeness: Exploring Some Elusive Concepts," 10.

285. "Spiritual Roots of Disease," *Be in Health*. Date of access: December 20, 2022 (https://www.beinhealth.com/spiritual-roots-of-disease). Quoting Dr. Henry Wright.

understanding of the source of sickness and healing. He came to understand that marrow is found in the bones and marrow is the center of the human immune system. So if the marrow of the bone is dried up, the immune system goes down with it.[286]

Sickness is a means of the enemy's attack, and the apostle Paul believed that affliction is a messenger of Satan, whose aim is torment us (2 Corinthians 12:7). Like Satan, it is like a prowling lion, seeking someone to destroy.

Again, sickness can occur in any of the three human domains—body, soul, or spirit—and according to James, the treatment for a problem in the household of faith is both individual prayer and the PCPM. A fervent prayer of faith is a resisting force that keeps the devil on the run (1 Peter 5:8).

In describing disease and sickness from a biblical perspective, Elwell reminds us that the people of those times knew nothing of germs, bacteria, viruses, or anesthesia. They didn't understand the organs of the body or their functions. Scripture also describes conditions like "wasting disease," which refers to tuberculosis, or "fever," which relates to maria. The term "scorching" describes skin conditions like eczema or skin cancer. The list could go on.[287]

In the area of mental health, we read descriptions of King Saul's depressive state (1 Samuel 16:14–23) and delusions suffered by Nebuchadnezzar (Daniel 4: 6–25). Also, social distancing is not a uniquely twenty-first-century therapeutic idea. In biblical times, it was enforced in cases of leprosy, tuberculosis, smallpox, and psychosis.[288]

In acknowledging the tendency of illness to afflict everyone, author Susan Sonntag states,

> Everyone who is born holds dual citizenship, in the kingdom of the well and in the kingdom of the sick. Although we all prefer to use only the good passport, sooner or later each of us is obliged, at least for a spell, to identify ourselves as citizens of that other place.[289]

## II. PURPOSE OF A CRISIS

Although we all face challenging and unpleasant experience in this life, God oversees their cause and controls our destiny for the good. Two instances in the Bible illustrate this character of God: the case of Job in the Old Testament, and the case of the blind man in

---

286. Ibid.

287. Elwell, *Baker's Evangelical Dictionary of Biblical Theology*.

288. Ibid.

289. Susan Sontag, *Illness as Metaphor* (New York, NY: Farrar, Straus & Girons, 1978), 3.

the New Testament. In both stories, the purpose of the affliction was to exalt God's might and sovereignty over human affairs (John 9:24).

No one consciously chooses pain or illness, yet the experience of dealing with these challenges can lead us on a journey that ultimately delivers excellent rewards. I have heard many people with cancer and other life-threatening diseases describe their illness as one of the greatest blessings in their lives because it forced them to reshuffle their priorities and pursue a new path that produced profound fulfillment. The illness permitted them to make choices they would not have considered otherwise.

When the presbytery crisis prayer does not gain the divine favor of God and turn a negative situation into a positive, the presbytery and the crisis member must arrive at the conclusion that God is holy, righteous, and excellent in all his ways. He never merits a curse from his creation, but always a blessing.

Psalm 145:10–21 reads,

> *All of your works will thank you, Lord, and your faithful followers will praise you. They will speak of the glory of your kingdom; they will give examples of your power. They will tell about your mighty deeds and about the majesty and glory of your reign. For your kingdom is an everlasting kingdom. You rule throughout all generations.*
>
> *The Lord always keeps his promises; he is gracious in all he does. The Lord helps the fallen and lifts those bent beneath their loads. The eyes of all look to you in hope; you give them their food as they need it. When you open your hand, you satisfy the hunger and thirst of every living thing. The Lord is righteous in everything he does; he is filled with kindness. The Lord is close to all who call on him, yes, to all who call on him in truth. He grants the desires of those who fear him; he hears their cries for help and rescues them. The Lord protects all those who love him, but he destroys the wicked.*
>
> *I will praise the Lord, and may everyone on earth bless his holy name forever and ever.* (NLT)

## THE RIGHTEOUS FEAR OF THE LORD

When believers ask for healing, they desire healing and wholeness—and God has promised to grant such a wish on one condition: we must fear him. This means acknowledging him and doing his will. Fearing God demolishes human pride and arrogancy.

Isaiah 42:10 says, *"...fear not, for I am with you; be not dismayed, for I am your God; I will strengthen you, I will help you, I will uphold you with my righteous right hand"* (Isaiah

42:10, ESV). It is impossible to be upheld in the righteous hand of God and also be subject to the torment of disease and sickness.

What would hinder the miraculous healing of the presbytery? An absence of the love of God in the believer's life and practice. Knowing the depth, height, width, and strength of God's love for us will grant us victory over every affliction.

John wrote precisely this: *"There is no fear in love. But perfect love drives out fear, because fear has to do with punishment. The one who fears is not made perfect in love"* (1 John 4:18, NIV).

## III. GODLY PURPOSE OF SICKNESS

The questions regarding illness remain. Does sickness have any positive aspect? What is the purpose of sickness? To the faith community, the truth inform us that sickness does have a positive side.

### SICKNESS INCREASES OUR DEPENDENCE ON GOD

We have acknowledged that sickness was not in God's original plan for humanity. In other words, God does not cause illness. However, he can allow it—and he does this to increase our dependence on his sovereignty.

It is in this spirit of dependency that Paul gladly honored God's decision on his situation:

> *But he said to me, "My grace is sufficient for you, for my power is made perfect in weakness." Therefore I will boast all the more gladly about my weaknesses, so that Christ's power may rest on me. 10 That is why, for Christ's sake, I delight in weaknesses, in insults, in hardships, in persecutions, in difficulties. For when I am weak, then I am strong.* (2 Corinthians 12:9–10, NIV)

### SICKNESS IMPROVES OUR PRAYER LIFE

Nothing motivates faith and growth more than the practical results of prayer. Believers pray more when they come to understand that prayer is a type of divine authorization that places them over the activities of the power of the darkness.

### SICKNESS STRENGTHENS ONE'S FAITH IN GOD

God will be swift to act if he knows that the presbytery has strengthened the faith of believers through the use of persistent prayer. When God knows that these local church leaders will not be silent when it comes to standing in the gap on behalf of sick members of their congregation, he will not delay in responding.

# THE PRESBYTERY CRISIS MINISTRY

The parable of the unjust judge and the persistent widow demonstrates the strength of continuous prayer:

> *Jesus told his disciples a parable about their need to pray all the time and never give up. He said, "In a city there was a judge who didn't fear God or respect people. In that city there was also a widow who kept coming to him and saying, 'Grant me justice against my adversary.' For a while the judge refused. But later, he told himself, 'I don't fear God or respect people, yet because this widow keeps bothering me, I will grant her justice. Otherwise, she will keep coming and wear me out.'"*
>
> *Then the Lord added, "Listen to what the unrighteous judge says. Won't God grant his chosen people justice when they cry out to him day and night? Is he slow to help them? I tell you, he will give them justice quickly. But when the Son of Man comes, will he find faith on earth?"* (Luke 18:1–8, ISV)

When the presbytery persistently seeks the Lord in a crisis, even the demons that stood in Daniel's way will obey the righteous prayer. Likewise, the more that the presbytery and the victim of sickness sees God in an action answering the prayer of faith, the more their mountain of trust in the Lord will increase. In this case, faithlessness is the only obstacle between righteous prayer and the presbytery.

## SICKNESS REVEALS GOD AS THE GREAT HEALER

One of the main aspects of Jesus's earthly ministry was taking authority over pain, infirmity, and all manner of sickness. Without disease and ill health, we wouldn't know the Lord's healing power and control. In short, we would know him as God the Healer, Jehovah Rapha. This godly credential of our Lord has not changed; it has only been transferred and conferred to the presbytery.

## SICKNESS HELPS US MAINTAIN OUR INNER INTEGRITY

Job maintained his integrity amidst affliction. The Bible describes his goodness:

> *The Lord said to Satan, "Have you considered My servant Job? For there is no one like him on the earth, a blameless and upright man fearing God and turning away from evil. And he still holds firm to his integrity, although you incited Me against him to ruin him without cause."* (Job 2:3, NASB)

Even when his wife tried to encourage him to disown God's faithfulness and their incredible blessings from God, Job would not go down that road. Instead he maintained his integrity to his dear wife and closest associates, demonstrating his steadfast faith.

> *Then his wife said to him, "Do you still hold firm your integrity? Curse God and die!" But he said to her, "You are speaking as one of the foolish women speaks. Shall we actually accept good from God but not accept adversity?" Despite all this, Job did not sin with his lips.* (Job 2:9–10, NASB)

In the same spirit, he rejected the ungrateful mindset of his associates.

> *Far be it from me that I should declare you right; until I die, I will not give up my integrity. I have kept hold of my righteousness and will not let it go. My heart does not rebuke any of my days.* (Job 27:5–6, NASB)

When faithful elders believe that the greatness of God is broader than the earth and more comprehensive than the sea (Job 11:9), there will be nothing to stop them from standing in the presence of God until healing takes place.

Illness intensifies the maintenance of our integrity and the praise of God's faithfulness in bestowing his abundant blessings.

## SICKNESS MAKES US MORE ADAPTABLE

Adaptability is a state of mind wherein believers declare that they can do all things through Christ who strengthens them. God's peace and strength keep a believer through every life challenge (John 14:17, Philippians 4:13). Adapting to changing circumstances helps a crisis member derive peace and power from the inside-out during the crisis.

## IV. WHY DO PEOPLE GET SICK?

Why do people get sick? Our response to this question is more theological than medical or psychological. In this section, we will discuss some contributing factors.

## THE EFFECT OF ORIGINAL SIN

Generally, the human system is cursed, weak, and susceptible to attack. As we read in Genesis 3:17–19,

> *And unto Adam he said, Because thou hast hearkened unto the voice of thy wife, and hast eaten of the tree, of which I commanded thee,*

> *saying, Thou shalt not eat of it: cursed is the ground for thy sake; in sorrow shalt thou eat of it all the days of thy life; thorns also and thistles shall it bring forth to thee; and thou shalt eat the herb of the field; in the sweat of thy face shalt thou eat bread, till thou return unto the ground; for out of it wast thou taken: for dust thou art, and unto dust shalt thou return.* (KJV)

This passage reveals two types of curses: the curse of the human system and the curse of the human environment.

## CORRUPTION OF THE HUMAN SYSTEM

In discussing the effect of sin on the human system, we need to ask several important questions.

Why did Christ have to become human to provide his blood as a restitution for sin? How do Christians get purification from the blood of Christ? What does the blood of Jesus Christ purify in a sinner? What is the extent of the cleansing of sin? Why does modern scientific medicine depend so much on laboratory tests of blood, urine, saliva, stool, skin, and other body fluids to look for disease?

Disease, sickness, and pain exist in our bodily fluids, and we have the same fluids which have been passed down to us from our first human parents. Even evolutionists agree that humans don't carry the same types of bodily fluids as animals. Therefore, the idea of there being a distinction between higher and lower animals is not biblical. God did not describe humans as animals created in his image and likeness. Animals such as chimpanzees, gorillas, baboons, and dogs are not made in the image and likeness of God; they were created for the benefit of humanity (Genesis 1:24–30).

## THE ROLE OF BLOOD IN THE CORRUPTION AND HEALING OF THE HUMAN SYSTEM

It is revealed in Scripture that God is Spirit and Christ is God. Christ was with God the Father from the beginning of all creation.

> *For in him all things were created: things in heaven and on earth, visible and invisible, whether thrones or powers or rulers or authorities; all things have been created through him and for him. He is before all things, and in him all things hold together.* (Colossians 1:16–17, NIV)

He did not have a body. In fact, Christ never had blood before becoming a man. Blood is the source of a living and active soul. God's breath creates a living soul.

So Christ took on a human nature and lived in this sinful and broken world. He ate, slept, felt pain, and got tired—however, he never sinned or acted unrighteously. Why? Because there was no seed of sin running through his human veins. Disease, sickness, and death did not occur to him. The blood in his system did not come from the will of man, and therefore it had no contamination or defilement.

Man's blood has the seed of sin and deceit. Whether man understands that the problem of human affliction is connected to blood, the blood of Jesus Christ is powerful to provide mortal healing. This is possible because Christ's uncontaminated blood can clean and purify contaminated human blood.

## SEPARATION BETWEEN GOD AND MAN

Mankind's sinful behavior not only caused enmity between God and man; it also caused a separation between man and his fellow creatures. After the fall, man became overwhelmed with fear. And hostility and fear have ruled ever since. Fear controls every man's actions and reactions, inside and out.

Fear can positively or negatively affect a believer's life. It is the seat of many problems because man's knowledge is limited. For example, man is terrified of the unknown. What about the uncertainty about poverty, the loss of a relationship or job, or the death of loved one? What about moral indiscipline, relational indecency, social embarrassment ill health, or unexpected death? All of these trigger fear and anxiety.

Such uncertainties lead to unanswered questions and fear. Fear is a pre-existing condition in us. When Adam and Eve discovered the loss of their righteous relationship with God, fear overtook them. They became emotionally sick, spiritually inadequate, and physically ashamed. This loss of connection has impacted humanity ever since, causing hatred, bitterness, and selfishness. The broken relationship with God has destroyed our physical, mental, and spiritual systems. The result is human affliction.

## SIN CAUSES HUMAN AFFLICTION

Therefore, sin and sickness are the fruit of the same tree. In other words, what you sow is what you reap.

The Bible teaches the interconnection of sin and sickness. Sin is at the very core of human genetics. It isn't something we picked up on the street; we inherited it from our parents. It is part of human existence. It is who we are. As Psalm 51:5 tells us, *"Surely I was sinful at birth, sinful from the time my mother conceived me"* (NIV).

In both the Old and New Testaments, the product of sin is sickness, pain, and death. In many instances, God the Father and God the Son made a statement about sin and sickness. Christ's instructions to those who came to him for physical healing also left with spiritual healing. The records given by Mark and John attest to this truth.

> *Some men came, bringing to him a paralyzed man, carried by four of them. Since they could not get him to Jesus because of the crowd, they made an opening in the roof above Jesus by digging through it and then lowered the mat the man was lying on. When Jesus saw their faith, he said to the paralyzed man, "Son, your sins are forgiven."* (Mark 2:3–5, NIV)

We find a similar scenario in the gospel of John:

> *Then Jesus said to him, "Get up! Pick up your mat and walk." At once the man was cured; he picked up his mat and walked…*
>
> *Later Jesus found him at the temple and said to him, "See, you are well again. Stop sinning or something worse may happen to you."* (John 5:8–9, 14, NIV)

Many other scriptures reveal that sickness directly affects the sin committed by individual believers. James was speaking from this angle when he declared, *"Therefore, confess your sins to one another [your false steps, your offenses], and pray for one another, that you may be healed and restored"* (James 5:16, AMP). This passage portrays our apparent need to diagnose afflictions and provide clear direction for the presbytery crisis prayer.

## GOD ALLOWS SICKNESS AS A CORRECTIVE MEASURE

Satan inflicts people with disease and sickness, locking them up as prisoners of illness: *"So ought not this woman, being a daughter of Abraham, whom Satan has bound—think of it—for eighteen years, be loosed from this bond on the Sabbath?"* (Luke 13:16, NKJV)

Earlier, in Exodus, God said,

> *If you diligently heed the voice of the Lord your God and do what is right in His sight, give ear to His commandments and keep all His statutes, I will put none of the diseases on you which I have brought on the Egyptians. For I am the Lord who heals you.* (Exodus 15:26, NKJV)

God will heal his children through his abundant grace, and Christ's grace makes healing even more accessible in the church age.

## AN UNWORTHY ATTITUDE TOWARDS THE LORD'S SUPPER

Besides the original sin that affects all of society, sin and sickness in the lives of believers has a lot to do with our obedience and respect for the blood of Jesus and his broken body, commemorating the Lord's Supper. Paul wrote:

> *Everyone ought to examine themselves before they eat of the bread and drink from the cup. For those who eat and drink without discerning the body of Christ eat and drink judgment on themselves. That is why many among you are weak and sick, and a number of you have fallen asleep.* (1 Corinthians 11:28–30, NIV)

When someone participates unworthily at the Lord's Table, there can be damning consequences. It's a flagrant abuse of the Lord's body and blood and can attract physical and spiritual illness

Unworthy participation involves guilt, a violation of law—in this case, a violation of the body and blood of the Lord.

Eating the body and drinking the blood of Christ signifies communion with a sinless God. The result of participating in this practice in an unworthy manner is death. Pay attention again to the words of 1 Corinthians 11:30: *"That is why many among you are weak and sick, and a number of you have fallen asleep"* (NIV).

## THE PRESSURE OF LIFESTYLE

We live in a world with all kinds of pressure being exerted on us from the outside (2 Peter 1:2–4). It is a materialistic world, and the stress of materialism can lead us into lust and the desire to acquire more and more. It manifests in our lives as greed and gluttony.

Consider the story of a little fish in the deep ocean. The fish has enough pressure within itself to withstand the external pressure. The power and strength which is inside is stronger than the power and strength which is outside.

This same truth applies to the PCPM. When the presbytery prays over a crisis member, God creates more internal pressure in the form of peace, comfort, and encouragement to overcome the external pressure of anxiety, illness, pain, and sorrow.

Poor mental health management can cause sickness, especially stress, anxiety, and depression. Uncontrolled negative emotions and worry can result in poor mental health.

The feelings we experience strongly impact how we function in a social setting. When our negative emotions are more substantial than our positive emotions, they affect our access to God's righteousness and impair our spiritual function.

Poor eating habits also can lead to eating disorders. Such a condition results from how an individual thinks about food. As believers, an eating disorder could impact what we eat in a body that is indwelled by the Holy Spirit. It may involve the consumption of alcohol and the abuse of drugs.

Sometimes believers engage in unhealthy eating to cope with something deeper within them, such as low self-esteem or the stress of maintain their relationships, covering marital abuse, or suppressing their inner struggles.

An eating disorder is a severe illness that can be life-threatening. It is accompanied mainly by depression and anxiety. For example, sufferers of anorexia nervosa may also be bulimic. They may binge and then purge to minimize the amount of calories they absorb.[290]

Eating disorders defy classification solely as mental illnesses, however, as they also involve considerable physiological impairment and are associated with wide-ranging medical complications that can affect every major organ in the body. In addition, many people with eating disorders also present with depression, anxiety, personality disorders, or substance abuse problems.[291]

When an eating disorder becomes an addiction, it qualifies as an affliction. The victim of such a condition needs the grace of God, presbytery crisis prayer, and sometimes therapeutic intervention for healing to occur.

A believer in this situation has got to reach out for attention. The woman with the issue of blood for twelve years in Mark 5:34 had to reach out and touch Jesus Christ. Bartimaeus, the blind beggar in Mark 10:47, had to cry out to help for his healing to happen.

God has given local church elders the mandate, as well as the authority and power, to execute divine intervention. No believer should live with affliction in silence.

## A NEGATIVE ATTITUDE TOWARDS RIGHTEOUSNESS

Having a negative attitude toward godly righteousness creates bitterness and pain. The apostle Paul listed bitterness alongside other negative attitudes that can lead to emotional sickness.

> *Let all bitterness and wrath and anger and clamor [perpetual animosity, resentment, strife, fault-finding] and slander be put away from you, along with every kind of malice [all spitefulness, verbal abuse, malevolence]. Be kind and helpful to one another, tender-hearted*

---

290. Richard J. Gerrig and Philip G. Zimbardo, *Psychology and Life, Sixteenth Edition* (Boston, MA: Allyn and Bacon, 2002).

291. "What Is an Eating Disorder?" *National Eating Disorders Collaboration*. Date of access: May 9, 2023 (https://nedc.com.au/eating-disorders/eating-disorders-explained/whats-an-eating-disorder).

[compassionate, understanding], forgiving one another [readily and freely], just as God in Christ also forgave you.* (Ephesians 4:31–32, AMP)

Bitterness is a result of acting wrongly about things that happen to you. These are negative thoughts you hold that cause you to blame God or others for your misfortune, failure, and disobedience. Acts of ill will arise from angry thoughts.

Three different sets of people in the Old Testament reacted differently to their grief and loss: Naomi and Ruth, Job and his wife, and Saul and David.

**Naomi and Ruth.** Naomi became bitter about losing her husband, two sons, and property. She expressed her bitterness this way: *"Don't call me Naomi… Call me Mara, because the Almighty has made my life very bitter"* (Ruth 1:20, NIV). Note that the name Naomi means "pleasant," whereas Mara means "bitter."

**Job and his wife.** Similarly, Job's wife became very bitter about their family's loss of children, wealth, and her husband's terrible sickness. She also expressed her bitterness: *"Are you still maintaining your integrity? Curse God and die!"* (Job 2:9, NIV)

**Saul and David.** As per King Saul and his relationship with David, we read,

> *As they danced, they sang: "Saul has slain his thousands, and David his tens of thousands."*
> *Saul was very angry; this refrain displeased him greatly. "They have credited David with tens of thousands," he thought, "but me with only thousands. What more can he get but the kingdom?"* (1 Samuel 18:7–8, NIV)

Bitterness is a sickness unto itself. It has been noted that bitterness does more damage to the one who is bitter than to the other person. The noted pastor C.H. Spurgeon once wrote, "Sin is the gall of bitterness; a drop of it would turn an ocean of pleasure into wormwood."[292]

Paul wrote, *"See to it that no one falls short of the grace of God and that no bitter root grows up to cause trouble and defile many"* (Hebrews 12:15). So having a negative attitude towards righteousness causes not only bitterness but also emotional and spiritual illness.

---

292. Charles Haddon Spurgeon, "Healing and Pardon," *Spurgeon.org*. June 20, 1886 (https://www.spurgeon.org/resource-library/sermons/healing-and-pardon/#flipbook).

## PRESERVING THE SANCTITY OF THE BODY

The name of Jesus Christ signifies his nature to make the imperfect perfect, to make a sick body health and whole. The body needs to be protected. For example, if you have unprotected sex, you will contract a sexual disease; if you engage in drugs and intoxicating wine, you will develop addiction. King Solomon asked:

> *Who has woe? Who has sorrow? Who has strife? Who has complaints? Who has needless bruises? Who has bloodshot eyes? Those who linger over wine, who go to sample bowls of mixed wine. Do not gaze at wine when it is red, when it sparkles in the cup, when it goes down smoothly! In the end it bites like a snake and poisons like a viper. Your eyes will see strange sights, and your mind will imagine confusing things. You will be like one sleeping on the high seas, lying on top of the rigging. "They hit me," you will say, "but I'm not hurt! They beat me, but I don't feel it! When will I wake up so I can find another drink?"* (Proverbs 23:29–30, 35, NIV)

Therefore, keeping oneself pure from drunkenness is a preventive medicine.

## WORRIES ABOUT THE ISSUES OF LIFE

The parable of the sower, especially the seeds that fell among the thorn bushes, teaches about the danger of worry (Matthew 13:5, 22). Worry is a major factor leading stress, anxiety, and depression, and the state of depression is characterized by deep sadness, emptiness, and restlessness. Worry makes us ill because it attacks and weakens our immune systems.[293]

Henry Wright writes that all autoimmune diseases have a possible spiritual root of self-hatred, self-bitterness, and guilt.[294] Worrying about life issues could lead the soul into conflict, deep sorrow, mental and physical sickness, and even death (James 4:1).

## V. HOW TO RESPOND TO ILLNESS

People respond to illness in a variety of ways. We have discussed elsewhere in this book that different practitioners view a crisis through the lens of their own professions. Theologians and ministers should respond to illness through the lenses of God's word.

---

293. "Causes of Sickness," *Miracle Valley*. Date of access: May 9, 2023 (https://miraclevalley.net/subpage15.html).

294. "Spiritual Roots of Disease," *Be in Health*. Date of access: December 20, 2022 (https://www.beinhealth.com/spiritual-roots-of-disease). Quoting Dr. Henry Wright.

The following statements of truth should be taken into consideration in a believer's response to ill health.

LIFE IS MORE VALUABLE THAN ILLNESS
Your illness should not steal your value. Do not allow family members, friends, or society to devalue you because of disease. You are valuable to God even amidst affliction.

A renowned British philosopher and scholar, Havi H. Carel, has been teaching about the correlation between subjective well-being and objective health. She underscores that one can have a high degree if well-being even in an ill health situation. Subjective well-being is about how people feel about their health and function in daily life; the feelings are emotional and can be expressed at different levels by different people with the same ill health condition depending on their awareness, the severity, informational data, and personal experience. On the other hand, objective health is based on medical testing and professional observation.

Carel emphasizes that ill health should not determine one's well-being. In other words, sickness should not take away one's happiness, joy, or peace. It is possible to have a high quality of life amidst your affliction.

Because there is no correlation between emotional well-being and objective health, somebody can be healthy yet unhappy, and another person sick yet happy. Carel believes that an individual can live life to the fullest without physical wellness, and vice versa.[295]

Although her position is purely philosophical, it echoes the biblical teaching on how a believer should respond to objective health. Our strength in health and sickness is centered on Christ through the ministry of the Holy Spirit. Jesus lived with godly emotional strength amid objective health.

Hezekiah rejected the certificate of death presented to him by the prophet of God, and he returned to God, the author and controller of disease, sickness, and health. He prayed and asked God for more years because of what he had done and what he would accomplish for God's glory.

What does Hezekiah's scenario teach believers in crisis about being in the presence of God amidst ill health? In weakness, a believer should be able to say, "The Lord is my strength, and I can do all things through Christ who strengthens me! God is working all things to my benefit. His plans for my situation are good and prosperous."

---

295. Havi H. Carel, "Illness and Authenticity," *Art and Authenticity* (City, State: Australian Scholarly Publishing, 2010), 197–204.

## THE PRESBYTERY CRISIS MINISTRY

### MAINTAIN A POSITIVE ATTITUDE AND ASK GOD FOR THE GIFT OF SATISFACTION IN AFFLICTION

Believers are encouraged to give thanks for everything. Maintaining a positive attitude leads us to praise, offer thanksgiving, look up, strengthen our faith, see healing on the way, and appreciate God as he operates in his faithfulness.

All forms of treatment put a patient into the care of others; a patient's health fails when their caregiver fails. Alternatively, when a patient fails to follow the treatment regimen, their treatment can either fail or have reduced effectiveness.

In the presbytery, the Healer does not fail. The Lord does not sleep, nor does he act unfaithfully. He is unlimited in understanding our conditions and his authority and power can heal every disease. Therefore, we should ask God for the gift of satisfaction amidst our own affliction and completely trust him for a change in our situation.

### GLORIFY GOD IN YOUR BROKEN SITUATION

Since every plan of God for his child is good, God is awake at all times to watch over his word to ensure that it comes to pass. As the Lord said, *"You have seen well, for I am [actively] watching over My word to fulfill it"* (Jeremiah 1:12, AMP). God is wakeful and ready to perform his word on behalf of his child.

The role of God is to ensure the performance of his word; the crisis member's role is to be ready to glorify God in a broken situation. Psalm 146:2 states, *"I will praise the Lord as long as I live; I will sing praises to my God while I have my being"* (ESV).

As we close this chapter, let's look at a few quotes about living life to the fullest. May they encourage you as you walk through your affliction.

> Dance. Smile. Giggle. Marvel. TRUST. HOPE. LOVE. WISH. BELIEVE. Most of all, enjoy every moment of the journey, and appreciate where you are at this moment instead of always focusing on how far you have to go.[296]
> —Mandy Hale

> Life is a bowl of cherries. Some cherries are rotten while others are good; its your job to throw out the rotten ones and forget about them while you enjoy eating the ones that are good! There are two kinds of people: those who choose to throw out the good cherries and wallow

---

296. Mandy Hale, "Dance. Smile. Giggle..." *Goodreads*. Date of access: June 2, 2023 (https://www.goodreads.com/work/quotes/22371540-the-single-woman-life-love-and-a-dash-of-sass-single-lady).

in all the rotten ones, and those who choose to throw out all the rotten ones and savor all the good ones.[297]
—C. JoyBell C

Keep your mind open. The meaning of things lies in how people perceive them. Therefore, the same thing could mean different meanings to the same people at different times.[298]
—Roy T. Bennett

---

297. C. JoyBell C., "Life is a bowl of cherries…" *What Should I Read Next?* Date of access: June 2, 2023 (https://www.whatshouldireadnext.com/quotes/c-joybell-c-life-is-a-bowl-of).

298. Roy T. Bennett, "Keep your mind open…" *Goodreads*. Date of access: June 2, 2023 (https://www.goodreads.com/quotes/tag/keep-your-mind-open).

CHAPTER SEVENTEEN
# The Name of Jesus in the PCPM's Efficacy

Prayer lays hold of God's plan and becomes the link between His will and its accomplishment on earth. Amazing things happen, and we are given the privilege of being the channels of the Holy Spirit's prayer.[299]
—Elisabeth Elliot

Prayer is the exercise of drawing on the grace of God.[300]
—Oswald Chambers

Leaders must be released from the idea that they must be great prayer warriors before they can begin to call others to prayer.[301]
—David Bryant

## I. FRESH REVELATION IN UNDERSTANDING CHRIST'S GREATNESS

THEOLOGIAN A.W. TOZER once said,

> If Bible Christianity is to survive the present world upheaval, we shall need to have a fresh revelation of the greatness and beauty of Jesus… He alone can raise our cold hearts to rapture and restore the art of true worship.[302]

This quote ushers in discussion on the PCPM. Prayer is one of the major themes in Christian doctrine and it means different things to different people. It is just an intellectual exercise to some, but to others it means engaging in worship and declaring one's trust in God for expectations beyond the ordinary.

---

299. David Jeremiah, "Maybe We Should Take a Moment to Pray," *David Jeremiah*. Date of access: May 20, 2023 (https://www.davidjeremiah.ca/magazine/article/maybe-we-should-take-a-moment-to-pray-283). Quoting Elisabeth Elliot.

300. Oswald Chambers, "Drawing on the Grace of God—Now," *Utmost*. Date of access: May 20, 2023 (https://utmost.org/drawing-on-the-grace-of-god%E2%80%94-now).

301. David Bryant, "Leaders must be released…" *AZ Quotes*. Date of access: May 24, 2023 (https://www.azquotes.com/quote/55403).

302. A.W. Tozer, "If Bible Christianity is to survive…" *AZ Quotes*. Date of access: January 1, 2022 (https://www.azquotes.com/quote/550385).

The focus in this chapter is to briefly describe what prayer is in the light of our dependency on God as it relates the PCPM.

The reader needs to understand that prayer has a lot to do with reminding himself of whom God is and reminding God of who he is to Him – Father-child, Creator-creature, and Holy God-sinner relationships. The local church needs to address any specific sin that would hinder the recapitulation of the promises of God. The phrase "reminding God" does not suggest that God can forget, neglect, ignore, or not know what his children need. It does, however, put us in a position of revisiting the promises of God and making them alive and effective in our present time of need.

Prayer is what occurs when believers ascend to the mountain of God's promises and take him at his word. Each time believers pray, they remind themselves about God's nature, acts, power, authority, mercy, favor, grace, and promises to the church. Prayer reveals our dependency on what he has said he will do in his word.

Prayer is all about God and his relationship to his creation. It puts him in control of the seen and the unseen and makes known his sovereignty over all so that know fully well that he is *"one God and Father of all, who is over all and through all and in all"* (Ephesians 4:6, NIV).

It is incredible to read about how King David prayerfully worshipped him in his splendor: *"For the Lord is the great God, the great King above all gods"* (Psalm 95:3, NIV). Likewise, God said to the apostle Paul that Christ is

> *...far above all rule and authority, power and dominion, and every name that is invoked, not only in the present age but also in the one to come. And God placed all things under his feet and appointed him to be head over everything for the church...* (Ephesian 1:21–22, NIV)

I believe that the phrase *"all things"* here refers to God's unimaginable power and mercy to attend to his children's prayers, even though we stand before him as filthy rags. His response to all the prayers we present to him are made possible through the righteousness of his begotten Son, the Lord Jesus Christ.

Therefore, the purpose of presbytery crisis prayer is not to announce something, but rather to declare that God is the supreme Ruler over all, including sickness. The PCPM's purpose is to express our dependency on God by inviting him to control every displeasing situation. It reminds God of his promises and affirm that he honors his word more than his name.

Reminding God of his promises makes sense because Scripture affirms this to the apostle Matthew:

*When you pray, don't babble on and on as the Gentiles do. They think their prayers are answered merely by repeating their words again and again. Don't be like them, for your Father knows exactly what you need even before you ask him!* (Matthew 6:7–8, NLT)

The presbytery should pray with their understanding of the mind and the realm of the spirit. Their prayer should be spoken with knowledge and specific in focus.

## II. SICKNESS

What is sickness? We discussed the definition of sickness in the previous chapter, but sickness is the direct opposite of health. It's also not necessarily physical.

Author Richard K. Thomas sees sickness as a public or social component of ill health. He understands that illness is transformed into a sickness when the sick condition becomes publicly known through an announcement by the affected person, observation by significant others, or professional diagnosis.[303]

Thus, while illness is primarily a biological state, sickness is also a social state. It has implications for one's social roles and interpersonal interactions.

An illness or sickness is related to wickedness, depravity, immorality, unpleasantness, disagreeableness, and hurtfulness.[304] So when James talks about sickness, he is referring to several things, ranging from the physical and social to the mental and spiritual.

**The physiological.** It can be difficult to define a disease. Mervyn Susser writes that illness does not define a specific pathology. Instead he describes illness in a subjective sense of feeling unwell or experiencing unhealthiness, such as discomfort, tiredness, or general malaise. While disease focuses on the pathological processes that could or could not lead to symptoms, he says that sickness refers to dread or any mental illness or stigma that affects a patient.[305]

**The psychological.** This aspect of dealing with sickness has very little to do with spiritual health. Instead its main issue concerns mental and moral sickness. It also deals with emotional and mental illness.

Before the emergence of health psychology in the twenty-first century, disease was viewed primarily in the light of biology and associated with medicine. Common conditions included asthma, headaches, ulcers, colds, and constipation. Research proves that

---

303. Richard K. Thomas, *Society and Health: Sociology for Health Professionals* (New York, NY: Springer US, 2003), 23.

304. Boyd, "Disease, Illness, Sickness, Health, Healing and Wholeness."

305. Mervyn Susser, *Causal Thinking in the Health Sciences: Concepts and Strategies of Epidemiologies* (New York, NY: Oxford University Press, 1973).

the principal killer diseases circa 1900 were contagious diseases like polio, smallpox, tuberculosis, typhoid fever, malaria, influenza, and pneumonia.[306]

Today, these are no longer threatening issues, especially in the developed world. People in developed nations are most likely to die of psychological illnesses rather than medical ones.

Those who live in developed nations believe that the struggles against such sicknesses are no longer a risk. Heart disease, cancer, strokes, and even HIV/AIDS are preventable.[307] The American Psychiatric Association has identified and classified more than two hundred mental disorders that cause illness.[308] Moreso, it is believed that many sicknesses caused by mental disorders may not respond to medical treatment but could respond to presbytery prayer.

**The spiritual.** From a biblical perspective, sickness does not necessarily fit a scientific definition. It is sometimes related to abstract, spiritual experiences. That is why medical and scientific provisions don't always address spiritual conditions, which don't respond to medication or psychotherapy.

On the other hand, presbytery prayer is capable of treating spiritual disease. Moreover, it solves any kind of sickness.

The limits of medical and psychological treatments are the result of human fallibility. A disease's spiritual pathology may not be identifiable by science. In fact, that which is impossible to do scientifically, medically, or psychologically is very possible through presbytery prayer.

Both the Old and New Testaments emphasize the truth of the power of God in accomplishing the impossible. God healed Sarah's barrenness through natural means (Genesis 21:6–7). God healed Hezekiah through the fervent prayer of faith and added fifteen years to his life (2 Kings 20:1–6). Daniel acknowledged that God could do the impossible: *"He reveals deep and hidden things; He knows what is in darkness, and light dwells with Him"* (Daniel 2:22, NKJV).

That is why presbytery prayers can handle spiritual warfare and physical disorders. The prayer of a faithful man brings the impossible to God and changes our destiny (2 Kings 19:1–7).

The Bible says that our God specializes in accomplishing the impossible. Jesus says, *"With man this is impossible, but with God all things are possible"* (Matthew 19:26,

---

306. Saul M. Kassin, "Internalized False Confessions," *The Handbook of Eyewitness Psychology, Volume One: Memory for Events* (Mahwah, NJ: Lawrence Erlbaum Associates, 2007), 175–192.

307. Ibid.

308. Gerrig and Zimbardo, *Psychology and Life, Sixteenth Edition*.

NIV). Matthew suggests that the prayer of the righteous presbytery is powerful. The intercessory work of Christ Jesus is supreme over all sickness.

King David reiterates the testimony that there is beauty and confidence in the intercessory work of Christ. Only Christ knows how we have been created, and only he knows the power behind our formation. In Psalm 139:13–16, David speaks of God from an anthropological perspective:

> *For you created my inmost being; you knit me together in my mother's womb. I praise you because I am fearfully and wonderfully made; your works are wonderful, I know that full well. My frame was not hidden from you when I was made in the secret place, when I was woven together in the depths of the earth. Your eyes saw my unformed body; all the days ordained for me were written in your book before one of them came to be.*

The work of Christ brings us healing, laughter, happiness, joy, and freedom from our inner sorrow and pain. James was very familiar with Yahweh's teachings and miraculous works in the Old Testament, including those of Jesus Christ and the apostle Paul. Their miracles went beyond the mere healing of a fever. People with blindness received their sight. Disabled persons walked. Lepers were cleansed. Demons were driven out. The dead rose!

So when James proclaimed the PCPM, he knew what the name of Jesus Christ of Nazareth had done and could do. He knew that nothing on the earth could stand against the name of Christ Jesus (Philippians 2:9). Jesus himself reiterated that his Father would answer any prayer offered in Christ's name (John 16:23–24).

## III. THE ROLE OF DIAGNOSIS

Diagnosis deals with finding or assessing the cause of a sickness—physiological, psychological, or spiritual. It is critical to diagnose a sickness before seeking a solution through prayer, for ascertaining the problem will guide presbytery prayer.

The Bible tells us that certain behaviors can cause sickness. Author A.A. Allen states,

> It is a well-known fact that, when a good physician starts to work on a case, the first step is to find out, if possible, the cause of the sickness. Then he works to eliminate that cause. So it is when we come to God for healing. We find that He deals not so much with symptoms as with causes. It is important to know the causes of sickness. The pain of an attack of acute appendicitis may be eased by administering narcotics.

But, while the person is unaware of pain, the appendix may burst and death may result. Carelessness about finding the cause of suffering has resulted in great damage and even the loss of lives. Many people have lost confidence in God's promises to heal, failing to understand that there are conditions that must be met before healing can occur. They fail to remove the cause of sickness and thus fail to meet God's conditions for healing.[309]

John understands how we should get healing from both sins of commission and sins of omission.

> *If we claim to be without sin, we deceive ourselves and the truth is not in us. If we confess our sins, he is faithful and just and will forgive us our sins and purify us from all unrighteousness.* (1 John1:8–9, NIV)

The presbytery needs to diagnose the sickness and get the victim to confesses of their sin. God will heal the sickness, as well as those that are hidden, through the righteous prayer of the presbytery. That was the perspective James had in mind.

The presbytery must know that it is not only medical and psychological professionals that diagnose their clients' cases to ascertain the pathology of a sickness, as well as it extent and effects. The presbytery too should diagnose the case of each church member who calls for a prayer of intervention. Such diagnoses will help them understand the sickness.

For example, some mental health sicknesses cannot be treated satisfactorily with the scientific method but rather through a psychotherapeutic approach. These same sicknesses can be identified and treated through biblical counselling and the fervent prayer of the presbytery. James says, *"Make this your common practice: Confess your sins to each other and pray for each other so that you can live together whole and healed"* (James 5:16, MSG).

The presbytery must engage in soul-searching to ensure that their righteousness is not at stake, for without righteousness their prayers will not be effective. The Bible teaches that if believers have iniquity in their hearts, the Lord will not hear their prayers (Luke 13:27, 16:8, Acts 8:23, 1 Corinthians 13:16, James 3:6).

God does not accommodate unrighteous living, which is the state of not having right standing with God, according to the standard of his holiness, or with man, according to what man knows to be right by his conscience.

---

309. A.A. Allen, *God's Guarantee to Heal you* (San Francisco, CA: Bottom of the Hill, 2012), 9.

The crisis member must diagnose their relationship with Christ. They need to check whether any unrighteousness or sin is hindering God's perfect healing.

Therefore, the practice of assessing spiritual sickness and investigating the spiritual standing of the presbytery is not just James's idea; a similar principle is applied by Luke and the apostle Paul. It has been stated that presbytery prayer must involve praying with the mind and with the spirit. As Paul explained,

> *For if I pray in a tongue, my spirit prays, but my understanding is unfruitful. What is the conclusion then? I will pray with the spirit, and I will also pray with the understanding. I will sing with the spirit, and I will also sing with the understanding.* (1 Corinthians 14:14–15, NKJV)

## CHAPTER EIGHTEEN
# The Caller's Strength in the Faith Authenticates Healing

Christ is the Good Physician. There is no disease He cannot heal; no sin He cannot remove; no trouble He cannot help. He is the Balm of Gilead, the Great Physician who has never yet failed to heal all the spiritual maladies of every soul that has come unto Him in faith and prayer.[310]

—James H. Aughey

Fear imprisons, faith liberates; fear paralyzes, faith empowers; fear disheartens, faith encourages; fear sickens, faith heals; fear makes useless, faith makes serviceable.[311]

—Harry Emerson Fosdick

THE FAITH OF the sick member who calls for presbytery crisis prayer reveals an expectation for healing. It also reveals their desperation to put their faith into action. There will be no change, no healing, except through prayer. This kind of call reveals a deep cry for relief.

Men of high integrity, such as Job and King David, have taught us that God loves to be called upon to rescue his children when they face an affliction (Job 5:8, 33:26, Psalm 18:6, 20:1, 22:23, 27:5, 77:2, 81:7, 86:7). Calling for presbytery prayer is a sign of faith.

## IT HAS A HISTORY OF HEALING THE AFFLICTED

Several scriptural passages teach about the divine history of healing. It is clear from God's Word that God identifies his name by what he does. He expressively indicates his desire for the well-being of his children.

God has also demonstrated his healing power in the lives of afflicted people in the Old and New Testaments. In the Old Testament, he offered proof of his name as Jehovah Rapha: *"I am the Lord who heals you"* (Exodus 15:26, NKJV).

Part of God's divine character is healing. So healing is part of who God is and what he does. God's plan includes the wellness of his people.

---

310. James H. Aughey, "Christ is the Good Phyisican…" *Bible Portal*. Date of access: May 20, 2023 (https://bibleportal.com/bible-quote/christ-healing-christ-is-the-good-physician-there-is-no-disease-he-cannot-heal-no-sin-he-cannot-remove-no-trouble-he).

311. Harry Emerson Fosdick, "Fear imprisons…" *AC Quotes*. Date of access: May 24, 2023 (https://www.azquotes.com/quote/532442).

King David laid out his experience regarding the condition of calling and rescuing the acts of God:

> *"Call on me in times of trouble. I will rescue you, and you will honor me." But God says to wicked people, "How dare you quote my decrees and mouth my promises! You hate discipline. You toss my words behind you. When you see a thief, you want to make friends with him. You keep company with people who commit adultery. You let your mouth say anything evil. Your tongue plans deceit. You sit and talk against your own brother. You slander your own mother's son. When you did these things, I remained silent. That made you think I was like you. I will argue my point with you and lay it all out for you to see. Consider this, you people who forget God. Otherwise, I will tear you to pieces, and there will be no one left to rescue you. Whoever offers thanks as a sacrifice honors me. I will let everyone who continues in my way see the salvation that comes from God."* (Psalm 50:15–23, GW)

Yes, God desires that his child to call for intervention, but he equally loves for such a call to come from clean lips. You cannot default on God's holiness and character and expect a miraculous intervention in your troubled moment.

When you call the elders to the scene of your trouble to pray, it speaks volumes about your heart's desire for salvation. So check what defilement is in your lips before you call for the presbytery prayer of intervention.

## IT INDICATES FAITH IN JESUS

A sick member of the body of Christ should understand God's promise about fulfilling the desire of their heart. The afflicted person needs to realize that God is eager to bring to pass the righteous desires of a spiritual heart. He has promised that the desire of the righteous shall not be cut off (Proverbs 23:18).

The caller also needs to know the dialogue between God and the prophet Jeremiah: *"For I know the plans I have for you… plans to prosper you and not to harm you, plans to give you hope and a future"* (Jeremiah 29:11, NIV). God has put in place a righteous plan to fulfill the honest desire of those who call on him.

God's plans and purposes for his children are brimming with goodwill, optimism, and hope. His plan is one of total wellness. Some aspects of God's plan may seem challenging for the church to comprehend, but Scripture teaches that all He does is for a good purpose. Scripture reminds us that *"God causes everything to work together for the good of those who love God and are called according to his purpose for them"* (Romans 8:28, NLT). This verse gives us two reasons that God responds to our need in times of trouble: our faith in him and our love for him.

James writes of a case involving a sick man to teach us that healing is God's desire for his church. John made similar a declaration about the heartbeat of God concerning the physical well-being of his children: *"Dear friend, I pray that you may prosper in every way and be in good health physically just as you are spiritually"* (3 John 1:2, HCSB).

Emily Dotson asserts,

> Others believe God heals, but they don't know how to activate His healing power. So they do not believe God will heal them. But I would rather believe that God could not heal me, rather than think He would not heal me. As that is to doubt God's integrity, so He cannot heal that person.[312]

## IT DEFEATS WEARINESS

The act of calling defeats our physical, psychological, and spiritual weariness. A biblical example is the story about a woman with an issue of blood, which is recorded in three gospels (Matthew 9:20–22, Mark 5:25–34, Luke 8:43–48).

In Leviticus, we learn more about the Jewish perspective on women with bleeding problems:

> *When a woman has her regular flow of blood, the impurity of her monthly period will last seven days, and anyone who touches her will be unclean till evening.*
>
> *Anything she lies on during her period will be unclean, and anything she sits on will be unclean. Anyone who touches her bed will be unclean; they must wash their clothes and bathe with water, and they will be unclean till evening. Anyone who touches anything she sits on will be unclean; they must wash their clothes and bathe with water, and they will be unclean till evening.* (Leviticus 15:19–22, NIV)

This text reveals that the woman spoken of in the gospels was carrying spiritual, physical, emotional, psychological, and social sickness. This profoundly motivated her

---

312. Emily Dotson, "God Wants to Heal Your Spirit, Your Soul, and Your Body," Sid Roth. March 7, 2006 (https://sidroth.org/articles/god-wants-heal-your-spirit-your-soul-and-your-body).

to touch Jesus to be made whole. She believed that if she felt the Lord Jesus Christ, his power and authority would instantly neutralize the power of her sickness.

In Matthew 9:21, the woman's confesses the Lord's power and authority to heal her: *"If I only touch his cloak, I will be healed"* (NIV). Through her touch of faith, immediate healing was transferred to the woman. We read in Mark 5:29, *"Immediately her bleeding stopped and she felt in her body that she was freed from her suffering"* (NIV).

It's interesting to note that when the touch occurred, Jesus immediately realized that something had gone out of him: *"At once Jesus realized that power had gone out from him. He turned around in the crowd and asked, 'Who touched my clothes?'"* (Mark 5:30, NIV).

The lesson here is that the woman's unyielding faith in the control and power of Jesus Christ superseded her relentless bleeding and ushered in her healing. All the caller needs to understand is that the presbytery has been given the power and authority of Christ to relieve them of their afflictions through prayer in Jesus's name.

## IT INDICATES A DESIRE FOR EMOTIONAL WELLNESS

We have acknowledged that God is interested in his creation's physical wellness. Except for instances in Scripture where God allows sickness for his own glory, he beholds our beautiful bodies that have been made in his image and likeness. The original masterpiece of God's creation was considered good (Genesis 1:31).

We have also established that the state of absolute perfection in the world was afflicted by sin. Although God allowed disease as a penalty for man's disobedience, he has also provided a radical remedy: Jesus Christ. But this solution is not appreciated by all.

Health and wellness are among the excellent blessings God has given to man from the time of creation. Biblical writers like Moses, Solomon, and John all expressed and promoted this. The Lord told Moses of his passion for the Israelis to live and enjoy physical wellness:

> *If you listen carefully to the Lord your God and do what is right in his eyes, if you pay attention to his commands and keep all his decrees, I will not bring on you any of the diseases I brought on the Egyptians, for I am the Lord, who heals you.* (Exodus 15:26, NIV)

Our obedience to God's instruction is key here. We need to obey what he says we should do. If he instructs the sick to call the presbytery for prayer, anointing, and the laying on of hands, then we must do it. If we do, he promises that he will heal. With obedience to the instruction of the Lord, the presbytery can pray anything into effect. Yes! With God, all things are possible.

The act of obedience to God's instruction is one of the central themes in the writings of Solomon. And the result of observation is health and prosperity.

> *My son, do not forget my teaching, but keep my commands in your heart, for they will prolong your life many years and bring you peace and prosperity… My son, do not forget my teaching, but keep my commands in your heart, for they will prolong your life many years and bring you peace and prosperity.* (Proverbs 3:1–2, 8, NIV)

Disease needs to be confronted with the prayer of the presbytery. My experience teaches me that each time I am physically sick, each time my body is soar, it affects my spiritual well-being.

## IT LEADS TO PHYSICAL BREAKTHROUGH

Whenever a sick member in the body of Christ invites the church elders for prayer, it is a crystal-clear indication of a person's deep desire for a physical breakthrough over the power of sickness. Physical healing is one of the benefits of Christ's atonement, and the good news is that this atonement was completed at Calvary. Christ was wounded and the church was given the divine provision for healing. This is the healing power which frees us from the bondage of sin and sickness. Christ took the sorrow, and the church received the joy (Isaiah 53:4–5, Psalm 103:2–4).

The psalmist has encouraged us to never forget the blessings we receive when God makes us whole through placing our faith in the finished work of Christ. These benefits aren't limited to being pardoned of our iniquities and adopted as God's children; they include physical healing.

Jesus made it abundantly clear that the prophecy of Isaiah 53 provides spiritual and physical wellness. He said, *"This was to fulfill what was spoken through the prophet Isaiah: 'He took up our infirmities and bore our diseases'"* (Matthew 8:17, NIV). The church can confidently trust in the propitiator of our souls.

The blessing of our salvation is extended to us because Christ took those infirmities away and nailed them on the cross. Christ's victory there did noy only apply to the forgiveness of sin and the offer of salvation; it is a package of many blessings, including the power to be healed.

So when a believer calls for the church leadership for prayer, it showcases a deep desire to experience a physical breakthrough over the power of sickness.

## THE PRESBYTERY CRISIS MINISTRY

### IT INDICATES COMPLETE TRUST IN GOD'S PROMISES

The issue of trust rests in the hope of what God has said he would do for his church. Any hope that focuses on the unchanging promises of God is a hope that does not disappoint, because the God's love for the church is more robust and significant than the hope found in life challenges (Romans 5:5).

Calling for the presbytery's prayer means challenging God to action. It tells God, "I have done my part by acting in response to what you said you would do." God's promises are his Word, and he has said that he honors his word more than his name.

Calling for payer also demonstrates trust in our church leaders as God's representatives. It is an act of total dependency on God and his chosen servants. A caller knows that God's living authority is found in the board of elders, who have been vested with the authority to act on behalf of God.

### IT AFFIRMS THE CALLER'S FAITH

Messages of salvation and deliverance can emerge from the prayer of faith of the righteous presbytery. James 5 is translated in numerous ways:

> *Is anyone among you suffering? Let him pray. Is anyone cheerful? Let him sing psalms. Is anyone among you sick? Let him call for the elders of the church, and let them pray over him, anointing him with oil in the name of the Lord. And the prayer of faith will save the sick, and the Lord will raise him up. And if he has committed sins, he will be forgiven. Confess your trespasses to one another, and pray for one another, that you may be healed. The effective, fervent prayer of a righteous man avails much. Elijah was a man with a nature like ours, and he prayed earnestly that it would not rain; and it did not rain on the land for three years and six months. And he prayed again, and the heaven gave rain, and the earth produced its fruit.* (James 5:13–18, NKJV)

> *Is anyone among you suffering? He must pray. Is anyone joyful? He is to sing praises [to God]. Is anyone among you sick? He must call for the elders (spiritual leaders) of the church and they are to pray over him, anointing him with oil in the name of the Lord; and the prayer of faith will restore the one who is sick, and the Lord will raise him up; and if he has committed sins, he will be forgiven. Therefore, confess your sins to one another [your false steps, your offenses], and pray for one another, that you may be healed and restored.*

*The heartfelt and persistent prayer of a righteous man (believer) can accomplish much [when put into action and made effective by God—it is dynamic and can have tremendous power]. Elijah was a man with a nature like ours [with the same physical, mental, and spiritual limitations and shortcomings], and he prayed intensely for it not to rain, and it did not rain on the earth for three years and six months. Then he prayed again, and the sky gave rain and the land produced its crops [as usual].* (James 5:13–18, AMP)

*Is anyone among you in trouble? Let them pray. Is anyone happy? Let them sing songs of praise. Is anyone among you sick? Let them call the elders of the church to pray over them and anoint them with oil in the name of the Lord. And the prayer offered in faith will make the sick person well; the Lord will raise them up. If they have sinned, they will be forgiven. Therefore confess your sins to each other and pray for each other so that you may be healed. The prayer of a righteous person is powerful and effective.*

*Elijah was a human being, even as we are. He prayed earnestly that it would not rain, and it did not rain on the land for three and a half years. Again he prayed, and the heavens gave rain, and the earth produced its crops.* (James 5:13–18, NIV)

*Are you hurting? Pray. Do you feel great? Sing. Are you sick? Call the church leaders together to pray and anoint you with oil in the name of the Master. Believing-prayer will heal you, and Jesus will put you on your feet. And if you've sinned, you'll be forgiven—healed inside and out.*

*Make this your common practice: Confess your sins to each other and pray for each other so that you can live together whole and healed. The prayer of a person living right with God is something powerful to be reckoned with. Elijah, for instance, human just like us, prayed hard that it wouldn't rain, and it didn't—not a drop for three and a half years. Then he prayed that it would rain, and it did. The showers came and everything started growing again.* (James 5:13–18, MSG)

The wordings is more down to earth in The Message, but all of these passages portray the physical effects of the PCPM.

These different expressions authenticate the importance of presbytery prayer. The prayer of faithful elders can move God to release his divine mercy, considering what Christ did at Calvary, and change the physical and spiritual states of members of the church. sick member of his body, the church.

The active verbs used here—to make, to save, to restore, to heal—all carry the meaning of repairing damage, bringing something back to its original state, returning what was lost. In the same context, we get phrases like "raise up," "be forgiven," and "put you on your feet," etc.

## IT RECOGNIZES GOD'S ABUNDANCE

Healing is an act of God's mercy, an extra display of a blessing we do not deserve. We aren't qualified to approach the throne of God, nor are we good enough to obtain the gift of merciful healing. The writer of Titus 3:5 says, *"Not by works of righteousness which we have done, but according to his mercy he saved us, by the washing of regeneration, and renewing of the Holy Ghost"* (KJV).

God is full of mercy, and his mercy endures from generation to generation. No wonder Psalm 103:11 acknowledges, *"For as the heaven is high above the earth, so great is his mercy toward them that fear him"* (KJV). Psalm 86:5 echoes this idea: *"For thou, Lord, art good, and ready to forgive; and plenteous in mercy unto all them that call upon thee"* (KJV).

When a crisis member calls the elders for prayer, they establish their trust in God's mercy for healing. God responds to these difficult situation based on his great mercy because he is our helper in times of need.

Jeremiah 3:12 records a powerful statement about God's mercy:

> *Go and proclaim these words toward the north, and say: "Return, backsliding Israel," says the Lord; "I will not cause My anger to fall on you. For I am merciful," says the Lord; "I will not remain angry forever."* (NKJV)

James says, *"And if he has committed sins, he will be forgiven"* (James 5:15, NKJV), because God's mercy abounds.

When God is called upon to show mercy, he responds by taking away his anger and bestowing forgiveness. Therefore, the prayer of righteous elders can transform God's anger into forgiveness through the abundance of his mercy.

Daniel 9:9 says, *"To the Lord our God belong compassion and forgiveness, because we have rebelled against Him"* (NASB). And the apostle Paul summarized God's great mercy when he wrote, *"But God, who is rich in mercy, because of His great love with which He loved us…"* (Ephesians 2:4, KJV)

## IT REPORTS THE ENEMY TO JEHOVAH RAPHA

The act of calling is a step toward denying the devil from dominating your health, for the Holy Spirit dwells in a believer's body, even during illness. However, the disease can weaken the body—the house of God—and reduce its effectiveness. And sometimes the situation can lead to the grieving of the Holy Spirit.

Job's wife was not physically involved in her husband's pain and agony. Still, after carefully observing what he was experiencing, she declared, *"Do you still hold fast your integrity? Curse God and die"* (Job 2:9, ESV). However, Job believed that the giver of good things is not dead. Why would he curse God just because he had gotten sick? He held to the fact that his Redeemer lived; he could face his crisis triumphantly, whatever the sickness brought to his life.

The act of calling for prayer is akin to reporting the enemy of good health and prosperity to God and his church. It is a redirection of a pathetic situation to the author of health and goodwill, denouncing the bringer of ill health and affliction.

Sickness shouldn't make you lose your integrity while your Redeemer lives. When you hold on to your integrity and focus on the faithfulness of God, he will restore your losses in the fullness of time. He did it for Job and he will do it to you.

## IT DEMONSTRATES OBEDIENCE TO GOD'S WORD AND FREEDOM FROM BONDAGE

When a suffering church member calls for the prayer of the clergy, it shows that he is obedient to God and his word. This encourages us to pray with supplication and make our burdens known to God.

When a sick person calls for prayer, it is a healing step toward attaining freedom from the bondage of sin, disease, and pain. We all know that sickness can take a sick person captive. It can steal our joy and make us less effective in our lives and ministries. It can also shipwreck the faithful and move a sick person into a state of hostility.

Calling for prayer opens the door of freedom and leads on from the grip of sickness into the abundant life.

## IT RECOGNIZES THE SOVEREIGNTY OF THE HOLY SPIRIT

Ungodliness in our lives increases the chance of weakness and disease developing in us. So when a sick calls for presbytery prayer, it shows their recognition of the sovereignty of the Holy Spirit to take control of the situation and give them strength.

The Spirit of the Lord quickens, strengthens, and increases the power of the weak. Any healing starts with the faith of the sick through their persistent hope in God's ability to act unusually under challenging circumstances.

> *He gives strength to the weary and increases the power of the weak. Even youths grow tired and weary, and young men stumble and fall; but those who hope in the Lord will renew their strength. They will soar on wings like eagles; they will run and not grow weary, they will walk and not be faint.* (Isaiah 40:29–31, NIV)

In his commentary, Matthew Henry explains that a person's healing is affected by the prayer of faith of the righteous presbytery. Therefore, when an honest person presents an effectual and fervent prayer, wrought in his heart by the power of the Holy Spirit, it avails much. A righteous person is a true believer, justified in Christ, who walks in grace before God in holy obedience.[313]

I firmly believe in the power and efficacy of pastoral ministry. However, their prayer—accompanied by faith, oil, and the laying on of hands—must also be spoken in the name of Christ.

When a crisis member calls the elders for prayer, it fulfills God's instruction to James. Note that sickness, in James 5, is not limited to physical symptoms; it includes all forms of ill health. But it is important to note that physical sickness could be a symptom of a broken relationship between the crisis member, the local church, and God. Thus, we arrive at James's conclusion that intentional pastoral prayer can bring about an effective result.

It seems that intentional pastoral prayer of intervention makes God temper his justice with mercy. This is a use of legal language. In the Canadian judicial system, whenever an individual confronts a traffic offence, the case is referred to a judge. The first question a judge will ask, after reviewing the offence, is a simple one: "Guilty or not guilty?" The individual must first admit to their guilt before offering an explanation or offering a plea for justice.

It seems fitting that effective prayer amounts to invoking God for intervention. We should always come before God with an attitude of confessing sin, seeking forgiveness before we present our petitions to him.

---

313. Matthew Henry, "Matthew Henry's Commentary, James 5," *Bible Hub*. Date of access: May 11, 2023 (https://biblehub.com/commentaries/mhc/james/5.htm).

# Conclusion

IN CONCLUDING THIS book, it is worthwhile to recap its main themes and ideas. The central point of discussion is the healing ministry that God handed over to elders of the local church. The PCPM is a continuation of Christ's third ministry, healing, with preaching and teaching being the other two. He won souls to himself through preaching, and he taught believers how to live holy and victorious Christian lives. Through his healing ministry, he ministered to the physical crises of his followers. People with problems came to him and he attended to their needs.

God created man without the presence of sin. He intended mankind to live free of evil, disease, and suffering, which was not part of his original plan.

But mankind chose to disobey the rules that enabled them to be deposited with his image and likeness. Their disobedience caused separation, which the Bible calls sin. Sin is the root cause of all forms of spiritual and physical human misery. Sickness and suffering resulted from God's penalty for man's choice to go against God's righteousness.

In his divine plan to restore humanity to a perfect eternal state, God put in motion a process of restoration through his sinless Son, Jesus Christ. He also instituted the presbytery and invested them with the authority and power of Christ to heal people with prayer spoken through the righteousness and faith of Christ.

The withdrawal of God's righteousness gave Satan access to carry out his mission in the world, including the suffering of humanity. The Bible summarizes the mission of Satan in John 10:10: *"The thief comes to steal and kill and destroy"* (NIV). The Bible teaches that the consequences of sin include human suffering and death.

Since mankind could no longer access the Creator, they searched for remedies for suffering within creation itself. Using their God-given wisdom and intelligence, they created four methods by which to deal with the problem of sin:

- Traditional medicine
- Scientific medicine
- Mental healthcare
- Religious/spiritual healing

These four human methods of healing need to be practiced through an understanding that sin is the cause of all suffering. No crisis takes place apart from sin and mankind's original act of disobedience.

In the current age of explosive knowledge, mankind is piecing together the puzzle of the curse of sin and human suffering, especially as it pertains to modern scientific medicine. Despite many revelations about the nature of disease, sin continues to be a great mystery.

In dealing with the tyranny of evil and suffering, the PCPM serves as our divine provision for handling every type of crisis. It brings us hope for every human problem, freeing us from mental, physical, and spiritual agony.

God gave the clergy the divine mantle of speaking healing prayer through the authority, power, and righteousness of Jesus Christ in the local church. Although the other four healing methods enjoy the gift of God's common grace, the presbytery operates according to his grace and promise to minister healing to crisis members. The local PCPM is not in competition with other God-given gifts of healing. Rather, it is complementary.

Jesus Christ, the divine Son of God, came:

- to destroy the power of sin, for in Him there is no sin.
- to destroy the works of the devil.
- to demonstrate that earthly healing.

Throughout human history, people have been asking, "If God is God, why do we suffer disease, pain, misery, poverty, and even death?" God is the God of transformation, restoration, and healing. Instead of returning to God and trusting in the blood of Jesus Christ for a complete recovery, however, man has placed his dependence on creation, rejecting the Creator.

There are many treatments and practitioners of medicine in the world, but true divine healing comes only from the living God, the Creator of the universe. It is God who heals all manner of suffering. The other treatment approaches struggle to provide cure for disease. Only Jesus offers transformational healing—physically, mentally, socially, spiritually, and relationally.

# Transforming Faith Healing Scripture

JESUS IS OUr Great Physician and Healer. He always fulfills his promises to heal our disease and sickness. So call your righteous elders today. You've got to taste and see whether the Lord will continue to fulfill his promises.

> He said, "If you listen carefully to the Lord your God and do what is right in his eyes, if you pay attention to his commands and keep all his decrees, I will not bring on you any of the diseases I brought on the Egyptians, for I am the Lord, who heals you." (Exodus 15:26, NIV)

> Worship the Lord your God, and his blessing will be on your food and water. I will take away sickness from among you... (Exodus 23:25, NIV)

> The Lord will keep you free from every disease. He will not inflict on you the horrible diseases you knew in Egypt, but he will inflict them on all who hate you. (Deuteronomy 7:15, NIV)

> See now that I myself am he! There is no god besides me. I put to death and I bring to life, I have wounded and I will heal, and no one can deliver out of my hand. (Deuteronomy 32:39, NIV)

> He sent out his word and healed them; he rescued them from the grave. (Psalm 107:20, NIV)

> My comfort in my suffering is this: your promise preserves my life. (Psalm 119:50, NIV)

> My son, pay attention to what I say; turn your ear to my words. Do not let them out of your sight, keep them within your heart; for they are life to those who find them and health to one's whole body. (Proverbs 4:20–22, NIV)

> A cheerful heart is good medicine, but a crushed spirit dries up the bones. (Proverbs 17:22, NIV)

*...but those who hope in the Lord will renew their strength. They will soar on wings like eagles; they will run and not grow weary, they will walk and not be faint.* (Isaiah 40:31, NIV)

*Nevertheless, I will bring health and healing to it; I will heal my people and will let them enjoy abundant peace and security.* (Jeremiah 33:6, NIV)

*Jesus called his twelve disciples to him and gave them authority to drive out impure spirits and to heal every disease and sickness.* (Matthew 10:1, NIV)

*Peace I leave with you; my peace I give you. I do not give to you as the world gives. Do not let your hearts be troubled and do not be afraid.* (John 14:27, NIV)

*But he said to me, "My grace is sufficient for you, for my power is made perfect in weakness." Therefore I will boast all the more gladly about my weaknesses, so that Christ's power may rest on me.* (2 Corinthians 12:9, NIV)

*"He himself bore our sins" in his body on the cross, so that we might die to sins and live for righteousness; "by his wounds you have been healed."* (1 Peter 2:24, NIV)

# About the Author

REV. DR. PETER Bawamakadi served as a minister of the Gospel of Christ Jesus and a teacher of the Bible for many years. He obtained his first Doctor of Ministry in Conflict Management from Trinity Theological Seminary in Newburgh, Indiana. Later he received his second Doctor of Ministry in Contextual Leadership from Providence Theological Seminary in Otterburne, Manitoba. He accepted his Master of Divinity in Christian Theology from Free Lutheran Seminary in Minneapolis, Minnesota. He obtained a second Master of Arts in Counselling Psychology from Yorkville University in New Brunswick and a Bachelor of Arts in Theology/Education from ECWA Theological Seminary in Jos, Nigeria.

www.ingramcontent.com/pod-product-compliance
Lightning Source LLC
Chambersburg PA
CBHW060654100426
42734CB00047B/1650